THE PILGRIM ROUTE TO COMPOSTELA

2ND REVISED EDITION

ACKNOWLEDGEMENTS

This guide is the work of many enthusiasts, too numerous to name.

Special thanks go to Justin de Menditte for this new edition, and to the walkers who accompanied Georges Veron for the initial reconnaissance of the route; notably Robert Mangon, Gilberte Veron, and Danielle and Yves Maze. We are grateful for comments from those who have used the first edition, Bernard Bailly, Yan L Crispel, H D Van Gelder, and Roger Verin.

ABBE G. BERNES   GEORGES VERON   L. LABORDE BALEN

THE PILGRIM ROUTE
TO COMPOSTELA

IN SEARCH OF ST. JAMES

2ND REVISED EDITION

Robertson McCarta

CONTENTS

- *Preface by His Excellence Monseigneur Archbishop*
  of Santiago de Compostela   6

- *Introduction from:*
  La Société des Amis de Saint-Jacques de Compostelle   8
  Los Amigos del Camino de Santiago   9
  Note from Monsieur l'Abbé Georges Bernés   10
  The History of a Great Pilgrimage
  by Louis Laborde-Balen   11
  General information   26

- *Stage 1: Saint-Jean-Pied-de-Port to Burguete*   37
- *Stage 2: Burguete to Zubiri*   43
- *Stage 3: Zubiri to Pamplona*   49
- *Stage 4: Pamplona to Puente la Reina*   55
- *Stage 5: Puente la Reina to Estella*   61
- *Stage 6: Estella to Los Arcos*   67
- *Stage 7: Los Arcos to Logroño*   71
- *Stage 8: Logroño to Nájera*   77
- *Stage 9: Nájera to Santo Domingo de la Calzada*   83
- *Stage 10: Santo Domingo de la Calzada to Belorado*   89
- *Stage 11: Belorado to San Juan de Ortega*   94
- *Stage 12: San Juan de Ortega to Burgos*   99
- *Stage 13: Burgos to Castrojeriz*   103

- Stage 14: Castrojeriz to Frómista   109
- Stage 15: Frómista to Carrión de los Condes   113
- Stage 16: Carrión de los Condes to Sahagún   119
- Stage 17: Sahagún to Mansilla de las Mulas   123
- Stage 18: Mansilla de las Mulas to León   127
- Stage 19: León to Hospital de Orbigo   133
- Stage 20: Hospital de Orbigo to Astorga   139
- Stage 21: Astorga to Acebo   143
- Stage 22: Acebo to Ponferrada   147
- Stage 23: Ponferrada to Villafranca del Bierzo   151
- Stage 24: Villafranca del Bierzo to El Cebreiro   155
- Stage 25: Cebreiro to Triacastela   161
- Stage 26: Triacastela to Sarría   165
- Stage 27: Sarría to Portomarín   169
- Stage 28: Portomarín to Palas de Rei   175
- Stage 29: Palas de Rei to Arzúa   179
- Stage 30: Arzúa to Labacolla   187
- Stage 31: Labacolla to Santiago de Compostela   195

- The Aragon Road   199
- Bibliography   206
- Maps   207 – 239
- Index   240

Preface by His Excellence Monseigneur Antonio M. Ronco Varela,
Archbishop of Santiago de Compostela.

PREFACE

*How could the Archbishop of Santiago de Compostela offer anything less than
a warm welcome to this new guide? It is a worthy addition to the many
remarkable handbooks to this route issued over the centuries.*

*The editors deserve every encouragement for their work and their enthusiasm
in stimulating the expansion of the pilgrimage.*

*There is much to indicate that the unique and historical values of Compostela
are appreciated as much today as at any time in its history.*

*The footsteps of today's growing number of pilgrims echo with age-old
resonance along the many branches of the Road to Compostela. The pilgrimage
has universal relevance; but it is primarily and supremely European in its
social significance and its cultural and religious aspects. When UNESCO
recently recognised Santiago de Compostela as a World Heritage site, I was
moved to write: `pilgrims beyond number are reviving the route to Compostela,
bringing their belief in Christ from all of Europe and the New World, men of
goodwill approaching a haven of reconciliation and of peace.'*

*The pilgrim who stands in the crypt beside the actual tomb of the Apostle
must be aware, surely with strong personal emotion, that his westward path
to Compostela has been a rediscovery of his own origin as a European. The
words of Pope John-Paul II, himself a pilgrim, are there to be read on the
commemorative plaque: `As Bishop of Rome and priest of the Church throughout
the world, I pronounce this loving appeal from Santiago in ancient Europe:
look within yourself, be true to yourself, return to your origins, renew your
roots, live once more according to the true values which were the glory of your
history and the blessings you brought to other continents. Renew your spiritual
unity in a climate of total respect for other religions and true freedoms.'*

*The purpose of this guide is to help the pilgrim with the strictly practical
aspects of walking the French route. These are equally important, and have
their own Christian significance. The great Cathedrals undoubtedly manifest
the powerful faith of our ancestors; but, as has been stated with typically French
perception, the cathedrals were built because there was faith and because people
understood geometry. Physical materials make their own demands which a
mature religious faith not only respects but clarifies and develops to the full.*

The Lord said that a cup of cold water given to the humblest of men would not pass unrewarded (Matthew 10.42). This example of the value of the simplest things, the precise detail of the fresh water, is highly significant. We hope that as the pilgrim follows his arduous and meritorious path this book will bring similar refreshment.

Santiago de Compostela
1 January 1986
Antonio M. Ronco Varela
Archbishop of Santiago de Compostela

Centre Européen des Etudes Compostellanes,
4 Square du Pont de Sèvres,
92100 Boulogne-sur-Seine

Among the Routes of European Culture currently under preparation, the Roads to Santiago across the whole of Europe must be at the forefront.

It is important that as part of this great movement in contemporary cultural and artistic development, today's pilgrims, seeking to follow in the footsteps of their predecessors, not only have the privilege of doing so but can also benefit from whatever help is available to guide them.

This implies the outstanding importance of the premier Road to Santiago, the `CAMINO FRANCÉS' in Spain.

We therefore congratulate the Randonnées Pyrénéennes for their initiative in re-issuing Abbé Bernès' well-known work, bringing it up to date and improving the presentation of this excellent guide: it is now even better suited to the needs of today's pilgrims.

The Société des Amis de Saint-Jacques and its regional affiliates are confident that this edition answers a genuine need, and are delighted to give their warm support to this guide for the Santiago enthusiasts.

René de La Coste-Messelière

*President of the Société des Amis de
Saint-Jacques de Compostelle*

Los Amigos del Camino de Santiago
apartado de Correos, 20,
Estella (Navarra)

To contribute to the cultural, social and religious resurgence of the Road to Santiago, to open up to tourists the ancient pilgrim ways where so many Christians of all social and cultural backgrounds have shared their common faith as they shared their travels, fostering communication between Spanish traditions and other nations of Europe and the world, to share in the restoration of the route - such were the Society's aims, formulated when it was established in 1959.

We were therefore delighted to see the new publication of the Randonnées Pyrénéennes association, which is entirely in accord with our objectives; it confirms the universality of our motto: `The Road to Santiago, the European Road'.

We have been promoting the Road to Santiago for 16 years, organising first a `Medieval Studies Week' and then a debate in the pages of our magazine, and various other means of communication - books, maps, audiovisual series - and excursions.

Various proposals were adopted recently during the first Assembly of Parishes of the Road, with His Eminence the Archbishop of Santiago as President, and to which we were invited. They included the restoration of hostels, waymarking along the route, the establishment of diocesan associations concerned with the future of the Road, distribution of a `Pilgrim's Certificate', all decisions which attest to the effectiveness of our efforts.

It should be noted that Los Amigos des Camino de Santiago led the way by publishing the first map of the route and an audio-visual presentation including Gregorian chants, Mozarabic and popular songs, and to work on waymarking - setting up cairns - and on establishing alternative routes avoiding tarmac surfaces.

We wish to encourage the efforts and sustain the hopes of all who are moved by a vocation to pilgrimage and by artistic, sporting and humanistic motives, as are all friends of the Randonnées Pyrénéennes.

Fransisco Beruete
Presidente de los amigos del Camino de Santiago

When in 1973 I published the first modest edition of THE PILGRIMS' GUIDE, with the support of the Comité Gascon d'Etudes Compostellanes, I was convinced that the pilgrimage to Santiago was about to flourish once more. Indeed, every year hundreds of pilgrims undertake this great walk on foot, and their numbers are increasing.

This is the fourth edition of the Guide. Thanks to the Randonnées Pyrénéennes and their magnificent work, the sacred Way to Compostela has been opened up to so many more pilgrims. I hope that both along the Road and in the Apostle's chosen city they will discover celestial light to illuminate their lives with a new Star, the Star of Compostela, through the intermediary of St James, the Son of Thunder, the Apostle with the fiery heart.

Georges BERNES
Priest

THE HISTORY OF A GREAT PILGRIMAGE

Pilgrimages are not exclusive to Christianity; they are known in all lands, in all ages - the temples of Delphi and Solomon, the tombs or sanctuaries of Confucius, Buddha, or Muhammad... Today there are secular pilgrimages which are no less popular - to Montségur, Lenin's tomb, even the tomb of General de Gaulle. Nothing could be more reasonable or more natural than this instinctive return to our roots.

But the distinguishing mark of the pilgrimage of faith which concerns us here lies in its profound contribution to Christianity over many generations.

JERUSALEM, ROME AND COMPOSTELA

Christian pilgrimage developed early. As early as the 4th century a route from Bordeaux to Jerusalem was published: ITINERARIUM A BURDIGALA JERUSALEM USQUE; and at more modest levels of province or parish, local pilgrimages took as their goal the relics of a martyr or a saint from the early days of the Church. This was one cause of the trade in relics which was condemned by the Church.

The three most highly prized and meritorious pilgrimages, however, were those to Jerusalem, to Rome, and before long to Compostela: the tombs of Christ, St Peter, and St James. The Spanish language has different names for pilgrims on the three routes: the pilgrim to the Holy Land was a *palmero*, he who went to Rome was a *romero*, and the traveller walking to Compostela was a *jacobeo* or a *jacobita*.

The Gascons, too, distinguished between *lous Roumiûs* and *lous Jacqués* - in theory at least: since in practice the *Camis Roumiûs* marked on the IGN maps head for Spain and across the frontier, while any annual pilgrimage to a hidden mountain *ermita*, is called *romeria*.

SANTIAGO AND SPAIN

We are concerned here with Santiago de Compostela.

The `Santiago' in question has been established as the Apostle St James (in Spanish Sant Iago) the Great who died in the year 44, thus 10 or 12 years after the death of Christ. According to tradition, he tried during this period to evangelise Spain, though many historians have expressed doubt, and no contemporary text mentions it. On the other hand, there is nothing to contradict the tradition. The Acts of the Apostles do not claim to be exhaustive, and cover only the missionary work of Paul, Luke, Peter and Mark. Today these texts would be regarded as reports on specific tasks. There is no mention of the other Apostles although they too, according to the opening lines, received the same commission and the same gift of speaking foreign tongues; in the words of Jesus, `Ye shall receive power ... and ye shall be witnesses unto me ..in all Judaea, and in Samaria, and unto the uttermost part of the earth'. (Acts 1.8.) Subsequently (Acts 9.1), Luke reveals that there were already Christians in Damascus when Paul arrived there, without indicating who had brought Christianity to Syria.

WHO WAS ST JAMES?

St James was one of Christ's Twelve Apostles, brother of John the Evangelist, son of Zebedee, related to Jesus according to the early Fathers of the Church. Reading between the lines of the New Testament, it is possible to picture him as loyal and impulsive.

He should not be confused with another James, the brother of Jesus who, as head of the Christian Church in Jerusalem, was to be thrown from the top of the Temple and clubbed to death in the year 68. To distinguish between the two, the latter is known as James the Less, the son of Zebedee being known as James the Great.

The Acts of the Apostles (12.1-2) describes the death of James the Great: `Now about that time Herod the king stretched forth his hands to vex certain of the church. And he killed James the brother of John with the sword'.

This cannot refer to Herod Antipas of the Gospels, but to one of his successors, Herod Agrippa I, who reigned from 41 to 44, the year in which James was put to death.

Whatever the facts may be, it was not until the sacred writers of the 4th century, such as St Jerome or Didymus of Alexandria, that there was any mention of James having been to Spain. He was said to have landed in Andalusia, crossed the peninsula without much success, along a Roman road and to have finally reached Galicia, the land of Celtic mysticism.

After his death on his return to Jerusalem, his disciples Theodorus and Anasthasius stole the body by night from the executioners and, `guided by an angel', brought it by boat to Iria Flavia, the modern Spanish town of Padrón, to bury James in his chosen land.

As described later in this book, legend tells of their encounter with Queen Lupa, of her conversion, and the gift of her palace as a place of burial.

THE DISCOVERY OF THE TOMB: 813

Whether real or mythical, the tomb was neglected as the burden of persecution increased - but not by all. It was mentioned by a 7th century Irish monk, St Adelhelm, and by the Spanish monk Beatus de Liébana, author of the text of the `Apocalypse of Saint-Sever', in the 8th century.

It was early in the 9th century, however, before the whole of Europe was stirred by news of its rediscovery.

About 813 the hermit Pelayo, who lived in San Fiz de Solovio near the sanctuary that we see today, saw a strange light shining every night from a small hillock, like that from a star - hence the name of Compostela.

Informed in a dream that it was from the Apostle's tomb, he gave the news to Theodomir, the Visigoth Bishop of Iria Flavia, and the remains of the Saint and his disciples were discovered.

"THE FIELD OF THE STAR"

From the mysterious light seen by Pelayo popular etymology derives the name of Santiago de Compostela: 'CAMPUS STELLAE' means 'the field of the star'. More exigent historians prefer an erudite linguistic connection, deriving 'Compostela' from 'COMPOSITUM' - 'prepared, made ready' - which in low Latin had acquired funerary meaning. A possible alternative could be 'COMPOSTUM', 'placed together'. In all cases, the tomb was certainly the origin of the name.

THE BIRTH OF THE PILGRIMAGE

Alfonso II, King of Asturia and Galicia, who died in 842, ordered a small church to be built on the site, and spread the news to the great men of his day, particularly Charlemagne, who apparently received one of the Saint's shoulder-blades, and to Pope Leo III.

The pilgrimages now began. As early as 950 one Godescalc, the Bishop of Puy-en-Velay, came from the very heart of Gaul.

Such stirrings displeased the Moors who then ruled most of Spain. The Moorish king Al Manzor, or Almanzor, destroyed this first church in 997 and brought his horse to drink in the baptismal font. He had the bells carried away on the backs of Christians to the Mosque at Cordoba;

in later years a Christian king had them brought back - on the backs of Moors. Al Manzor did not disturb the tomb: it was Christianity that he opposed, not the companions of a prophet called Jesus.

The church of Compostela was rebuilt after 1078, more beautiful than before, increasing in size down the centuries until it became the vast monument we see today. Deep within the heart of this ever growing building the tomb lay in the crypt, visited at first by all pilgrims, then increasingly kept concealed from view. In the 16th century it was hidden, from fear of the English pirates along the Coruña coast, in the wake of the famous Sir Francis Drake. Eventually the secret of its precise location was lost.

SANTIAGO PEREGRINO AND SANTIAGO MATAMOROS

St James appears in painting and in sculpture in two very different forms.

The most traditional, well known in other countries, is that of St James the Pilgrim who, as pictured by his followers, has the broad-brimmed hat, staff, cape and scallop-shell.

The second is peculiar to Spain and recalls his appearance beside King Ramiro I at the battle of Clavijo in 844. In this the saint is shown as a galloping knight, with sword in one hand and cross in the other. Then he is called 'SANTIAGO MATAMOROS', literally 'St James the slayer of the Moors'.

COMPOSTELA SEEN BY A MOOR IN 845.

The Moorish poet and philosopher Algazel, born in the Spanish city of Jaen, wrote the following strange lines in 845 to explain the growth of the sanctuary at Compostela, indicating clearly the coexistence, not to say syncretism, existing in Spain in those early days before the beginning of the Reconquest:

'Their Kaaba is a colossal idol at the centre of the church: they swear by this. And from the most distant lands, starting from Rome as well as other countries, they come in pilgrimage, claiming that the tomb inside the church is that of St James, one of the Twelve Apostles, the most beloved of Isaiah; blessings be

on him, and the grace of God, and on our Prophet'

THE FERRYMEN AT SORDES L'ABBAYE

It is at Sordes l'Abbaye, between the Landes and the Basque country, that Aymery, or Aymeric, Picaud complains bitterly of the ferrymen on the Gave d'Oloron: 'Curses on their boatmen. Their boat is small, made of a single tree-trunk and barely able to carry horses; so that on getting in one must be careful not to fall in the water. Frequently, when they have taken their money, the ferrymen put so many pilgrims on board that the boat overturns and the pilgrims are drowned. And then the boatmen are wickedly delighted, and strip the dead.'

ARCHAEOLOGICAL CONFIRMATION: 1879 AND 1946

In 1878 the Cardinal of Compostela commissioned several months of research, and remains were discovered on the night of 28 January 1879. Scientists and doctors confirmed their authenticity, proclaimed solemnly by Pope Leo XIII in his Papal Bull 'Deus Omnipotens'...

Digging of a more scientific nature was undertaken in 1946, with surprising results: this time, not only was the Saint's tomb rediscovered, but also a complete first century necropolis and, lying beside a 9th century tomb, the tomb of Bishop Theodomir, who died in 847.

Controversy flared up. In the eyes of some historians `these are the remains of Galician nobles of the first century, who worshipped Jupiter, Mercury and local gods ...'

This may indeed be true, but there is no proof. And the fact of Bishop Theodomir's existence, regarded as legend by other historians, has since been confirmed.

More disturbing is the thesis of Jacques Chocheyras, a medievalist at the University of Grenoble: he suggests that the tomb was in fact that of the heresiarch Priscillian, whose body was certainly brought back to Galicia and buried by his disciples. The veneration in which his tomb was held for 200 years would have been 'absorbed', consciously or not, by Catholicism at the time of the Reconquest. This too is possible, though unproven; either way it is a question of faith rather than of science.

We may therefore assume that when archaeology confirms a 700-year-old tradition it is reasonable to believe it unless it is proved wrong... If we are honest we should acknowledge that many believers, even when they come as pilgrims, doubt the presence of the Apostle's body. But is its presence the important thing? What matters is the powerful surge of faith which makes Compostela one of the poles of Christianity, it is seven centuries of prayer and meditation of pilgrims as they walk.

THE COMPOSTELA PILGRIM

In any case, the pilgrims approaching along the paths of Europe were not concerned with such doubts. The simple faith of the day held that all are only pilgrims on this earth, and a hard journey to venerate a relic is one of the `works' which ensure salvation. They arrived in their thousands. In the 13th century, 30,000 meals were served each year in Roncesvalles, and in 1434, 63 ships brought 3,000 pilgrims to Coruña.

They travelled from one rest-house to the next, wearing the costume familiar to us now from statues and altar-pieces. Nothing to do with fashion, it was functional, the result of practical experience.

If the crowds of 20th century pilgrims were to come to Lourdes today on foot, they would surely be wearing shorts or jeans, and trainers, perhaps a cape, and carrying rucksacks.

The medieval pilgrim walking to Santiago wore thick shoes capable of standing up to footpaths strewn with flints and thorns; a broad-brimmed hat or leather-hooded cape for protection from rain and sun; a coat thick enough to give protection from the cold, and short enough not to catch on bushes; an unbreakable water container, with a carrying loop at its neck; a wallet attached to the belt, with money to pay for shelter at inns, and in which to hide any alms received; a scrip for bread and modest belongings; and finally the staff, the heavy stick for use in walking and, if necessary, as a defensive weapon.

The only luxury was the St James's scallop-shell, the 'concha' or 'vieira'; this was originally a souvenir of Galicia, where it abounded on the sea-shore, but it was quickly adopted as an emblem carved on churches and 'hospitals' - 'hospital' is the term used over the centuries, and throughout this guide, for the hostels and hospices specially set up to provide rest and hospitality for pilgrims.

THE PRISCILLIAN THEORY

Said to have been born in Betica in Andalucia about the year 340 and a student in Bordeaux, Priscillian was the leader of an obscure religious sect. He led an ascetic life and had many disciples. He appears to have been influenced by Manicheism and Adoptionism (briefly, God, the principle of Good and opponent of Satan the principle of Evil, adopted Christ as his Son at his death; no doubt Priscillian's beliefs were more subtle). Although a Council at Saragossa refuted his beliefs he was elected Bishop of Avila. At Trier, where he went to justify himself, the secular advisers of the Emperor had him put to death for magic and wicked practices, together with six of his disciples, including a woman. This was the first recorded execution of a heretic in history. St Martin, St Gregory and the Pope Siricius himself protested: despite his errors, the spirituality of Priscillian was beyond doubt. His disciples brought his body back to Galicia, where he had many adherents. Professor Chosseyras suggests that his corpse may have been brought by water, down the Rhine and then along the coast to Padron.

RICH AND POOR, PENITENTS AND ENTHUSIASTS

The crowds of pilgrims included rich men on horseback. In the 13th century Alfonso II the Chaste, King of Aragon and Catalonia, was the first to come with all his court, bringing generous donations.

The poor came on foot. There were beggars who made

a career of the pilgrimage. The Middle Ages suited them well: 'Christ's poor' had their place within society. More secular times were to suit them less well: a suspect pilgrim in Louis XIV's days was less likely to be imprisoned if he could show a passport-letter acquired in advance from the Governor or the senior administrator.

Motives varied too. There were forced pilgrimages, ordered by a church tribunal in expiation of some sin; there were proxy pilgrims, travelling in the name of some powerful individual, a city, or a community. The great majority of pilgrims, however, set out on their own account, having made a vow and often a will: for 'nothing is more certain than Death, and nothing is less certain than the day and the hour of our Death'.

THE FIRST TOURIST GUIDES

Recognised itineraries were fully developed from the 11th century onwards, notably by the Cluniac order, which established 'hospitals' in monasteries along the roads; the Knights of the Holy Sepulchre kept the roads safe, there were Augustinian canonries and monasteries of all orders. The pilgrim would go from one stopping place to the next, certain of finding board and lodging at the end of each stage which might often have its dangers - snow, wolves, or bandits, anyone who took advantage of the circumstances. For it was not only begging pilgrims or *coquillards* who did so. Aymery Picaud warned his readers against ferrymen who overturned or even drowned their passengers; against touts who, twenty leagues from Compostela, would direct travellers to dishonest hostels; against lodging-houses which overcharged and arranged for their staff to empty pilgrims' water containers so that next day they could sell poor wine at a high price.

It was now, indeed, that true guides were written and passed from hand to hand, often just a few pages, but sometimes real books full of detailed information. There were dozens, written by Germans, English, Italians, and French, and their use continued for many years.

The 18th century Béarn historian Christian Desplats was surprised to discover Brotherhoods of Saint-Jacques in the little villages of Béarn, in south west France, in the full flowering of the Age of Enlightenment; membership was dependent on making the pilgrimage, followed by presenting a written account of it.

AYMERY PICAUD AND THE CODEX CALIXTINUS

The 1140 route was included in a larger Latin work known as the CODEX CALIXTINUS, from its false attribution to Pope Calixtus II, a fervent devotee of Compostela.

The work was in fact the fruit of team work led either by Cluny or, more probably, by Vézelay. Aymery, or Aymeric Picaud, the priest of Parthenay-le-Vieux in Poitou, appears to have contributed the most precise description of all the stages; often impassioned (he was shocked by the Gascons and held a grudge against the Basques), sometimes unfair, always very lively.

This, however, is only one part of the CODEX, which consisted of five sections:

The revision of the liturgical chants, canticles, hymns and pilgrim songs in use at Compostela;

A compilation of the miracles attributed to St James, particularly the most recent;

The account of St James's evangelisation of Spain, and the repatriation of his body;

An apocryphal chronicle by Archbishop Turpin, one of Charlemagne's Peers, describing the legendary campaigns of the Emperor with the white flowing beard;

The list of the Roads to Compostela, divided into stages (long stages of 80 kilometres), the 'hospitals' providing shelter, the rivers to be crossed, dangers to be avoided, relics to be worshipped along the way.

Some of these sections are of historical interest only. The first and last, however, are valuable for their insight into the Middle Ages; the first because it provides knowledge of very ancient religious music, some of it Visigoth, and the last because it constitutes the 'Pilgrims' Guide' itself.

Two works are famous and are frequently referred to because they offer information on the pilgrim's daily routine at different periods:
- in 1676, the work of the Italian priest Domenico Laffi,

of Bologna;
- 1140, that of Aymery Picaud in the Codex Calixtinus.

PRINCIPAL AND SECONDARY ROUTES

The *Codex* describes four major pilgrim routes across France:
- the Toulouse route, from Arles to Somport;
- the Le Puy route to Roncesvalles;
- the Limousin route, from Vézelay to Roncesvalles;
- the Tours route, from Paris to Roncesvalles

The Toulouse route continued into Spain along the *Camino Aragones* to Puente la Reina, while the other three met at Ostabat to form the *Camino Navarro*. From Puente la Reina, as indicated on its monument 'there is only one Road', the one followed in this book.

Although these were the most frequented routes and the best supplied with lodgings, they were not the only ones available.

There was initially an older fifth route of equal importance; starting from Bayonne, it followed the coast of Cantabria through Oviedo.

Subsequently many secondary routes were developed. The pilgrim was often urged to make a detour to sanctuaries in possession of a relic or consecrated spring, as might happen today through a Tourist Information Office. According to inclination, advice, or experience, he could choose between the following:
- Narbonne, le Perthus and Catalonia;
- Andorra and Lérida;
- Saint-Gaudens and the Val d'Aran;
- the foothills of the Pyrenees, Saint-Bertrand, l'Escaladieu, Lourdes, Mifaget, Gabas and the Col des Moines;
- Lescun, the Col de Pau, and the Hechó valley;
- the Saint-Blaise 'hospital', through Sainte-Engrâce and the Roncal valley;
- Béhobie and Vitoria; and there were others.

Finally, there were the wholly Spanish routes:
- from Barcelona via Saragossa or San Juan de la Peña;
- from Seville and Salamanca through Zamora (via the Plata and the Mozarabic *camino*);

- or directly from the ports of Galicia: Coruña, Padrón, etc.

And of course, a Portuguese Road traversed the country from south to north.

Apart from the coastal routes, all the others joined up with the *Camino Francés*, thus swelling its traffic considerably.

MONUMENTS ALONG THE WAY

Four main periods succeeded one another between the birth of the pilgrimage and its peak:
1. Until the 8th century Spain was a Visigoth kingdom.
2. From 709 to 1,000, the greater part of the country was under Moorish, rather than Arab, domination, an Islam reasonably tolerant and syncretic, and highly civilised. But, particularly in the north, Christian resistance brought into being several small mountain kingdoms in the Visigoth tradition.

THE FOUR GREAT ROADS
TO SANTIAGO ... AND THE FIFTH

The four main routes set out by Aymery Picaud went through the following places:
The *Via Tolosana,* or Provence Road
Arles, Saint-Gilles du Gard, Castres, Toulouse, Auch, Morlas, Lescar, Lacommande, Oloron, Sarrance, the Col du Somport.

This route, to be followed by the GR653 long-distance footpath now under preparation, was the route for pilgrims from Provence as well as from Italy, Switzerland, Austria, and Bavaria.

Originally it, too, had to join the other routes through Ostabat, but after the 12th century, and particularly after the recapture of Saragossa in 1118, the roads of Aragon were open and the Vicomte de Béarn, Gaston IV, did much to develop the route through the Aspe valley. Sainte-Christine (or Santa Cristina) du Somport was considered one of Christendom's three main 'hospitals'.
The *Via Podensis,* or Le Puy Road
Le Puy en Velay, Aubrac, Conques, Cahors, Moissac, Condom, Eauze, Nogaro, Aire-sur-l'Adour, Garlin, Sauvelade, Navarrenx, Saint- Palais, Ostabat.

This, the modern GR65 long-distance footpath, is the route taken by Bishop Godescalc.
The *Via Lemovicensis* (from the Limousin area), or the Vézelay Road
Vézelay, Nevers, Neuvy, Saint-Léonard, Limoges, Périgueux, La Réole, Bazas, Mont-de-Marsan, Saint-Sever, Orthez, Sauveterre, Saint-Palais, Ostabat.

This was the route for pilgrims from Burgundy, Lorraine, the Rhineland, and northern Germany.
The *Via Turonensis* (from Tours), or the Paris Road
Paris, Orléans, Tours, Poitiers, Sainte-Blaye, Bordeaux, Dax, Arthous, Sordes l'Abbaye, Saint-Palais, Ostabat.

This was the principal French route, also used by pilgrims from northern Europe.
The old Coast Road
Finally, this route should not be thought of as secondary, but rather as very ancient; the route along the Cantabrian coast, though not mentioned in the Codex, must surely date from earlier times when the Moorish occupation made it impossible to cross León and Castile.

Touching Bayonne, Bilbao, Santander and Oviedo, its antiquity followed by relative neglect has left it rich in pre-Romanesque monuments.

3. In the 11th and 12th centuries the situation was reversed; the south fell into disarray and political anarchy, then Berber domination. The north turned towards Europe, notably with the arrival of the Cluniac monks; this was the great Romanesque period of the Road to Santiago and the Reconquest.

4. The battle of Las Navas de Tolosa in 1212 was the first step towards the political unity of Christian Spain, achieved with the completion of the Reconquest in 1492 and the annexation of Navarre in 1512.

The effects of this long history are evident in Spanish architecture and art, although the oldest masterpieces must be sought off the route as the pilgrim churches were rebuilt in Romanesque or Gothic periods.

The following architectural periods may be identified:

Visigoth, simple (with only a hint of an apse), although more delicate than Merovingian architecture of the same period, with the marvellous plant or animal decoration and horseshoe-shaped arches which were to influence Islamic architecture; see the church of St John the Baptist at Baños de Cerrato (661, near Palencia), and Quintanilla de las Viñas (7th century, near Burgos).

Pre-Romanesque Asturian was a continuation of Visigoth architecture in this small Christian kingdom, with twin-columned arches and beautiful lacy stone carving. Near Oviedo, see the church of Santa María de Naranco and San Miguel de Lillo (9th century); also San Salvador de Valdedíos (893). Pre-Romanesque and 'Lombard' styles also flourished in the mountains of Aragon and Catalonia.

Mozarabic is the name given to Christians in Islamic lands, as *Mudéjar* or *Moorish* is given to Muslims living in Christian countries. Between the 9th and 11th centuries Mozarabic architects brought the delicacy of Islamic architecture to Christian churches. Visigoth origins are certainly apparent, but much developed, with the widespread use of horseshoe arches, multilobed arches, and then ribbed domes. Not far from the route, see San

Miguel de la Escalada (913, near León).

Romanesque (the equivalent of Norman architecture in Great Britain), is seen finally in its flourishing brilliance everywhere along the Road to Santiago, bringing Spain back into European harmony. Pilgrims can see it at Jaca, San Juan de la Peña, Leyre, Frómista, Silos, and Compostela itself. Later came *Gothic* architecture (Pamplona, Burgos, León, etc.).

These monuments will be described as the guide takes you along the various stages of the route, together with practical information and suggestions on meals: now we are ready to start.

L.L.-B.

GENERAL INFORMATION

TELEPHONES

Public telephones may not be seen as frequently as in some other countries, but they are usually in working order. Take plenty of 25-peseta coins. It is often possible to use the telephone in bars and restaurants where one is eating.

Each region has its own area code, to be used in front of the subscriber's six-figure number. Following the route taken in this guide:

Province of Navarre: 948, from Roncesvalles to Viana inclusive;

Province of Logroño:
   941 from Logroño to Santo Domingo de la Calzada;

Province of Burgos:
   947 from Recedilla del Camino to Castrojeriz;

Provine of Palencia:
   988 from Boadilla del Camino to Ledigos;

Province of León:
   987 from Sahagún to Vega de Valcarce;

Province of Lugo:
   982 from Cebrero to Palas de Rey;

Province of Coruña:
   981 from Melide to Santiago.

ACCOMMODATION

Spain provides accommodation in establishments as varied as their charges, but which are in general comparable with standards in other countries; as elsewhere, there are happy and disagreeable surprises.
The range is approximately as follows, with the normal star-rating:

Parador (P) - rooms at about 35 per night in 1989. For the prosperous pilgrim!

Hostal Résidencia (HsR) or *Hotel Résidencia* (HR), with rates varying between those of a Parador and those of a good standard hotel in France (probably cheaper than the equivalent standard in Great Britain). They do not generally have a restaurant but will provide breakfast (except for those who wish to set out very early indeed).

Hostal (H) - with the number of stars varying according to the standard of comfort.

Fonda (F) - a modest establishment, similar to a small hotel with bar and restaurant or family 'pension'; less luxurious but usually very reasonably priced;

Posada (P) - either an inn or a variety of Fonda;

Casa de Huespedes (CH) - bed and breakfast in private houses.

In most Spanish villages, even if there is no hotel sign it is generally possible to find a room in a private house; enquire in bars or shops for suggestions.

FREE LODGING, REFUGES, PILGRIM SHELTERS

Usually by application to the parish church (Parroquia) or the town hall (Ayuntamiento).
Specific places are usually indicated at the end of each section of the guide.

PRACTICAL SUGGESTIONS

Rucksack, made of waterproofed nylon, with side pockets, camera pocket, and a pocket inside the flap. Its capacity should be at least two cubic feet, particularly for those carrying a sleeping-bag. Do not hesitate to take a very large rucksack; it is a bad habit - and very risky - to hang clothing and other objects on the outside, although a tent can be tucked beneath the flap.

Shoes: mountain walking boots seem unsuitable. Having walked this route in all seasons we recommend:

- tennis shoes, or better still, trainers with anti-skid soles, for the minor roads, the interminable footpaths and many tracks, in dry weather;

- waterproof boots, or ankle-boots with anti-skid soles, large enough to wear two pairs of socks, or boot-liner socks. We consider such boots or ankle-boots essential for winter walking, and very useful in summer for the final third of the route.

- *Socks* made of finely looped wool, without any elaborate stitches which might cause rubbing;

- *Ankle socks* of wool, and tennis ankle socks in summer;

- *Coloured cotton underwear*, and a swimming costume;

- *Trousers*, one pair of jeans and one of walking breeches; the latter are practical with or without boots, and are preferable to ordinary trousers when walking through damp grass;

Track suit trousers would also be suitable. The basic rule is two pairs of trousers, one being relatively smart to wear in the evenings;

- *Shorts*, best of all athletics shorts, for all circumstances and seasons: comfortable to wear in summer, and useful in rainy weather: trousers can remain dry, in the rucksack!

- *Coloured cotton T-shirts;*

- *Shirts/blouses*, light and sleeveless or short-sleeved in summer, with front pockets;

- *Handkerchiefs* and pieces of old cloth, always useful;

- *Sunglasses;*

- *Hat*, essential in summer and frequently useful in winter;

- *Cagoule* or anorak or large cycling cape, to provide generous cover for walker and rucksack. Walkers' overtrousers made of proofed nylon, gussetted and very light, are strongly recommended except in summer;

- *Stick* (referred to as a 'staff' by pilgrims), essential, if only to discourage dogs;

- *Identity papers,* such as current passport, note of blood group and Rhesus factor; who to contact in case of accidents. Money, chequebook, stamps;

- *Notebook,* pen/pencil;

- *Compass,* essential;

- *Map,* Michelin sheet 442 followed by 441.

- *Miscellaneous:* battery torch, candles, matches, stamped envelopes, tin-opener, knife, spoon, shoe-laces, string, thread, needles, buttons, plastic bags, rags, paper tissues.

- *Medical pack* with antiseptic, bandage, razor-blade, sticking-plaster, aspirin, fine tweezers and small scissors, vitamin C. Because anti-snakebite serum should be kept cool, (and its use increasingly questioned) take Calciparine instead or calcium heparin.

- *Toilet articles:* minimum requirements, face-cloth, toothbrush and toothpaste, soap, battery razor, etc.

For campers:

- specialised shops can provide excellent tents sleeping three which, complete with tent-poles, flysheet, inner tent, and tent-pegs, weigh no more than 3 or 3.6 kilogrammes. Avoid all-nylon tents; cotton inner tent and waterproof nylon flysheet would seem a sound compromise.

- *Sleeping-bag,* zipped and synthetic-filled for the summer, remembering that nights can be very cool, even cold, in summer. 'Arctic' bag in winter.

- *Camping gas,* pans, small plastic bowl (more useful than the usual mug), water bottle or simple bottle made of strong plastic with a good screw top.

NIGHT-TIME DISTURBANCE

Like most southern races, the Spanish enjoy going out in the evening, and frequently at night-time.

A road which is deserted in the afternoon may be full

of bustle and noise after dark. Such agreeable habits may disturb those who like to go to sleep early.

Consequently, avoid rooms opening onto the main street or the central town square, also rooms directly over bars or restaurant dining-rooms. Take earplugs; they may prove invaluable.

HITCHING

This is not a widespread custom in Spain, but may be worth trying; lorry drivers and even the police often helped us back to our car when we reconnoitred the routes in 1985.

BUS SERVICES

Medium-sized towns along the route are often connected by bus services, which are relatively very cheap.

PETROL

Petrol stations are sometimes far apart or closed in the early morning; drivers are advised to fill up whenever possible.

TIME DIFFERENCE

Spanish time is one hour ahead of GMT. Lunch is not generally served before 2.30 p.m.
- Evening meals are not usually available until 9.30 or 10.00 p.m.
- Breakfast: not easily obtainable before 9.00 or 9.30 a.m.

Shops and offices are generally open from 9.30 a.m. - 1.30 p.m., and from 4.30-8.00 p.m. The siesta is sacrosanct, and often necessary because of the heat.

Monuments and museums are usually open to visitors from 10.00 a.m. - 1.00 p.m., but in the afternoon rarely reopen before 4.00 p.m.

It is sometimes necessary to seek out the key-holder.

Cinemas and theatres often have two performances, one before and one after the 10.00 p.m. meal.

It is easy to adapt to this pattern of timing; indeed it has its advantages. By starting out early, in the cool of the morning, walkers can cover a considerable distance before lunch-time.

Thus it is possible to eat in a restaurant and rest to avoid the furnace heat of summer afternoons, before walking further for some hours later in the day; or exploring the area, doing some late shopping, and enjoying the liveliness and freshness of the evening before dinner. Pay your hotel bills in the evening and make arrangements for breakfast - for example, by having a thermos flask filled by the hotel staff.

CLIMATE

Winters are cold along the whole of this route, most of which lies at an altitude of about 800m.

The sharp dry cold weather is pleasant for walking, but the damp chill of Navarre and Galicia is less agreeable.

Rain can be expected at any time of year along the first and last thirds of the itinerary, but particularly in spring, as is normal with an Atlantic climate.

Weather is generally pleasant in summer; but particularly
dry then in the middle section (the Meseta of the Burgos - León region) where the afternoons are very hot and the nights chilly.

THE BEST TIME OF YEAR

The pilgrimage can be undertaken at any time of year, and each season offers some advantages.

Summer is undoubtedly not the best time, for those who can choose when to go on holiday. There are crowds of tourists, heavy traffic on the melting tarmac of the main roads, crowded hotels and restaurants. The heat of the afternoons may be too much for some. Happily the days are very long, and it is possible to do most walking early in the day, continuing if necessary in the relative cool of the evening.

Winter is tempting, despite the sharp chill of the Meseta and the rains of Navarre and Galicia; this is the best season for appreciating the grandeur and immensity of the landscape.

The cold, often accompanied by dampness, would not be a drawback if one could be absolutely certain of finding somewhere comfortable and well heated for the night ..

The spring, which is often damp and mild, is not our choice; we would undoubtedly suggest autumn as the best time of year.

MEALS

Most Spanish restaurant meals are fairly rich in oil and protein (charcuterie, fish, meat with chips), but may offer less choice of salads, green vegetables, cheese, yoghurt, and fruit.

However, it is possible to obtain well-balanced meals by requesting, for example:

Verduras - cooked vegetables, often in the form of a thick vegetable soup;

Ensalada - raw vegetable salad with tomatoes.

It is also possible to buy yoghurt and fruit to complement or balance the meals available.

Another suggestion: have a light snack an hour earlier; one of the wide variety of *'tapas'* served in bars with aperitifs, which an be eaten with a glass of wine or beer, or a *'café cortado'* (white coffee).

Since breakfast is served late by our standards, you can make your own arrangements, for example, by asking the hotel staff to fill a thermos flask with coffee at the end of the evening meal.

Be wary of Spanish wines, which often have a high alcohol rating - but they are very good!

In summer, because of the heat, it is wise to respect elementary rules of hygiene and care: peel fruit, be careful with ice-cream, drink mineral water (usually very cheap) rather than tap-water, which is often highly chlorinated.

PLACE-NAMES

The spelling of Spanish place-names tends to differ from one set of published maps to another. Even the Spanish equivalent of the British Ordnance Survey maps are not entirely innocent of variation, and minor differences may be noted between the two sets of maps from the French edition which are reproduced in this
guide. This is not likely to cause serious confusion. But for the sake of consistency, and for the convenience of travellers wishing to see their pilgrimage within the wider context of Northern Spain as a whole, we have matched the spelling of place-names throughout the text with that of the Michelin 1:400,000 series recommended above, which are widely available in the UK and most European countries.

DISTANCES AND ALTITUDES

Throughout this guide the words 'kilometres' and 'metres' spelt out in full indicate distances to be covered or e.g. the lengths of buildings, etc. Where the abbreviation 'm.' is used for metres it relates specifically to altitude.

BEFORE SETTING OUT

T he distance from the Col de Roncesvalles to Santiago de Compostela is about 580 kilometres as the crow flies, and about 800 kilometres on foot. For this reason a Béarn farmer in Sauvelade, accustomed to seeing walkers on the GR65 long-distance footpath crossing his land, was nonetheless taken aback to hear a young German commenting: 'We've been on the road for six weeks now; another six weeks and we'll be there.' If you come from Le Puy, or along any of the other ancient tracks across France, you are already thoroughly hooked. If you start from Saint-Jean-Pied-de-Port (Saint-Jean at the foot of the pass), arm yourself with courage and patience; but remember that this expedition through space and time, across frontiers and centuries, is so spellbinding that even if you set out to cover only part of the route, after a few stages you will have only one dream in mind: to complete the whole of this magnificent pilgrimage ... or to come back and complete it another day if time is short. Certain stages are as beautiful as any of the waymarked footpaths of France; others so insistently monotonous that in the end they acquire their own strange beauty. All are so laden with monuments, ancient stones, historic reminders, legends, and paving worn by the tread of sandalled feet, that in your solitude you will seem to walk with a crowd of ghosts, the ghosts of the millions of pilgrims who have walked the route before you.

Stage 1 - 28 kilometres - 7 hours 30 minutes

SAINT-JEAN-PIED-DE-PORT (181M)
TO BURGUETE (893M)

The distances and times indicated along each day's route are merely suggestions: you may walk faster or more slowly; you may prefer other stopping places to suit your pace or individual plans. In this first stage, for example, travellers seeking the original spirit of the pilgrimage will appreciate the welcome at the Roncesvalles monastery, which deserves a full day of exploration and meditation. The timings and breaks suggested should however help you to know exactly where you are and how much more ground can be covered before nightfall. The mountain route from Saint-Jean-Pied-de-Port to Roncesvalles is magnificent, usually free of snow, and always open from May to December; it will present no problems to anyone used to mountains, nor to the fit cyclist. As almost all the route is suitable for cycling in dry weather, we have included detailed distances as well as the usual timing.

Walkers unused to hills are warned that this stage involves climbing a total of 1,300m; however, you will be rewarded by magnificent views of the mountain peaks, and the descent to Roncesvalles.

Reminders of Julius Caesar, Charlemagne and Napoleon are constant companions along these tracks where the final red and white markings of the French GR65 long-distance footpath meet the first yellow signs of the Spanish waymarking. Charlemagne is the only one of the three who probably came here in person, but after Caesar's lieutenant, Crassus, had conquered the Basque region of Aquitaine, the town of Imus Portus was established near Saint-Jean-le-Vieux. Our path lies through mountains which echoed to the sound of Roland's horn announcing the death of the gallant knight. And although Napoleon's ill-fated expedition to conquer the Spanish kingdom set out from Bayonne, his retreating and defeated armies must have returned along the route which has borne his name ever since.

IF YOU CHOOSE THE VALCARLOS ROUTE

Although the Route Napoleon is the one followed by Aymeric Picaud and is the best for the modern walker, the main road from Saint-Jean-Pied-de-Port to Roncesvalles has its own honourable Santiago ancestry. Used by pilgrim chroniclers such as Nompar, Caumont, Munzer and Laffi, this route follows approximately the modern C135 road. Even before you reach the frontier bridge at Arnéguy, the left bank of the River Nive is Spanish, and bridges offer access to the 'markets' on the other side for tourists tempted to try a little smuggling. Beyond Arnéguy the road changes banks, and countries. The Nive divides the bustling commercial Spanish village of Valcarlos from the rural French district of Ondarolle: but here too there are sturdy footbridges across the river, and many French Basques are baptised in the Spanish church.

Two houses, one in the village and the other a little farther on, in the hamlet of Gañecoleta, retain the name of old pilgrim 'hospitals'- the term used over the centuries, and throughout this guide, for the hostels and hospices specially set up to provide rest and hospitality for pilgrims.

SURVIVING TRACES OF THE OLD ROAD

- On the way into Saint-Michel there was a Monastery and the 'hospital' of Saint-Vincent in 1072. The Arbalaenia house still has a 1617 door-lintel with an abbot's crook and Roncesvalles cross.
- At Orisson the Priory of Sainte-Marie-Madeleine was exempted from taxes by Charles III of Navarre, in recognition of the help it offered to pilgrims.
- The fortress at Château-Pignon was built by Ferdinand the Catholic when he took possession of Spanish Navarre.
- The Elizacharra hermitage belonged to the Roncesvalles monastery.

THE BELL OF
SAN SALVADOR DE IBAÑETA

The very modern chapel of San Salvador (St Saviour) at Puerto (or Col) de Ibañeta was built in 1965; it replaced the now vanished chapel whose bell guided pilgrims from 1071 onwards through mist and darkness. The inscription in Basque, Spanish, and French on the column

0.00 - Saint-Jean-Pied-de-Port, Porte Notre Dame and the old bridge over the river Nive, altitude 170m. Climb the narrow and picturesque rue d'Espagne, heading south-south-west. Leave the town by the Porte d'Espagne; continue south-south-west along the tarmac road, passing on your right (west) the Rue de Mayorga and the red and white waymarkings of the French GR10 footpath, which we will rejoin above the Carrosse turn.

0.12 - Leave the D301 as it bears south-east, and climb up right, south-south-west, along the 'Route Napoléon' leading up to the Col d'Arnostéguy (1,256m, frontier marker 205), 18 kilometres ahead. Note the red and white waymarkings of the GR65 footpath, the Road to Santiago through south-west France, and the yellow markings which will be very important in future stages of the walk.

1.00 - On your left is the Etchebestea house, 312m. Ignore a 90-degree turning to the right, then two tarmac side roads to the left soon after, which come together further down.

1.10 - Ignore a turning to the left beside a very large tree, leading down Saint-Michel; continue upwards to the hamlet of Honto, and go through it.

1.40 - At an altitude of 540m, 200 metres beyond the final farm in Honto, leave the road temporarily as it makes a wide bend to the right, and take the old road through some tight hairpin bends up the ridge.

2.00 - Rejoin the tarmac road at 710m, and continue up it. The GR10 comes in again at 1,040m, above the Carrosse turning.

3.30 - At 1,095m, pass the Orisson Virgin and the GR10 on your left. Continue along the ridge road for

beside it invites travellers to pray to the Virgin of Roncesvalles.

THE REAL BATTLE OF RONCESVALLES

A monolithic monument near Ibañeta chapel is decorated with a wrought-iron 'Durandal', Roland's sword, dedicated to the hero who was conquered near here, probably at the Izandorre col.

Valcarlos means 'Charles's valley' - referring of course to Charlemagne. The well-known *Chanson de Roland* tells how this valiant knight, along with the twelve Peers, was killed by the Saracens at Roncesvalles. The *Chanson* is a legend, put into verse in the 12th century - some four hundred years after the event, which is more accurately described in the Latin chronicle of the monk Eghinard. The real politico-religious circumstances were much more complicated than the legend: the 'Moors' were frequently Spanish troops who rallied to Islam, and it was the 'Moorish King' of Saragossa whom Charlemagne sought to help, to draw him away from the protection of Abd-El-Rahman (or Abderrahman), the Emir of Córdoba. Since the army of the Franks had destroyed the ramparts of Pamplona when the town resisted them, the local Navarre people - the Vascones, i.e. Basques - set up their famous onslaught on his rearguard on 15 August 778. Modern historians think that the Franks are more likely to have followed the track along the ridges and through Blancpignon than the modern route; the two come together at the Col de Ibañeta. Here the Basques were waiting for them, on the heights of Astobizcar (1,606m), which is markedly steeper on the eastern slope.

RONCESVALLES: THE 'HOSPITAL' SERVING 30,000 MEALS

Roncesvalles today consists of a few houses clustered round a fortress-like monastery, with the path leading down to it. In olden times the path ran through the monastery, beneath two arches, but modern travellers have to go round the side, to ring and be admitted as visitors.

It was founded in 1132 by the Bishop of Pamplona, Sancho Larrosa, who was moved by the fate of the many pilgrims who fell victim to the snow and the wolves.

another 3.5 kilometres. It goes just to the south of the Pic d'Hostateguy, 1,142m; then below and west of the ancient fortress of Château-Pignon (1,177m). Ignore the tarmac road to Arnéguy on your right; go on up from the Col d'Elhursaro (1,152m), west round the Urdanasburu peaks, at 1,233m, and Urdanarre, 1,240m. After this the road follows the ridge.

4.30 - At 1,240m leave the road for the last time as it continues almost horizontally across the mountainside towards the Col d'Arnostéguy three kilometres away. Shortly before a cromlech which has unfortunately been knocked down to form a hunting-post, turn up to the right (south) along the old grass track, which disappears occasionally, heading for a col between the pyramid shape of Liezar Atheka and the oblong ridge north of the pass.

4.45 - Col at 1,300m in the ridge north of Leizar Atheka. Clearly marked, the track continues south - west and level, above the woods.

4.55 - Frontier marker 198, at 1,290m. Following a gully for 100 metres, the track crosses the ridge west of Leizar Atheka at 1,305m, and heads south-south-east beside a fence.

5.00 - Marker 199, 1,344m. Turn right, crossing the fence and ditch with wire netting, into Spain. At the time of writing this marked the end of the GR65 waymarking. The track bends to the right, passing close to the ruined Bentarte huts at 1,330m, and enters the beech-wood on the northern flank of Changoa.

5.25 - Ruin on your left (Elizacharra: possibly an old chapel or pilgrims' shelter); on the right, a small stock-yard and a stone hut.

5.35 - Col at 1,370m. Ignore a path down to your right just before a

Three years later the Augustinian canons made it one of Christendom's great 'hospitals'. Until the 18th century it would take in travellers for three days; they found meals, hot water and baths as well, a barber, and shoemenders - as important in those days as garage mechanics in the 20th century. The monastery served up to 30,000 meals a year, an average of a hundred each day.

VISITING RONCESVALLES

Inside the monastery the 14th-century cloister, damaged by an avalanche in 1600, leads to the chapel of St Augustine and the collegiate church.

In the *Capilla de San Agustín*, the 14th-century former chapter-house, visitors can see the tomb of Sancho the Great, 2.25 metres long, or 7ft 6ins, like his effigy on top, and on the walls two fragments of the chains used to secure the tent of a Muslim king, brought back from his victory at Las Naves de Tolosa; since then they have formed part of the Navarre coat of arms.

The *collegiate church*, built on his instructions in about 1200, is an outstanding example of French Gothic architecture in Spain. Its three naves, ten galleries and ten rose-windows are reminiscent of Chartres and the churches of Burgundy. Among other sights worth seeing is the 13th-century Virgin of Sorrows, with diamond tears.

Some exceptionally fine treasures are preserved in the museum in the south wing.

Outside, the *13th-century Capilla de Santiago* (St James's Chapel) holds the bell which used to ring for the pilgrims at the Puerto de Ibañeta. A little farther on, the pre-Romanesque *Capilla Sancti Spiritus* (Chapel of the Holy Spirit) was attached to the cemetery used for the burial of pilgrims who died there. A spring in a nearby meadow is known as 'the Virgin's Fountain'.

junction of tracks, an area often damaged by heavy machinery. Ignore another track down to the left, south-west, and continue along the track across the east flank of Mendi-Chipi, heading broadly south-west.

6.00 - Col Lepoeder, 1,430m. Go down the small tarmac road linking the Roncesvalles col to the Orzanzurieta television relay station; sadly, the road has destroyed the old track, although it is still visible in places.

6.50 - Puerto de Ibañeta or Col de Roncesvalles, 1,057m, on the watershed between the Atlantic and the Mediterranean. Modern chapel and monument to Roland. The C135 road goes through the pass, the Spanish road linking Pamplona (49 kilometres away) with Arnéguy (19 kilometres); this point is therefore 27 kilometres from St-Jean-Pied-de-Port. There is no need to stay on the tarmac to get down to the abbey; follow the yellow waymarking straight down through the woods, below the road.

7.05 - Roncesvalles, 925m. Abbey with collegiate church and cloister. The route goes through the imposing site and rejoins the C135, with a public telephone box beside it and a bar-restaurant which also has rooms available for part of the year. Continue along the road to Burguete.

7.30 - BURGUETE, 893m. Provisions and accommodation available.

ROLAND'S CROSS

The carved cross on the way out of Roncesvalles, of very antiquated appearance, dates in fact from 1880. It replaced the ancient *'Cruz de Roldán'* which was destroyed by the French revolutionary armies in 1794 as a 'tribute to the spirits of our ancestors'.

ACCOMMODATION

Saint-Jean-Pied-de-Port:
- Several hotels/restaurants open throughout the year.

Roncesvalles:
- An inn, Casa Sabina, tel. 76.00.12.

Burguete:
- H** Burguete, tel. 76.00.05
- H** Loizu, tel. 76.00.08
- H** Mendi Txuri, tel. 76.00.49
- H** Juandeaburre, tel. 76.00.78
- Bar-restaurant Asado Maritxu
- Campsite with bar Urrobi, 2 kilometres south of the village.

FREE ACCOMMODATION

Roncesvalles: Enquire at the monastery.

ACCOMMODATION OFF THE ROUTE

Valcarlos: Hotel and fonda.

ALTERNATIVES:
- Avoid 9 kilometres of tarmac by taking the very pleasant parallel route of the GR10 from St-Jean-Pied-de-Port to marker 1,095.
- You can easily reach the Col d'Arnostéguy and then the ruined Bentarte huts by following the frontier fence from marker 205 to marker 200. This is the route of the High Pyrenees long-distance footpath.
- For further details, consult the Randonnées Pyrénéennes map, scale 1:50 000, PAYS BASQUE EST.

NOTE

At the Lepoeder col (6.00) the waymarking cuts off the first two hairpin bends, and runs through a magnificent beechwood. This route, heading roughly south-west, is steep but well marked. The footpath becomes a track, less steep, leading straight to the abbey at Roncesvalles.

The only drawback to this attractive route is that it omits the famous Roncesvalles pass.

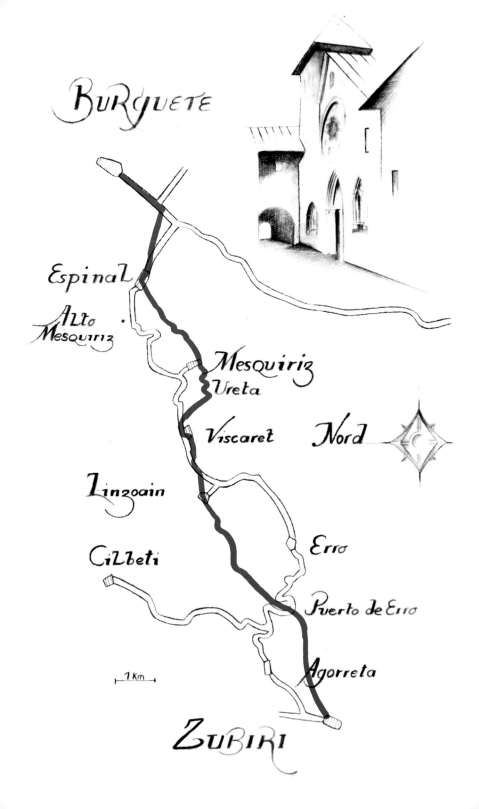

BURGUETE

Espinal

Alto
Mesquiriz

Mesquiriz

Ureta

Viscaret

Nord

Linzoain

Erro

Cilbeti

Puerto de Erro

1 Km

Agorreta

ZUBIRI

Stage 2 - 20 kilometres - 5 hours

BURGUETE (893M) TO ZUBIRI (526M)

T his is a short stage without any great challenges, except perhaps the risk of getting lost; after Linzóain, walkers are advised to follow the text, and the waymarking, with care. The route - which is a good example of the terrain to come - often follows the true Road to Santiago; there are recognisable traces and it is well-remembered, as can be learnt from conversation with people who live along the route. The waymarking, sometimes very intensive, generally enables walkers to avoid sections where the old track has been swallowed up and covered in tarmac. Cyclists can safely follow this route in dry weather, though otherwise they would be well-advised to stick to the road, which is peaceful apart from the summer holiday season. No important monuments still remain, but many stones bear heraldic markings and place-names are echoes of the past. This is our second day in the old Kingdom of Navarre, proud of its long independence; earlier it was the home of the turbulent Vascons who gave their name to Gascony.

THE HERALDIC HOUSES OF BURGUETE AND EL ESPINAL

Both places were created by Roncesvalles to extend its capacity. Three kilometres from the collegiate church, the 'Bourg' belonged to the French from Conques until 1151, then to the Sainte-Christine, or Santa Cristina, du Somport foundation until 1219, before becoming Burguete, a completely independent village. The great houses in the Pyrenean Basque style along the main street-itself part of the pilgrim Road-have stones carved with armorial bearings on their massive façades. Burguete's long history is visible in the boar which forms part of its coat of arms, and its traditions of 'hospitality'

0.00 - Burguete church, 893m. Follow the C135 road south-west for 1,900 metres.

0.25 - 100 metres beyond kilometre marker 43 turn right, north-west, on a gravel path; ignore a right turn 300 metres farther on.

0.45 - You reach the C135 again. Turn right, north-westwards, along it and through Espinal, 871m, with its modern church 500 metres away.

1.00 - Near the north-west end of the village turn left beside the Aunamendi house, along a small

are evident in the hotels and *pensions* for rural holidays. Espinal too has emblazoned doorways along its main street; the wrought-iron cross in the Santiago district is also worth seeing, and so, particularly, is the church of San Bartolomé; although modern it is none the less very attractive in its green setting.

OFF THE ROUTE:
A TRILINGUAL ROADSIDE COLUMN

If you follow the C135 instead of the old Road, you will find a modern trilingual column between Puerto de Espinal and Alto de Mezquíriz, inviting you in three languages - Basque, Spanish and French - to pray to Our Lady of Roncesvalles.

THE GASTRONOMIC PILGRIM
IN NAVARRE

Gastronomically speaking, Spain has two Navarres: the mountain and the plain.

Mountainous Navarre belongs to the 'sauce zone'. The wine is 'green' and quite light, known as 'Chacoli'.

Specialities include:
- 'Trucha a la Navarra', trout stuffed with a slice of ham;
- 'Calderete', 'Menestre de verdura', vegetable soup with mutton and chicken, seasoned with choriso sausage, snails and spices.

Southern Navarre, like Aragon, is part of the 'Chilindrón zone'; the wines here are the headier wines of Navarre.

Specialities include:
- 'Pollo a la Chilindrón' (chicken, although the recipe can also be used for kid, pigeon, rabbit, etc) served with a sauce of tomatoes and onions cooked in oil and seasoned with peppers; a southern version of the French Basque piperade.
- 'Pimientos rellenos' (stuffed peppers).

---

road which is tarmac at first.

1.05 - Junction of tracks: continue straight ahead, south-west, along a gravel path.

1.10 - Leave this track, turning right, west-north-west, beside a fence. After 200 metres go through a fence; follow the markings carefully, leading you through a col at 970m, approximately 1 kilometre south of the Puerto de Espinal on the C135, marked by the trilingual column, and continue along the footpaths.

1.30 - Join a larger track, with a barn 50 metres to your right, the Borda de Ademonia.

1.45 - Mesquíriz, 770m. From the centre of the village go south-south-west down a concrete-paved street, then westwards, leaving the church on your left.

1.52 - Fork: take the path to the left, south-west.

2.00 - Bear right, cross the bridge over a stream (mill on your right), then 100 metres farther on another bridge over a mountain stream (Rio Erro).

2.05 - Ureta, 750m. Take the hamlet's access road for about 100 metres north-eastwards, and turn left onto a path heading north-west.

2.12 - Close the gate behind you!

2.15 - Hilltop, 800m. Viscarret is clearly visible to the west and easily accessible; but the waymarking leads to the north.

2.25 - Rejoin the C135 and turn left, west, along it.

2.30 - Coming into Viscarret, 770m, the C135 skirts round on the north side. Take the first street to the left and through the village (follow the waymarking and if in doubt keep to the right).

THE CHI-RHO OF VISCARRET
AND THE CHURCH AT LINZOAIN

Superseded later by the expansion of Roncesvalles, Viscarret was a pilgrim staging-post in the 12th century. Some traces remain:

- A house in the virtually abandoned hamlet of Ureta, beyond the bridge at the mill, displays an escutcheon with the pilgrim's cross and scallop-shell.
- Viscarret - the Biscarretus of the *Codex* - still has a group of old houses; one with a Chi-Rho (the monogram of Greek letters used to represent the name of Christ) at the entrance must have been the 'hospital'. There is a small church with a Romanesque arch.
- at Linzóin, the modest church of St-Sernin is Romanesque in origin.

stamp here

ZUBIRI: FROM 'ROLAND'S STEPS' TO THE 'RABIES BRIDGE'

Here we are surrounded by the potent breath of legend .... some large stones 2 kilometres beyond Linzóain and its col are supposed to indicate the length of Roland's step, *los pasos de Roldan ;* he was undoubtedly a tall man!

On the way into Zubiri, in Basque, 'the village of the bridge', there is indeed a medieval construction crossing the River Arga. This was known as 'el puente de la rabia' for it was said that if an animal passed beneath it three times it would be cured of rabies. For some pilgrims it was also 'the bridge to Paradise', perhaps because of the delightful view of the Rio Arga valley ('the Esteríbar'), which the route now follows to Pamplona and even beyond, to Puente la Reina.

Zubiri's 13th-century church is transitional Romano-Gothic in style, the Urdaniz tower Romanesque. As early as 1042 there was a monastery here, connected with Leyre. The 'hospital' just before the bridge was probably a leprosarium.

AYMERIC'S DISLIKE OF THE BASQUES

We have already noted Aymeric Picaud's dislike or grudge regarding the Basque nation. The following extract from his narrative is significant:

2.35 - Heading west out of Viscarret follow the ancient Road, still clearly visible below and to the left of the road.

2.45 - Rejoin the C135 at the top of the slope (cemetery on your left). Go down the tarmac, westward, for about 500 metres.

2.50 - Follow a track along the right of the road (the track runs with water in wet weather) leading to Linzóain less than a kilometre to the west.

3.00 - Linzóain, 750m. Turn up a lane to the south-west, then a track to the west.

3.10 - Cross a broader track which you then join 300 metres further on.

3.22 - Leave the broad track and fork left, west-north-west.

3.25 - Ridge, 860m; junction of tracks. Cross a large one leading to Erro, and take another heading south-south-west. After 800 metres it crosses to the left flank of the ridge, and 600 metres farther on reaches the col.

3.45 - Col, junction of tracks. Follow the ridge track to the south-west, for 1 kilometre.

'They are a barbarous people, different from all others both in their customs and in their race, full of wickedness, dark in colouring, ugly, debauched, perverse, perfidious, treacherous, corrupt, dissolute, drunken, skilled in all violence, ferocious and savage, dishonest and false ... A man of Navarre or a Basque would kill a Frank if he could, for a penny.'

ACCOMMODATION

Espinal:
- Fonda Montain.
- Bar Jaso.
- Restaurant Basajaun.

Zubiri:
- Bar-restaurant Gau Txori, tel. 30.40.76.
- A grocery in the village has a few rooms to let.

OFF THE ROUTE

Erro:
- Fonda Oroz.
- Casa de Huespedes Cerdan.

FREE ACCOMMODATION

Zubiri: Enquire at the parish church.

4.00 - Puerto de Erro, 810m. Cross the C135 and take a broad track opposite, level at first, heading south-west.

After two fences it bears right, west, and 700 metres from the road reaches a half-ruined building used as a stable (Venta del Caminante, a former pilgrim hostel). Continue along the path which may be overgrown but is well marked. The roof-tops of Zubiri are soon visible. 5.00 - ZUBIRI, 526m. In a lane to the left on the way into the village, a bar and grocery, Casa Valentin, also arranges bed-and-breakfast accommodation. There is a restaurant, Gau Txori, 1 kilometre to the north, at the fork of the C135 and the Eugui road.

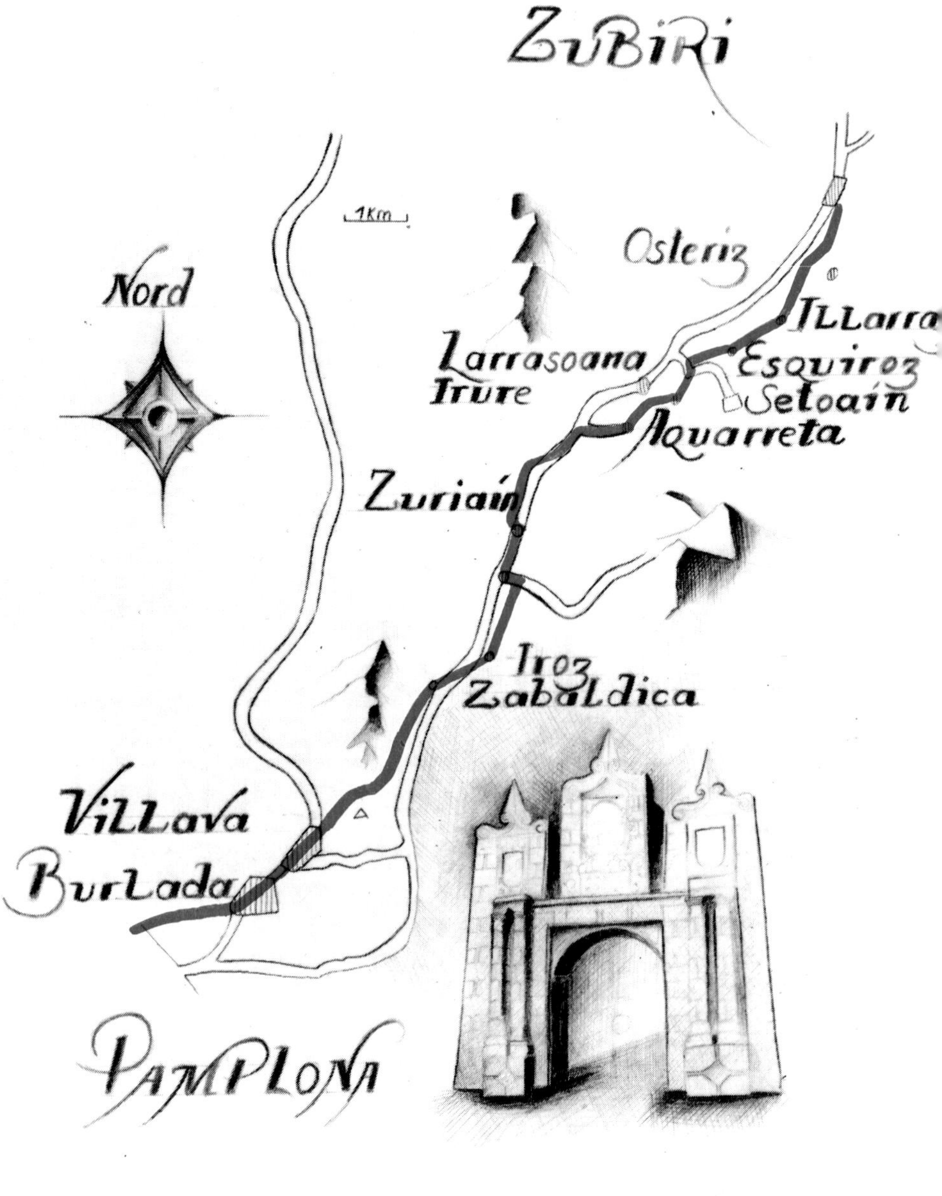

ZUBIRI

Nord

1Km

Osteriz

Illarra

Larrasoana
Irure

Esquiroz
Setoain

Aquarreta

Zuriain

Iroz
Zabaldica

Villava

Burlada

PAMPLONA

Stage 3 - 23 kilometres - 5 hours 30 minutes

ZUBIRI (526M) TO PAMPLONA (550M)

*A*n easy stage. For the first ten kilometres from Zubiri to Zabaldica, the Road to Santiago follows the ordinary motor road to Pamplona. This enables us to visit some picturesque little villages along the left bank of the Arga, which the waymarked route crosses.

After Zabaldica we continue on the Old Road to cross the ridge between the Arga and Ulzama river valleys, just to the north-east of Pamplona. Although the motor road and its traffic are not easily avoided between Villava and Burlada, our arrival in the capital of Navarre is a calm contrast. Leaving the traffic to find its way through the suburbs, we make a thoroughly stylish entry into the old city like the pilgrims of olden days, passing through the same gates and climbing the same ramparts, to reach the cathedral and the old streets lined with former pilgrim 'hospitals'. Pamplona is well worth a day's exploration.

THE 'CORTES' OF LARRASOAÑA

There are still armorially decorated houses and a fine 13th-century St Nicholas in the single street of Larrasoaña; there was an Augustinian monastery here in 1072 which was soon linked with Leyre. King Philip III of Evreux gathered the Cortes (the parliamentary assembly) of Navarre here in 1329, to swear his oath with Queen Juana II. There was a pilgrim 'hospital' and several hermitages. The old house on the right at the entrance, with the arch-stones, must have belonged to Roncesvalles.

0.00 - Zubiri, 526m. Thirty metres east of the old bridge over the Arga turn south along a tarmac lane which then becomes a track.

0.15 - 50 metres beyond a stream, at a crossways; continue straight ahead, south-west, with a fence on your right.

0.20 - 1 kilometre south of Zubiri, level with a factory (Fabrica de Magnesita) on your right and below the road, take the small tarmac road

REMAINS OF IROZ, ZABALDICA, AND ARLETA

Three modest places nearby, each with its own distinctive feature.

- in Iroz the River Arga bends to the west of the old road, which crosses it on an elegant Romanesque bridge.
- Zabaldica has a fine *statue of St James the Pilgrim in its church.*
- The Roman road from Bordeaux to Astorga passed through Arleta, where there are some disc-headed *burial stones;* one bears the cross of St James. The Santa-Marina church has a very plain Romanesque porch.

Off the waymarked route: the C135 road goes through Huarte, where the church has a 16th-century *white marble Virgin,* made in Paris.

THE SANTIAGO CROSSROADS AT TRINIDAD DE ARRE

Shortly before Villava we enter Trinidad de Arre across a three-arched bridge over the river Ulzama, a tributary of the Arga. The church is on the opposite bank. The N21 road from France via Velate, on the right, is also a secondary route to Santiago; hence the importance of the 'hospital' which existed here until the 16th century, and of which a few traces of the walls now remain.

to Esteriz, and follow it for 500 metres.

0.30 - Turn off it along a path to the right (south-west) for 600 metres.

0.40 - Cut across another path and go straight on down, beneath the high-tension wires. Continue down eastwards, skirting round to the left of two sedimentation pools, cross a cement footbridge, and turn along a track to the left, south.

0.55 - Iláraz farm, 560m. Follow its access road down for 600 metres.

1.00 - Turn off along a path to the left, south-west.

1.05 - Esquiroz. Continue southwest across a stream to a gravel road 500 metres farther on, and follow it for 200 metres to the south-west.

1.15 - Small tarmac road linking the C135 to the hamlet of Setoain; for once, leave the waymarking, which runs on down to Larrasoaña, and instead turn up the tarmac road for 400 metres to the left, south, then take the right fork, still going southwards, for Irure.

1.30 - Irure. Go through the hamlet and down a broad track to the west for 500 metres.

1.40 - Leave the bridge over the Arga and the village of Larrasaoña 30 metres to your right, north, and take the gravel track heading south-west.

2.00 - Hamlet of Aquerrete. Follow the narrow tarmac access road for 1,100 metres.

2.15 - Rejoin the C135, 150 metres north-east of the kilometre marker 'Pamplona 14', and follow this road for 700 metres, rejoining the waymarking.

2.25 - Turn right, south-west, on a track which runs parallel to the road.

2.30 - Note the kilometre marker 'Pamplona 13' 60 metres to the left. Continue along a footpath, then a

THE BRIDGES OF VILLAVA AND BURLADA

These are the last two towns before Pamplona.
- Villava has a restored five-arched bridge, and on its river bank the Romanesque chapel of the Trinity, with white-washed wooden decoration.
- Burlada, inhabited in 1184 by Sancho II the Wise, had a 12-bed 'hospital', in the 16th century, and a French priest. Its 'Puente de la Magdalena' is Romanesque, of the 13th century.

IRUÑA, POMPAELO, PAMPLONA

Three different names for the same city. Pamplona is the Spanish name, and Pompaelo its Latin original, for it was founded by Pompey in the 1st century BC to control a restless Basque people, the Vascones, who six centuries later gave their name to Gascony, invading and taking over the northern slopes of the Pyrenees. Iruña is the Basque name, witness to its enduring ethnic character through the centuries.

After its Visigoth and Islamic periods, a Basque 'king', Inigo Arista (died 851) was the first of the semi-legendary line of kings of Navarre which was to last for four centuries.

History in modern terms began around year 1000, with Sancho III the Great (El Mayor), whose kingdom ran from Pamplona to the Val d'Arán. During his reign the Cluniac reforms penetrated his lands, replacing the old Visigoth rituals and encouraging the expansion of Romanesque architecture.

Last in the line, Sancho VII the Strong (Sancho el Fuerte) was one of the Christian allies who defeated the Moors at Las Navas de Tolosa in 1212; it was he who brought back the famous iron chains from the camp of Emir Almohade which have figured since then in the arms of Navarre, and which appear at Roncevalles and in the cloister at Pamplona. He was succeeded by his nephew Thibaut IV of Champagne and I of Navarre - the first of a line of Franco-Navarrese kings. The last to reign over Pamplona was Jean d'Albret (Juan de Labrit), who lost his kingdom to Ferdinand of Aragon in 1512. The French 'Kings of Navarre' thereafter retained only the district of St-Jean-Pied-de-Port, and their title.

street, running from Zuriáin church down to the C135.

2.42 - You will reach the Pamplona road again 200 metres before kilometre marker 12; follow this road for 500 metres.

2.50 - Turn left, south, along the fork for Ilurdoz. After the bridge over the Arga continue along the footpath opposite, south, beneath the high tension cables. After a transformer, the waymarkings indicate the footpath to take, level at first, and very clear.

3.15 - The church at Iroz is on the right. Take a footpath heading initially south-south-west.

3.20 - Bridge over the Arga

3.22 - Return to the C135 near the 'Pamplona 10' kilometre marker, and follow the road for 600 metres.

3.30 - Zabaldica. Leave the C135 for the last time, heading west-south-west up towards the church along a broad track; turn left off this, south-west, after only 50 metres, aiming for a concrete high-tension line pylon 220 metres away. The track becomes clear and fully waymarked, although it passes high above Arleta, a hamlet which lay on the original Pilgrim Way.

3.50 - The waymarked route is liable to be interrupted here by a large area of ploughland; but the continuation of the track is visible to the south-west. Go round the field, either along its lower edge or by the ridge, with a view over Pamplona. In either case, continue southwards along the ridge.

4.10 - Col, 512m, north of Mont Miravalles, 597m. A small tarmac road drops gently down into Villava, less than 1 kilometre away.

4.25 - Bridge over the River Ulzama. Follow the road for 2 kilometres south-west towards Burlada, using the old

During Henri II d'Albret's final attempt to recapture Pamplona, Ignatius Loyola, captain of the Castilian army, was wounded beneath the ramparts, which led to his vocation to the religious life, and the foundation of the Jesuits.

During this long Franco-Navarrese period the 'Francos' arrived in great numbers, often from Aquitaine or Languedoc, following first in the footsteps of monks and pilgrims and later with their courts, choosing to live in the San-Saturnino and San Nicolás suburbs. They were granted privileged status in 1129 by the Fuero, or charter, de Jaca. During this time the Basque 'Navarreria', or Navarrese quarter, round the cathedral increasingly took on the character of a ghetto; hence the rivalries, as in 1276, when the Frankish 'burgueses' ravaged the 'Navarreria'. Finally a lasting peace was established. The Navarrese monarchy was deeply tolerant and did not agree to expel Jews until 1498, six years later than Castile.

CATHEDRAL, CLOISTER AND MUSEUM

- *The Gothic cathedral*, begun in 1497 and completed in the 18th century with a neo-classical façade, occupies the site of a Roman capitol, and later the first Romanesque cathedral. On its northern side the tower has the second largest bell in Spain - of twelve tons. Inside the church are several tombs including two very fine effigies, side by side for eternity: Charles III the Noble, builder of the church, and his wife Léonor. The choir is in the heavily ornamented 16th - century 'Plateresque' style.
- *The Gothic cloisters* of the cathedral are considered the finest in Spain, with some remarkable statues of the Virgin Mary.
- *The Diocesan Museum* in the former 'Hospital San Miguel' retains intact the refectory and the ancient pilgrims' kitchen with its four hearths open to the sky, forming an exterior tower. Each pilgrim received here a bowl of soup, a piece of meat, and a glass of wine.

PAMPLONA'S MONUMENTS

It is impossible to list here, even in summary, all the monuments in Pamplona; they deserve a whole book to themselves. Some comments, however, are relevant to the pilgrimage:
- The *Portal de Francia*, with fleur-de-lys.

route of the N121.

4.55 - Burlada. Just beyond the Renault dealer and the traffic lights, before No 11 of this 'Calle Mayor' and 200 metres before the bridge over the Arga, turn right, west, down a small one-way street. This crosses the modern route of the N121 and offers a quiet approach to the cathedral, which is clearly visible.

5.15 - Beyond a 'Ceda el paso' ('give way') sign, turn right then left, and cross the Arga by the Magdalena bridge.

5.20 - Traffic lights; cross an avenue, then head north-westwards across grass and through the trees towards the corner of the ramparts.

5.25 - From this north-eastern corner of the ramparts continue to the west.

5.28 - Portal de Francia.

5.29 - Portal de Zumalacarregui.

5.30 - Calle del Carmen, opposite, south.

5.33 - To the left, Calle de la Navarreria.

5.35 - The cathedral, which should certainly be visited. The pilgrims used to cross the city by the following route: Calle Curia - Plaza Consistorial - Calle de San Saturnino - Calle Mayor, and south-west towards the Avenida Pío XII; this comes into the fourth stage of our route.

- The *Zumalacaregui gateway* is named after a Basque leader in the Carlist war. The surviving fortifications date from the 16th century.

- The *church of San Saturnino:* 13th century, fortified, the oldest in the city; the north porch has a statue of St James with a pilgrim kneeling at his feet. Water from the well in front of the church was used by St Cernin to baptise Christians.

- The *Navarre Museum*, inaugurated in 1956 in the former 'Hospital de N.S. de la Misericordia' with its 16th-century porch, includes among the innumerable treasures in its 34 rooms the capitals of the first Romanesque cathedral.

- In the 11th-century Templo dei Castillo a baroque altar-piece depicts the legend of the pilgrim whose ass was stolen.

- *The Royal Chamber of Accounts and Deputation* holds immensely rich archives of the Kingdom of Navarre.

- Among the most famous pilgrim *'Alberguerias'* (inns for poor travellers), the Cofradia Santa Catalina, for the Spanish, was at 13 Calle Dormitaleria; and the inn for foreigners was at 3, Calle dei Obispo.

ACCOMMODATION

Villava:
- Restaurant Casa Sancho
- H Don Carlos, tel. 33.00.77
- for meals and information, enquire at the Centro Católico Espanol, 41 calle Mayor, tel. 11.03.61
- Circulo Carlista, 45 calle Mayor.

Pamplona:
Many hotels and restaurants, several near the Tourist Office, tel.22.07.42. We hear of a warm welcome at the Hostal Ibarras.

FREE ACCOMMODATION

Villava: Church of la Trinidad de Arre.
Pamplona: Apply to the Archbishopric, tel. 22.74.00.

PAMPLONA

Cizur Mayor

Nord

Cizur Me

GuenduLain

Galar

Astrain

Esparza

Zariquiegui

△ Perdon 1039m

1 km

Vterga

Murazabal

Adios

Obanos

Eunate

Eneriz

PUENTE LA REINA

Stage 4 - 28 kilometres - 7 hours

PAMPLONA (450M) TO PUENTE LA REINA (346M)

A lthough this is a long stage, it is not difficult and can be undertaken at any time of year. Crossing the Sierra del Perdón requires a climb of only some 330m, and brings the reward of a vast panoramic view in good weather. The rural route takes us through some very picturesque villages and past interesting monuments.

In particular, for those with energy and time, it is well worth making the 4- to 5-kilometre detour between Murazábal and Obanos to see the octagonal chapel at Eunate, one of the jewels of the Aragon route, which here joins up with our Navarre route to form the single 'CAMINO FRANCÉS'.

The stage ends by taking us through the beautiful medieval pilgrim town of Puente la Reina as far as the famous 'Queen's Bridge' itself, the starting point of the next day's walk.

THE COMMANDERY AT CIZUR MENOR

Visible from far off on its hill, Cizur Menor still has the ruins of a 12th-century Commandery of the Order of St John and a Romanesque church with an attractive porch, each of its three arches resting on its own slender columns, with a Chi-Rho. The former pilgrims' inn at No 1, Calle San Emeterio is still called 'Hospitalecoa'.

0.00 - Pamplona cathedral: go down the Calle Curia, south-west.

0.05 - Plaza Consistorial. Continue westwards down the Calle de San Saturnino.

0.08 - Next take the Calle Mayor, heading west-south-west.

0.16 - Cross the Avenida de

OFF THE ROUTE: GAZOLAZ, ASTRAIN, BASONGAIZ, EUNATE

- Three kilometres west of Cizur lies the Romanesque church at Gazolaz with an arcaded portico.
- Two kilometres west of Guendulain on the N111, Astráin still has its Virgin of the Pardon which originally came from the hermitage of the same name.
- At Basongaiz, also on the N111, beyond the col of Alto del Perdón, there is a Maltese cross above the doors of the chapel and of one of the houses, and statues of saints dating from the 12th century (John the Baptist) and the 14th century (Blaise).
- A small and easy detour on leaving Muruzábal leads to the splendid chapel at Eunate, the jewel of the 'Camino Aragonés' (see the chapter on that route, below).

Guipuzcoa, south-west into the Calle del Bosque Cello opposite.

0.20 - Avenida Pio XII, the urban section of the road to Logroño; follow it south-westwards.

0.45 - Pass the Clínica Universitaria, leaving it on your right. 100 metres beyond it, turn left off the Logroño road, down steps and along a path across the university campus.

0.50 - Follow a small road and cross a bridge over the River Sadar.

1.00 - 400 metres farther on, cross a bridge over the River Elorz.

1.05 - Where the road goes up to cross the railway, the waymarking guides you down and to the right to use the level crossing.

1.10 - At the crossroads 300 metres beyond the railway bridge, take the small road to Campanas.

1.25 - Cizur-Menor, 483m. Slightly to your left can be seen the Romanesque church of the old 'hospital' (and farther away, on the right, a restored chapel on the hill overlooking the village). From the crossroads at the top of the slope take the Campanas road for 200 metres to the south-west. Pass a drinking-trough and a sort of hollow on your left and turn right, south-west, along a track suitable for vehicles.

1.35 - After 500 metres ignore a tarmac road to the left, then a modern building-site on the right, and continue along the path parallel to the electricity cables.

1.40 - Carry on in the same direction (south-west) along a muddy track across the fields if they are fallow; if there are crops growing, go round to the north-west alongside a small hillock.

OLD HOUSES IN GUENDULAIN, ZARIQUIEGUI, UTERGA, MURUZABAL

- The village of Guendulain, now largely abandoned, still has its *Palace of the Counts.*
- Zariquiergui, with its Basque ornamental façade and cypress trees in the cemetery visible from afar, has a Romanesque church and armorially decorated houses with their eaves overhanging the paved roadway.
- Uterga has a fountain and emblazoned houses.
- In the lovely church at Muruzàbal St James is represented on the altar-piece in one of the side chapels.

OBANOS: THE MYSTERY OF SAN GUILLEN AND SANTA FELICIA

The church with its 13th-century Virgin from the hermitage, the Town Hall, and the seigneurial houses in Obanos, have all been impressively restored. The houses were the gathering places for the 'Infançones' of Navarre, gentlemen of the lesser nobility who, notably in the 13th and 14th centuries, provided an outspoken voice counterbalancing royal power.

Obanos is known today for the 'Mystery' play presented each year on 20 and 27 August, with 700 local inhabitants performing for 2,000 spectators in a well-equipped theatrical arena.

This is the 'Mystery of San Guillén and Santa Felicia'. Ste Felicité was a princess from Aquitaine who, after making a pilgrimage to Compostela, renounced her wealth and remained in Amocáin to take up a life of prayer there. Her brother Guilhem, unconvinced by the explanations of her retainers, sought her out and killed her; then, seized with remorse, he too journeyed to Compostela and returned to do penance at the sanctuary of the Virgin of Arnotegui, close by.

Let us hope that this tradition will continue down the years despite the interruptions it has experienced.

THE LINK WITH AQUITAINE: HISTORY AND LEGEND

Does the Obanos legend have any historical foundation? As so often, nothing is certain; but in view of attitudes at the time it is by no means improbable. Separate from the Gascony of the dukes Sancho, the Roman province

2.00 - 400 metres beyond a large metal high-tension line pylon the track goes over a hillock, passing under the high-tension lines.

2.10 - At the end of this follow the tarmac road towards Galar for 300 metres (the village itself lies 1,500 metres to the south); go beneath the high-tension lines and continue along a broad gravel track, still heading south-west. This track becomes grassy and muddy, but the route is clear, with Galar 800 metres away on a hillock to your left, south-east.

2.30 - After passing under two high-tension cables, and a few hundred metres before reaching a stream which is to be crossed, the old route becomes overgrown. The waymarking leads you slightly up and to the left, south-west, along the edge of a field, and across the stream on the right, 100 metres upstream from a large more or less ruined building. This stretch is the only slightly difficult part of this stage, and it is important to follow the markings carefully. On the left bank of the stream pass close to the large building, leaving it on your right; 50 metres farther on join a broad track, and turn left along it.

3.00 - Guendulain, 520 m: church

of Aquitaine (between the Loire and the Dordogne) had the dynasty of the Guillaumes (Guilhem/William), dukes of Poitiers and Aquitaine, with such picturesque names as William the Pious, William-Oakum-Head, William IV-Iron-Arm, William V-The-Great (who in about 1000 united Aquitaine and Gascony through marriage), William IX-The-Troubadour, etc. The only definite detail is that in 1984 calcined bones were found in a silver reliquary at Obanos in 1984, along with an old Compostela medallion.

'THERE IS ONLY ONE ROAD NOW'

On the way into Puente La Reina from Obanos a modern statue of a pilgrim, erected in 1965, bears a plaque recalling that the Aragon and Navarre pilgrim routes combined here to form a single 'French Road': *'Y desde aqui, todos los caminos a Santiago se hacen uno solo'.*

This inscription includes two minor errors:

- Firstly, it ignores various other lesser known routes to Santiago, such as the Cantabrian Road, or the 'Ruta Mozarabe' via Seville and Salamanca;

- Secondly, the reference to the start of the single 'French Road' is also incorrect, as it locates this at the modern junction of the main motor roads, whereas the true crossways were some 1,500 metres higher up the hill. The pilgrims arriving from Aragon joined the Navarre route on their way out of Obanos - to be precise, at the Hermitage.

PUENTE LA REINA, TOWN OF THE PILGRIMAGE

The town's development was entirely due to the pilgrimage and took its name from the bridge built in the 11th century on the orders of a charitable queen, as explained below. From then on a group of 'Francos' settled there to greet the pilgrims. It was however Alfonso the Quarrelsome, Aragon king of the Reconquest, who a century later gave it its 'bastide' shape, with the grid pattern of streets surrounded by walls and towers. The present ramparts date from the 13th century. The Road to Santiago runs in through a vaulted passage way between the church of the Crucifix and the old 'hospital', and becomes the main street of the town, the 'Rúa Maior' or 'Calle de los Romeus'. It still retains an impressive

and large building, partly ruined. Leave them on your left and continue along the track, which is suitable for vehicles, for about 200 metres, heading west. Then turn left, south, onto a track down through the fields to Zariquiegi, the village clearly visible 2 kilometres to the south-west.

3.10-Junction of tracks; turn right, south-west, on a broad track.

3.30 - Go past a small cemetery on a hillock to your left to reach Zariguiegui, 570m. Go through the village and take a wide gravel track heading south-south-west.

3.40 - Where the track forks, ignore the left turn and continue straight on, west, following the waymarking which sometimes indicates short-cuts along the twisting track.

3.50 - The route climbs along the hillside, reduced to a small path.

4.00 - It broadens out again.

4.10-Go underneath a high-tension line.

4.15 - Before reaching the edge of the wood turn right, to the west of the field. Spring on the left.

4.20 - You reach the ridge of the Sierra del Perdón, 780m, with a panoramic view. Cross the small ridge road, which links the Perdón pass, 2 kilometres to the north-west on the N111 to Logroño, with the 1,039m peak of the same name, 4 kilometres to the south-east, and go down to the south-west off the path. After 100 metres cross a level track to continue south-west down another broad track strewn with pebbles from the crumbling pudding-stone.

4.37 - Fork: bear left, south-south-east.

4.41 - Go through a gate.

4.43 - Take a track to the south-south-west.

5.00 - Continue along a footpath heading south.

medieval atmosphere - houses with gothic doors and capitals, the open stream down the middle of the roadway, and the many churches.

At the entrance the *Iglesia del Crucifijo*, square and topped with a substantial bell-tower pierced by semi-circular openings, still displays the sign of the Templars who built it and ran a 'hospital' here, succeeded in modern times by a school. The ogival porch is carved with scallop-shells and plants. The original plain Romanesque 12th-century nave was matched in the 14th century by another nave with three bays, with a figure of Christ nailed to a Y-shaped cross, no doubt of Rhenish origin.

Half-way along the Calle Maior, is the *church of Santiago*, rebuilt in the 16th century, but retaining its original Romanesque porch, one of whose five arches is 'multilobed', i.e. with a fringe of the small 'Mozarabic' arches we shall find again in Cirauqui and Estella. Inside, the baroque altar-piece illustrates the life of St James. Above all, facing the entrance, you will admire the magnificent carved cedar-wood statue of St James the Pilgrim, barefoot, staff in hand, scallop-shells on his hat, and his face emaciated and ecstatic. It was known as 'beltea', Basque for black, because of the darkening effect of candle smoke, and was only recently rescued from imminent danger of being thrown out for firewood.

ACCOMMODATION

Obanos:
- Hs** Hospederia Arnotegui, tel. 34.01.53.

Puente La Reina:
- H** Mesón del Peregrino, on the corner of the Campanas and the N111 roads, tel. 34.00.75.
- Fonda Lorca, in the village, tel. 34.01.27.
- Bar-restaurant-hostel, tel. 34.01.46

FREE ACCOMMODATION

Puente La Reina: Enquire at the Monastery of the Crucifix.

5.15 - Uterga, 495m. Carry on south-south-west from the village for 2.5 kilometres on a small peaceful road to Muruzàbal.
5.50 - Muruzàbal, 445m. Leave by the Obanos road, and 100 metres beyond the last houses turn right, west-south-west, off the tarmac road onto an overgrown thorny path, following the telephone wires. Then continue along the old grassy track, followed by a gravel path up to Obanos.
6.30 - Obanos, 414m. Restaurant. Leave the village by way of a concreted lane bearing west (FARMACÍA, (chemist), on the right). Beyond the last buildings go down a broad track heading west.
6.45 - Join the road from Puente la Reina to Campanas, and follow it westward for 500 metres.
6.52 - Rejoin the N111 (Pamplona-Puenta la Reina-Logro{n} o road): a modern statue of a pilgrim marks the junction of the two major routes, one from Somport and the other from Roncesvalles. Turn south-west along the N111.
7.00 - Puenta la Reina, 346m. The Pilgrim Way turns left off the N111 into a street leading between the monastery and the church of the Crucifix, then crosses the N111 which has taken a right-angle bend, and goes due west through the old town along the impressive Calle Mayor leading to the famous bridge over the River Arga. Provisions, restaurants, hotels, and garages are all available in this delightful small town.

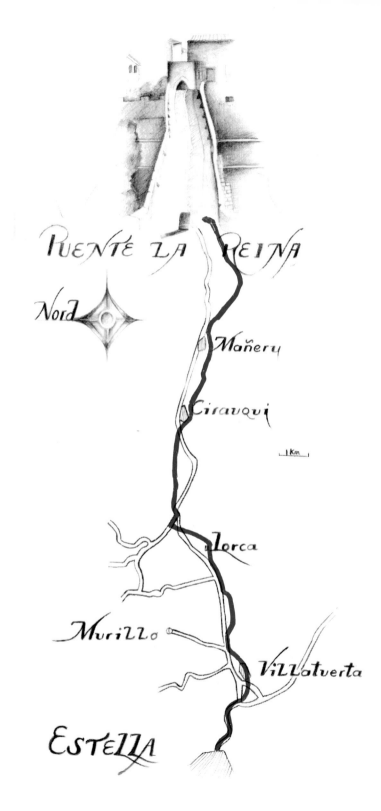

PUENTE LA REINA

Nord

Mañeru

Cirauqui

| Km |

Lorca

Murillo

Villatuerta

ESTELLA

Stage 5 - 20 kilometres - 6 hours

PUENTA LA REINA TO ESTELLA

O ur route along this easy stage runs very close to the N111 road, keeping off it as much as possible, although there are short stretches where it is unavoidable and it is impossible to evade tarmac over the final stretch. We have left the green Navarrese Pyrenees now, to cross ochre hillsides covered with crops and scented vegetation which is almost Mediterranean. Cirauqui, where the route skirts round below the town, is worth a stroll along the old steep streets up to the multilobed arches of its church porch. But walkers must keep enough time in hand to visit Estella, one of the most important places along the Pilgrim Way.

THE QUEEN'S BRIDGE AND THE BLESSING OF TXORI

The route leaves Puenta la Reina by the 'Queen's Bridge' which gave the town its name, crossing the River Arga, a tributary of the Ebro, for the last time. Until the year 1000 it had only a ford, much feared by pilgrims both for its sudden floods and its ferrymen. It is not known whether the queen who took pity on them was Doña Estefanía, wife of García de Nájera, or Elvira, known as Doña Mayor, wife of Sancho el Mayor. One or other had this fine hump-backed bridge built, with its six pointed arches and open pillars.

0.00 - Puente la Reina. Cross the River Arga by the famous bridge and at the western end turn left, cross the N111 and follow a road heading south-west.

0.10 - Wayside Calvary. Ignore the Old Road, the N111 and the Eunea buildings on the right, and take a small gravel road bearing west-south-west, followed by a broad track.

0.23 - Continue beside the Arga, on your left.

0.38 - Bend in the track; fork right,

The figure of the Virgin which used to stand on the parapet has been moved to the Romanesque church of San Pedro nearby. The Navarrese, who liked to share their joys with her, called her the Virgen del Txori (The Virgin of the Little Bird) because of a charming legend: when the birds flying upstream appeared to sprinkle water on her from their damp wings, it was a sign of a good year to come.

MAÑERU'S THIRTY ESCUTCHEONS

A stone cross on a polygonal base greets us on the way into Mañeru, where more than thirty armorial shields are displayed on the houses. The village belonged to the Order of St John; the round church of San Pedro, with its tower, is the work of the architect who was also responsible for the baroque façade of Pamplona cathedral.

THE 'CALZADA' AND THE MULTILOBED PORCH OF CIRAUQUI

Although the path skirts round the village, Cirauqui is worth a visit. The multilobed entrance to the church of San Román (13th century, like its neighbour, Santa-Catalina), in its high setting, is one of three which reveal Moorish influences; we have already seen one in Puente la Reina, and will see the third at Estella.

A typical medieval street leads up to the church, through arched gateways bordered with coats of arms and corniced walls with narrow steps leading up them. The way down, and out of the walled ramparts, is the 'Calzada', the ancient Roman road, which continues to the end of the hillside, crosses a hump-backed bridge, also of Roman origin, over the stream flowing down to the Salado, and then follows the road.

DYING HORSES AT THE BRIDGE OVER THE SALADO

Between Cirauqui and Lorca a bridge with two ogival arches crosses the 'Salado', a salt-marsh now drained following the establishment of the Alloz reservoir a little to the north. Aymeric Picaud, author of the Pilgrims' Guide, attributed the poisoning of his horses to the

west.

0.43 - Cross a small stream and take a footpath north-west up the right flank of a steep valley.

0.55 - Aim north-west for the col, also shared with the N.111.

1.08 - Col. The track rejoins the N111 200 metres farther on; follow the road for 100 metres.

1.13 - Turn left off the N111 onto a small road to Mañeru.

1.20 - Mañeru. Take the Calle de la Esperanza west (church 100 metres to your right, north).

1.25 - Plaza de los Fueros: bear left and then right, west: Calle Forzosa.

1.30 - Cemetery on your left. Continue along the track.

1.40 - Cross a path at right-angles (the N111 is 5 minutes away to the right) and follow the edge of the fields going towards the village of Cirauqui. The Old Road on the left, sunken, between low walls, is impassable. Drop gently down to the valley bottom.

1.50 - The Old Road becomes passable; continue north-west along it.

2.00 - Cemetery 100 metres to the left.

2.05 - Cirauqui. Leave the San Isidro co-operative 30 metres to your right, and go south-west down a street curving round the bottom of the village.

2.12 - Head north-west down the remarkable Roman road and cross the half-ruined bridge.

2.19 - N111, col, spring, kilometre marker 31 (Estella 13); take the track to the right, west-north-west.

2.25 - Ignore a turning off to the right.

2.33 - Bridge and fork; turn left, west.

2.40 - Fork; turn down to the left, north-west.

brackish water here; he also noted, however, that the horses were immediately cut into pieces by the Navarrese.

The time for an autopsy is long past and we shall never know the truth. On the one hand the author of the *Codex* bore a grudge against the Basques, and never lost a chance to put in a bad word about them; on the other hand, he witnessed the period of greatest rivalry between the native inhabitants and the *francsbourgeois*, who demonstrated their scorn for the Navarrese by conferring on them the fanciful etymology of *non verus* (untrue, illegitimate), and went on to pillage the 'Navarreria' district of Pamplona.

2.42 - Ignore a turning to the right, and four minutes later reach the hilltop.
2.49 - The track bears left; ignore an overgrown footpath down to the right, north-west, and instead follow the track past some ruins on your left, then under the high-tension cable.
2.52 - Cross a stream, and, by a turning space, take the track heading west-north-west.

THE BATTLE OF LORCA

The name of Lorca is said to be derived from the Arabic word *Alaurque* (battle), referring to the battle here in AD 920 when Sancho I of Navarre was defeated by the Moorish Mohamed Abenlope (doubtless at least as Basque as Sancho himself: this Ben-Lope being the Arabic form of the 'son of Lope', = Wolf, - i.e. of Otsoa, just like his Christian cousins, the Lopez family). The ogival church is very plain, with a Romanesque apse. Opposite is the former 'hospital'.

THE ROMAN VILLAGE OF VILLATUERTA

A new small ogival bridge with two spans over the River Iranzu leads to Villatuerta, rich in Roman archaeological remains, which was from 1175 a 'hospital' of St John. The restored remains include the monastic church of San Miguel (11th century) and a few traces of the San Román hermitage. The parish church, with an altarpiece, dates from the 14th century.

ESTELLA, THE CITY OF STARS

In Roman times Estella was 'Gebalda'. Its modern name is derived from a miracle in 1085; a shower of stars revealed to shepherds the statue of Our Lady of Le Puy. This would have been given the Basque name of Lizarra, Bella Stella in Latin, and Estella (for Estrella, star) in Castilian. Some linguists see its etymology as a pun in which Lizarra would mean 'the old church' and would refer to the original Basque hamlet.

3.07 - N111 road junction: turn north-west along the road to Alloz.
3.13 - Go under a modern concrete aqueduct.
3.15 - Leave the Alloz road to take a track to the left, south-west. Bridge and path on your left, south-west.
3.21 - Cross the N111 near kilometre marker 35. The track heads south then south-west.

Whatever the truth may be, the town was chosen by the kings of Navarre as their seat in the 12th century, and was so thoroughly gallicised that two hundred years later 'everyone there spoke Provençal' - meaning no doubt Occitan.

In 1492 Jean d'Albret offered a welcome here to the Jews expelled from Castile, because 'they are moderate and reasonable people'.

When Ferdinand of Aragon seized Navarre in 1512, his colonel Villaba blew up the castle at Estella, destroying with it part of the cloister of San Pedro de la Rúa.

In 1883 the Carlists proclaimed Don Carlos king of Spain, and since then they meet every year on May 7 at Montejurra.

The town is also the home of the society 'Los Amigos del Camino de Santiago', at Estella Town Hall, Estella.

MONUMENTS IN THE 'TOLEDO OF THE NORTH'

The Pilgrims' Guide was full of praise for Estella's treasures, calling the town the 'Toledo of the North'; we must be briefer.

This cluster of parishes, which have amalgamated over the years, consists of two main parts separated by the River Ega, with several bridges across it, including the hump-backed 'Pilgrims' Bridge', a 1971 reconstruction. The French quarter on the south side has the Rúa with its many monuments; on the north side is the Navarrese quarter, which is now the commercial sector.

San Pedro de la Rúa, a Romanesque church rich in furnishings, has the third multilobed porch along the route, following Cirauqui and Puente la Reina. Even if the church is closed, the carved cloister with its oblique pillars can be seen from the road above.

The adjacent *Palacio Real*, palace of the Kings of Navarre, is a fine example of Romanesque secular architecture with its twin windows and its capital depicting the combat of Roland and Ferragut.

The *façade of Santo Sepulcro*, on the opposite bank, is a homogeneous 12th-century church, endowed in 1328 with a magnificent carved Gothic porch.

San Miguel rears up on its height like a Navarrese challenge to the French quarter: this St Michael the Archangel, transformed in the Gothic period, retains

3.27 - Fork; turn right, south-west

3.30 - Cross a track suitable for vehicles.

3.34 - Small road and church at Lorca, right. Go through the village, heading south-west.

3.41 - Take the N111, keeping to the left.

3.56 - 400 metres beyond kilometre marker 37, take the gravel road to the left, south-south-east.

3.58 - Turn right, south-west.

4.10 - Turn right along a small road.

4.22 - Join the N111 again, passing kilometre marker 39 after two minutes.

4.30 - Turn left, south-south-west, along the road to Villatuerta.

4.45 - Villatuerta, church on the left. Unless you want to follow the yellow waymarks to Irache monastery, continue north-west along the street, which becomes a dirt track.

4.47 - Cross a small road and continue along the track, heading west.

4.50 - Rejoin the N111 near kilometre marker 41, with the San Miguel chapel 200 metres to the left; follow the road to Estella.

5.40 - Estella. Ignore the main road to Logroño, bear left, and continue straight on towards the centre of the town, which the pilgrims crossed as follows:

5.43 - Opposite the opening of the Calle de Julio Ruiz de Alda, turn left into the Calle de Asteria; cross the reconstructed hump-backed bridge, then turn right along the old street running parallel to the River Ega. At the end of this Calle de la Rúa, you reach:

5.50 - Plaza San Martin, with fountain, which marks the end of the timing for this stage.

from its Romanesque origins a richly storied north porch.

Other sights worth visiting include: the Rúa palace, the church of Rocamador (with a Romanesque statue of the Virgin), San Pedro de Lizarra (Romanesque, ogival apse), the Gothic monastery of Santo Domingo (founded in 1259 by Thibaud de Champagne), and the neighbouring Santa-María (Jus-del-Castillo), Romanesque apse with fine corbels.

Cross the River Ega again into the town centre. Estella is a delightful small town, very lively and interesting to explore, with all shops, hotels, restaurants, fondas, bars, coach station.

OFF THE ROUTE: CISTERCIAN IRANZU

Some 10 kilometres north of Estella, the 1176 Abbey of Iranzu is a fine example of the Cistercian style derived from Cluny, but taking much further the search for harmony based entirely on simplicity.

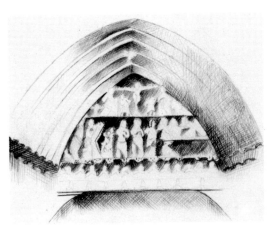

ACCOMMODATION

Estella:
- HR* San Andrés, tel.55.07.72.
- HR* Tatán, tel. 55.02.50.

- Pensión San Andrés, tel. 55.04.48.
- Fonda Izarra, tel. 55.06.78. - Fonda Maeztu, tel. 55.05.32.
- Fonda el Volante, tel. 55.39.75.
- Fonda Joaquin, tel.55.06.80.

FREE ACCOMMODATION

Estella: Enquire at the Town Hall

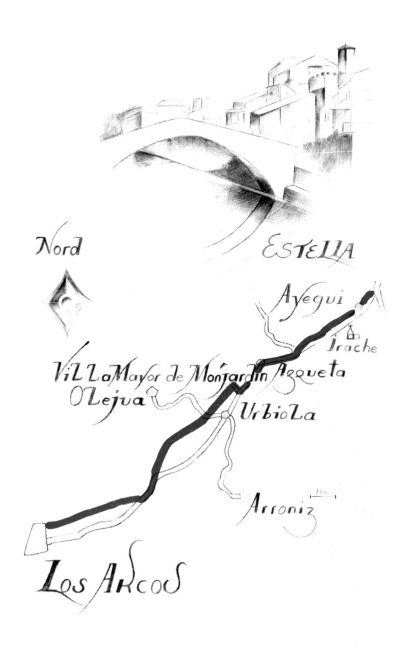

Nord

ESTELLA

Ayegui

Irache

ViLLaMayor de Monjardin Azqueta

OLejua

UrbioLa

Arroniz

Los ArcoS

stamp here

Stage 6 - 22 kilometres - 5 hours 30 minutes

ESTELLA TO LOS ARCOS

The only problem is to try and avoid the N111 main road from Pamplona to Logroño, linking Estella and Los Arcos virtually in a straight line and in many places engulfing the old Camino. Apart from a few kilometres around Azqueta, the route suggested keeps away from tarmac roads.

However, lovers of art and travellers anxious to follow in the steps of the old pilgrims will wish to visit Irache (see below), the oldest 'hospital' in the whole of Navarre, and Los Arcos itself is worth a stroll through the ancient streets while waiting for the evening dinner-hour to arrive.

THE SICK PILGRIM
AND THE BISHOP OF PATRAS

Estella is distinguished by two legends, apart from the one about the stars.

First, there is the story of the sick pilgrim, abandoned by his travelling companions and bereft of his staff. He prayed so hard to the Apostle that St James made a rhubarb stem grow in the cloister; and the man took it for his new staff when he continued on his way.

The second, more probable, concerns the Greek bishop of Patras who, in 1270, died and was buried here on the way to Santiago. The next day the sacristan saw a glimmering light above his tomb, which the priests immediately opened; they found on the body the two relics which the prelate had carried - a badge, and the shoulder-blade of St Andrew. His burial stone is in the cloisters at San Pedro de la Rúa, and the relics in one of the chapels.

0.00 - Estella, Plaza San Martín. Take the Calle de San Nicolás, heading south-west.

0.04 - Puerta de Castilla.

0.07 - Crossroads: take the Logroño road southwards.

0.12 - At the junction with the C123 (Lodosa 32), which you ignore, leave the N111 and turn right, south-west, onto a dirt road, Calle del Camino.

0.14 - Ignore a turning to the right and continue south-west along the track.

0.20 - Pass a warehouse on your left.

0.25 - Take a concrete path heading south and then veering south-west.

0.28 - Crossing of concrete paths; continue south-west.

0.30 - Ayegui. Bear left, south-west, to the N111, cross it near kilometre marker 46, and continue south-westwards to Irache. (This is a

IRACHE: NAVARRE'S MOST IMPORTANT HOSPITAL

On leaving Ayegui, 2 kilometres from Estella, many pilgrims made a detour south of the route to Irache. The monastery there, at the foot of Mount Montejurra, no doubt existed from Visigoth times; in any case its 'hospital', founded in 1050 by Garcia de Nájera, was the first in Navarre, pre-dating even Roncesvalles. After 1569 the Cistercian monastery housed a university which in 1824, on its decline, was moved to Sahagún. The transitional style church, dating from the late 12th century, has a Romanesque apse, three ogival aisles and a dome resting on pendentives, very similar to those at Salamanca and Zamora.

OFF THE ROUTE: DICASTILLO, VILLAMAYOR, MONJARDIN

The little village of DiCastillo, about 15 kilometres south of Estella on the Calahorra road, still has a 12th-century Virgin plated with silver, Santa María la Real, and the richly ornamented reliquary of San Veremundo, Abbot

heavily built-up area, but the detour is essential in order to see the monastery, which should on no account be missed.)

0.45 - Irache Monastery. Continue south-west and then west to rejoin the N111.

0.55 - Turn left, south-west, along the N111.

1.05 - Bear right towards the Hotel Residencia and continue west-south-west, passing first beneath a high-tension line and along a street which soon leads into a dirt track continuing westwards, with the N111 about 100 metres to your left.

1.15 - Cross a track and continue in the same direction, west.

1.18 - Fork: bear left, south-west, on a track across the fields.

1.21 - Corner of a wood, and fork: carry straight on, south-west.

1.28 - Col, junction of tracks: turn left, south.

1.31 - Rejoin the N111; turn right along the road, south-west, into Azqueta and through it.

2.00 - Azqueta. Coming out of the village, the old Road rejoins the new one, 50 metres beyond the tunnel. Follow the N111 again.

2.20 - Kilometre marker 52 - turn right on the fork to Villamayor, for 400 metres.

2.27 - Turn left down a gravel path to the south-west.

3.05 - Cross a minor tarmac road and continue along the gravel path, south-south-westwards.

3.45 - Ignore a left fork leading to the N111 and carry on up the path.

3.48 - Top of the hillside: on the right a ruined building and a modern one. Turn left, south, along a clearly marked track.

4.00 - N111, at kilometre marker 57. Turn right, south-west, along it for about 700 metres.

of Irache in the 11th century and royal counsellor.

Between Azqueta and Urbiola the small road on which we set out climbs to the right, towards the château of Monjardin (10th century, but mentioned as early as 833). At its foot lies the village of Villamayor and its Romanesque church with a capital representing two knights in combat - possibly Roland and Ferragut.

Farther on, the San Gregoria Ostienca sanctuary, on its height some 4 kilometres from Los Arcos, has a fine altar-piece.

LOS ARCOS, CITY OF JEWS AND FRANKS

Los Arcos, the 'Urancia' of Roman times, was granted a Frankish quarter by Sancho IV in 1175. In the Middle Ages it was known as the City of the Jews. The 17th-century gate opens into an arcaded square. The Church of the Assumption has a French 14th-century Virgin, a Gothic 15th-century altar-piece, polychrome stalls, and an elegant 15th-century flamboyant Gothic cloister. The village also has many emblazoned façades, particularly on the northern side, at the foot of the hill.

ACCOMMODATION

Irache:
- Large luxury HR***.

Los Arcos:
- H** Monaco, tel. 64.00.00.
- H** Ezequiel, tel. 64.02.96. 10% reduction for pilgrims.
- Shops, chemist, health-centre, post office.

4.10 - 300 metres before kilometre marker 58 bear right, west-south-west, on a broad track.

4.17 - Go along the edge of a field, leaving it on your left.

4.20 - Take a gravel path (which came off the N111 shortly after kilometre marker 58).

4.42 - End of the path. Turn left, south-south-west, on a track which soon veers to the right; keep straight on along it.

4.47 - Join a larger track and head south-west down it.

5.25 - You approach Los Arcos from the north; continue southwards through the village.

5.35 - Los Arcos, 447m, with the N111 running through it. Bus service to Estella and Logroño.

Note 1

It is possible to reach the Hotel Residencia from Ayegui without using the tarmac road, as follows:

0.30 - Ignore the left (south-westward) fork and go through Ayegui village.

0.34 - Main square on your left. Leave Ayegui on a path down to the west-south-west.

0.45 - Join a larger track and follow it for 30 metres to the right, west, then turn left on another track, with a pool on your left.

1.02 - Approaching the N111, leave the Hotel Residencia on your left. (This route avoids a stretch of the main road, but unfortunately misses out the monastery at Irache.)

Note 2 On leaving Azqueta you can continue towards Villamayor, leaving it above and on your right, by taking the gravel track:

2.00 - 50 metres beyond the tunnel turn down towards some straw silos.

2.05 - Take the yellowish track running parallel to the N111, along beside the high-tension cable. Turn right, west, onto a grassy path through the fields, leaving a low wall on your left.

2.10 - Make a U-turn for 100 metres to the south, then bear west towards a round cement tower. Carry on to the north-west facing a steep hillside, then west towards a bell-tower.

2.15 - The track goes past a wall on your right, then continues up between low walls.

2.22 - Rejoin the main route as described above.

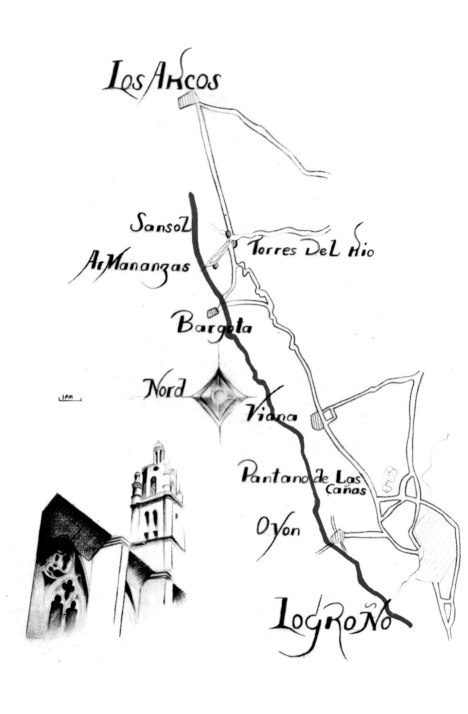

LosArcos

SansoL

ArManangas

Torres Del Hio

Bargota

Nord

Viana

Pantano de Las Cañas

Oyon

LoyRoño

1 Km

Stage 7 - 28 kilometres - 7 hours

LOS ARCOS TO LOGROÑO

The only problem with this long stage is, once again, the difficulty of dodging the N111, which has swallowed up the Old Road under its tarmac. Immediately after Viana we leave modern Navarre and enter the province of Rioja, now part of Castile - though it was not always so, as we shall see.

The octagonal chapel at Torres del Rio and the massive church in Viana, citadel of the Princes of Navarre, deserve more attention than Logroño, a fairly modest place in architectural terms.

THE OCTAGONAL CHAPEL IN TORRES DEL RIO

In Torres del Rio the Romanesque chapel of Santo Sepulcro (12th century) has the same octagonal shape, attributed to the Knights Templar, as the chapels at Eunate and the Sancti Spiritus at Roncesvalles; however, it retains its 'lantern-tower of the dead', a little turret where a lamp was lit at night. The stairs up to it face the oven-shaped apse. The Hispano-Arab dome with star-shaped vaulting is similar to those at Oloron-Sainte-Croix and the St Blaise 'Hospital', on the French-facing slopes. There are handsome capitals, and a stylised Christ.

VIANA, STRONGHOLD OF THE PRINCES OF NAVARRE

Still called 'Cuevas' by Aymeric Picaud, from the name

0.00 - Los Arcos. From the square to the north of the church, set off westwards through the gate, cross a road and a bridge and follow a street heading west; pass the public library on your right, and three minutes later, the cemetery.

0.08 - Chapel on your left, with the road to Logroño 30 metres to the left.

0.45 - Cross a stream by fording it.

0.52 - Dry-stone hut to your right.

0.55 - Junction of paths; take the grassy track to the west.

1.08 - Concrete bridge over the Arroyo de San Pedro.

1.12 - Rejoin the N111 between kilometre markers 67 and 68 and turn west along it for about 1,500

of its predecessor, the fortified town of Viana was founded in 1219 by Sancho the Strong to protect the frontiers of Navarre, of which it is now the last place along the Road to Santiago. It too had its 'hospitals'. In the 15th century Charles III made the Principality of Viana part of the fiefdom of the eldest son of the Kings of Navarre, a title revived by the Dauphins of France after Henri IV. In 1507 Cesare Borgia, generalissimo of the Navarrese armies, was killed in an ambush and buried near a side door of the church. The town gates and the old paved streets preserve its medieval atmosphere, and the Town Hall, built in 1688, with its two towers, is a fine example of municipal architecture. But above all, you should see the imposing church of Santa María, of the 15th and 16th centuries, as large as a cathedral with its 90 - metre triforium, its many chapels, its treasure, and its tall and richly ornamented façade. A few ruins remain of the earlier, 14th century, church of San Pedro.

LOGROÑO: THE CHILD CURED BY ST FRANCIS

Logroño is the capital of Rioja, a prosperous agricultural province watered by the River Ebro, land of the 1st-century Roman rhetorician Quintilian, the poet Prudentius (born in 348), the 12th-century Castilian poet Gonzalo de Berceo, and several saints and martyrs.

Originally a Navarrese town, Logroño is just a few kilometres from the legendary battlefield of 'Clavijo' - where there are castle ruins - said to have been fought between the great Abd er Rahman and King Ramiro I, who refused to deliver his tribute of a hundred virgins, and who triumphed in 844 with the aid of St James, armed with cross and sword. There was in truth such a battle, but in 938 and actually at Simancas, between Ramiro II and Abd er Rahman III. And in 1076 Alfonso I incorporated Logroño into Castile.

The modern industrial town is best known for its Rioja wines and its coffee caramels. However there are a few modest monuments:
- *The church of San Bartolomé* (12th-14th centuries), with a 'Moorish' tower of brick and enamel;
- *The 14th-century church of Santa María del Palacio,* with its Gothic spire oddly set on a lantern-tower;
- *The baroque church of Santa María la Redonda,* with two 18th-century towers, which no doubt derives its name from having replaced an ancient 'round' (or more

metres.

1.33 - Sansol, 505m.

1.35 - Kilometre marker 69; 50 metres farther on, leave the road as it bears right, and turn down south-west, below the road, where you find a waymarked footpath.

1.40 - You come to a small road; follow it to the south-west.

1.42 - 20 metres before a bridge turn down to the right, cross a bridge and climb up a street heading north-west.

1.47 - Torres del Rio. Leave the octagonal church of Santo Sepulcro on your right, and take the street to the north-west.

1.50 - Follow as it turns to the left, south.

1.51 - Turn along a lane to the right, west-south-west.

1.57 - Cemetery on the left. Follow the track south-west.

2.06 - Paths cross in the valley bottom; take the grassy track heading south-west.

2.08 - The road to Logroño (kilometre marker 71) is below on the right.

2.16 - Hilltop, with vines on the left; turn right, south-west, at the fork.

2.18 - Rejoin the N111 on a bend 200 metres before kilometre marker 72, and follow the road for 3.8 kilometres.

3.17 - 400 metres before kilometre marker 76, and just before a safety barrier, go down to the right of the road to take a dirt track heading south-west. This crosses the valley and skirts round the foot of a pinewood.

3.20 - Ignore a turning to the right.

3.25 - Another pine-wood. At a fork beneath a high-tension cable, climb up, off the track, beneath a telephone cable and between the two branches of the fork.

3.30 - Dry-stone hut to the left, and

probably polygonal) church similar to those in Eunate and Torres del Rio;

- The 16th-century Gothic church of Santiago el Real with a single large nave, and beside it the Pilgrims' Fountain. On its baroque porch, the work of Juan de Roan in 1662, can be seen a Santiago-Matamoros of great size, though somewhat clumsy; St James is dressed as a pilgrim with cape, but carries a curved sword in his right hand. He is mounted on a prancing war-horse trampling the heads of Saracens beneath its feet. The battle of Clavijo is carved on the main altar-piece;

- The monastery to the left of the stone bridge, on the way into the town, is said to have been founded by the grateful father of a child cured by St Francis of Assisi.

OFF THE ROUTE: CLAVIJO, AND THE VICTORIOUS APPARITION

The little village of Clavijo, with its 16th-century church, lies about 15 kilometres south of Logroño. It is dominated by the ruins of an imposing 10th-century castle, inaccessible on three sides and fortified on the fourth, overlooking the plains of the River Ebro and the site of the battle which bears its name. Its history and the conflicting legend have been mentioned above, the latter probably embroidered by the monks of San Millán. What cannot be denied, however, is the extraordinary influence on Spanish history of the combination of these two events - the one supernatural: the appearance of the saint during a semi-mythical battle, the other historical: the vow made by the victorious king to establish a 'Tributo de Santiago', a pious response that was only abolished centuries later by the Cortes of Cadiz. From that moment on, the Christians were sustained by an *idée-fixe* in their struggle for the Reconquest, somewhat comparable to the memory of Joan of Arc in France: a medley of regional civil wars was transformed into a definitive national crusade.

OFF THE ROUTE: ALBELDA DE IRUEGA, OR THE SCHOOL OF ARAB NUMERALS

Four kilometres as the crow flies from Clavijo, but without direct access, lies Albelda de Iruega, where there is little of interest to see: but its name should be known. In the high Middle Ages this was the site of the San Martin

farm to the right.

3.31 - You come to the N111, 200 metres before kilometre marker 77; cross the tarmac and take the track parallel with the road, running above it on the right.

3.38 - Hilltop; at a bend in the N111, turn west along it.

3.42 - Clay diggings on your left. Take the track heading west-south-west.

3.45 - Cross a track and continue straight on west-south-west.

3.48 - Rejoin the N111 and follow the road.

4.15 - Entry into Viana. Guardia Civil police-post on the right.

4.20 - Leave the N111, go to the left round and below Viana, and take the Old Road straight ahead, signposted to Aras.

4.25 - Pass a bar on your right, then another on your left, and go down to the west.

4.28 - Crossroads. Do not go down to the N111, a few hundred metres away, but turn right towards Aras.

4.32 - Go down a concrete lane to the left, west-north-west, and follow a dirt track to the west.

4.36 - Small bridge without parapets.

4.39 - Cross a small irrigation canal.

4.40 - Pelota court on the right.

4.41 - Bridge over the river. The track veers left and goes below a high-tension cable.

4.43 - Cross a small tarmac road and continue along the track between the fields.

4.50 - Pass a turning to the right, a dry-stone hut, and a metal gateway.

5.00 - Bridge across a small river; go under the high-tension cable and take the left fork, south.

5.20 - Pass a farm on your left, 300 metres from the N111, and turn right, south-west, on a path that goes beneath the high-tension cable.

monastery, receptive in about the year 900 to both French influences and Muslim scholars. It was here that the Arabic numerals, which then took the place of Roman numerals, appeared for the first time in Europe; and the invention of the zero opened the way to swift advances in mathematics.

OFF THE ROUTE: THE CITADEL OF LAGUARDIA

In the opposite direction lies the fortified city of Laguardia, 16 kilometres north-west of Logroño and off the Pilgrim Way. It has ramparts from which one can see as far as the Cantabrian Cordillera, ancient streets, and fine lacy stonework on the Gothic porch of its church of Santa María de los Reyes.

5.23 - Fork: ignore the left turn which rejoins the N111, and turn right, west-south-west, passing under the high-tension cable again.

5.28 - Hilltop. The path goes down a valley heading westwards, and separated from the N111 by a hill.

5.45 - After 1 kilometre bear left, south, without going up and without a path - but without any difficulties - and head south, passing a large factory on your left.

6.00 - Cross the N111 at a major crossroads, 30 metres beyond the 337 roadside marker, and take a track south-west, running at first through the cutting or embankment beside the road and then more distinct from it, with a small stream on your left.

6.04 - Cross this stream and climb up a broad grassy path to the south-west.

6.10 - Cross a tarmac road and take a broad gravel track straight ahead, south-west.

6.15 - Continue along the track as it drops down, with a view over Logroño.

6.25 - Warehouse and small house on the right. Next the path goes down between some dilapidated shanties of the scrapyard workers - beware of dogs!

6.40 - You reach a main road; turn right along it, following the left bank of the Ebro; cemetery on the right.

6.45 - Turn left, across the bridge over the Ebro.

7.00 - Centre of Logroño. The pilgrims used to take the following route through the town:

6.48 - After crossing the bridge, take the Calle de la Rúa Vieja, west-south-west, with the church of Santa María del Palacio on your left.

6.53 - Cross the Calle de Sagasta and take the Calle de Barriocepo.

6.55 - Church of St James, on the

NOTE

This long stage, monotonous for walkers, includes some tedious stretches of the main road which we have been unable to avoid, through lack of up-to-date maps or recent aerial photographs.

ACCOMMODATION

Viana:
- Pension Chavarri, tel. 64.51.36
- Bar-restaurant la Granja
- Restaurant Asador
- Restaurant Boria

Logroño: numerous hotels,restaurants, fondas
- HR**** Carlton Rioja, Gran Via, 5
- H*** Gran Hotel, 4 rue General Vara de Rey
- H*** Murrieta, 1 avenue Marques de Murrieta
etc.

FREE ACCOMMODATION

Torres des Rio: Sr. Ramon Sostre, casa Santa Barbara, tel. 64.80.06, offers hospitality to pilgrims. Walkers should leave a suitable contribution to cover expenses.

Logroño: Enquire at the parish church of Santiago, 6 calle Barriocepo, tel. 22.57.67

right.
6.58 - The road bears left.
7.00 - Leaving the Tobacco Board building on your left, turn right, west, into the Calle del Marqués de San Nicolás; note the old door 30 metres to the right.
7.02 - Cross the Calle Once de Junio, and head west along the Calle de los Depositos.
7.04 - On your left, a square and roundabout. Take the Burgos road, the Calle Marqués de Murieta, to leave the town.
7.15 - Bridge over the railway. The main crossroads, Saragossa-Soria, to the left, is 30 minutes farther on.

Stage 8 - 32 kilometres - 8 hours

LOGROÑO TO NAJERA,
via Navarrete, Sotés and Ventosa

A very long stage, but it presents no difficulties. The Old Road frequently coincides with the motor road to Burgos and its heavy traffic. Fortunately there are also some stretches of the old Camino which remain intact; and where the tarmac of the N120 has swallowed it up for ever, it is possible to find interesting alternatives.

We are now in Rioja, which was part of Navarre from its reconquest until it became part of Castile, i.e. for two hundred years. The names of Clavijo, Navarrete, Poroldán, even Nájera, are the names of historic or legendary battles, revealing the extent to which this flat region was fought over.

Clavijo, a little to the south, is particularly important, since the appearance of St James at the side of Ramiro I inspired the entire sacred tradition of 'Santiago Matamoros' - St James of the Sword.

At the end of this stage is the royal burial place of Santa María la Real at Nájera, one of the major monuments of the Road.

NAVARRETE AND THE DEFEAT OF DU GUESCLIN

Navarrete is a town of artisans - jewellery craftsmen - and wine-growers, spreading its emblazoned houses in a half-circle across the hillside and retaining its medieval atmosphere. The Pilgrim Way follows both the lower and the upper sections of the Calle Mayor.

- Immediately after crossing the motorway you pass the ruins of the old 12th-century 'Hospital' of St John of Acre.   - On the way into the town, in a niche near the Santiago Gate is a statue of Saint James as 'Matamoros', conqueror of the Moors.

- In the town centre the great 16th-century church of the Asunción has a baroque altar-piece, and in its sacristy a Flemish triptych attributed to Rembrandt.

- The most moving monument, however, lies on the way out of the town: a 12th-century Romanesque gateway has been reconstructed at the cemetery entrance by the devout and expert hands of an ordinary stone-mason;

0.00 - Logroño. From the square with its roundabout - see the end of Stage 7 - take the Burgos road, Calle Marqués de Murieta, out of the town, heading broadly westwards.

0.10 - Bridge over the railway lines. Continue along the avenue, still the Calle Marqués de Murieta.

0.16 - Turn left, south-west, into the Calle de Entrena.

0.20 - Continue onto a footpath.

0.23 - Cross a road and continue straight on, south-west, along a path (which in March 1985 had a rough surface).

0.28 - Cross a sort of main ring-road, and take a small road, south-west, which at first runs parallel with the ring road and then veers to the left.

it came originally from the Hospital of St John of Acre mentioned above.

- The battle known as Navarrete, in 1367, resulted in the temporary defeat of the famous French warrior Du Guesclin, who supported Henri de Transtamare and defeated the Black Prince, ally of Peter the Cruel. The site of the battle was in fact nearer to Nájera than to Navarrete.

stamp here

WHERE ROLAND BEAT FERRAGUT

The village of Ventosa between Navarrete and Nájera, to the left of the route, has a church dedicated to the French saint Saturnin de Toulouse. Next the route takes us past two peaks, also on the left:
- The *'Alto de San Antón'* - St Anthony's Height - where the ruins of a monastic 'hospital' still exist beside a farm;
- and the *'Poyo de Roldán'*, abbreviated to 'Poroldán' (Roland's Peak). According to legend, the gallant knight hurled an enormous rock from this hilltop onto the giant Ferragut as he sat outside his castle in Nájera; the rock struck him on the forehead and felled him, and thus his prisoners were freed.

0.35 - Just before the Gruas Casimiro building, the yellow waymarking leads you to the right through an area of rubbish tips and marshes. Go under a high-tension line, and follow a broad marshy track.

0.56 - Cross a small bridge on the left, with some stepping stones, over a small irrigation canal; the waymarked path bends left round an earth mound and then heads west.

1.03 - On a hairpin bend take a small road linking the N120 with the stretch of water about 100 metres ahead. Ignore the waymarking, which would lead you back to the N120, and go instead up the small road to the left, to the water, and skirt round it to the south. It is also possible to skirt round the northern edge.

1.32 - Pass a very tall radio-mast 100 metres to the north, and turn west along its access track to a building and the fenced area surrounding it.

1.35 - Turn left, south, on a broad gravel path, with the tarmac road going off to the right.

1.40 - At a fork turn right, west.

1.44 - Turn off the path to the left, south-west, up a track through the vines.

1.52 - The track bears left, south-west, above the vines, and with an area of heathland above on your right.

1.57 - Ridge overlooking the motorway; head west to the fence along the road.

2.02 - Turn right on a path along the fence beside the motorway, below the road at first and then very soon above it.

2.06 - On the left a large conduit will enable you to pass under the motorway without stooping too

NAJERA, FORMER CAPITAL OF NAVARRE

Nájera is said to be an Arab name meaning 'place between the rocks'; the Spanish literary critic and linguist Menendez-Pidal, however, believes that it is pre-Roman. In the 10th and 11th centuries it was the second court of the Kingdom of Navarre, until Rioja was incorporated into Castile in 1076. Here Sancho the Great minted the first known coins of the Renconquest; and the king Don Garcia was known as 'El de Nájera'.

- The existing bridge over the Najerilla (1886) replaced the seven-arched bridge built in the 12th century by San Juan de Ortega.

- The church of Santa Cruz (founded in the 12th century, with 17th-century porch) has a Gothic figure of Christ walking on the waters.

- Above all, the monastery of Santa María la Real should be visited.

much; either use this or wait till you reach a better way through:

2.22 - A good passage under the motorway. Follow a path which soon leaves the motorway and heads towards Navarrete.

2.35 - Go under the high-tension wires and down to the left, south-west, on a path following the line of the high-tension cable.

2.48 - Guardia Civil - police - post - on the left. Take the road LO864 to the left.

3.00 - Centre of Navarrete. Carry on to the N120 and turn left along it.

3.15 - Navarrete cemetery. Continue for another 120 metres along the N120, heading west-south-west.

3.17 - Continue south-south-west along this track suitable for vehicles and take the third turning after the cemetery - the first runs along beside the cemetery wall itself.

3.28 - Farm or large stable on the left.

3.43 - Another track comes in from the left. Continue westwards.

3.44 - Fork: bear left, south-west.

3.46 - Fork: turn left, south.

3.54 - Ignore a turning to the right, west, which five minutes later reaches the point where the roads to Sotés and Llornos fork. Continue straight on, south, towards a huge white shed.

4.00 - Cross the Llornos road. On the right of the white building take a track to the west.

4.15 - Bridge and the road to Sotés; turn along this road.

4.30 - Sotés; continue along the small Ventosa road, heading generally west.

5.00 - On the way out of Ventosa, with the village on your left, take a wide track going north-west.

5.05 - Note a small house with swimming pool, 50 metres to the right.

SANTA MARIA LA REAL, BURIAL-PLACE OF ROYALTY

The legend claims that in 1044, when King Don Garcia was hunting a dove, he found it alive in a cave, beside the falcon which had been pursuing it, both sitting peacefully in front of a statue of the Virgin.

In fact the statue which stands today in the crypt beneath the choir is Gothic, while there is a Romanesque Virgin in the choir itself. The buildings date from the 15th and 16th centuries, and form an imposing group, a royal pantheon containing some thirty tombs with effigies, the most important being that of Queen Blanche of Navarre, granddaughter of El Cid. Many pilgrimage scenes are depicted in the stalls and choir, and in the carvings in the 'Claustro de los Caballeros' - the Knights' Cloister, equally rich in tombs.

THE TOMB OF DOÑA BLANCA

The tomb of Doña Blanca (Queen Blanche) in the Royal Pantheon of Nájera merits a visit. She died giving birth to the future king of Castile, Alfonso VIII, and is shown on the tomb, surrounded by the king, servants, and mourners. Stretched out on her couch, she gives up her soul which is shown as a child carried up by angels. The other surfaces and the canopy display biblical scenes: Christ in Majesty with Apostles and monogram, King Solomon, the Epiphany, the Massacre of the Innocents, and the parable of the ten Virgins.

THE TOMB OF DIEGO DE HARO

The finest of the Chevalier tombs in the Pantheon at Nájera is that of Don Diego Lopez de Haro, lord of Viscaya and chief lieutenant of Alfonso VIII. The sides show monks covering the coffin, men tearing their hair, and women holding their hands to their eyes and weeping.

NAJERA FESTIVAL

Each year in July the Festival performed in the cloisters recalls Nájera's great historic occasions.

5.10 - Fork: turn right, north-west.

5.15 - Stone or cement shelter. Here the route rejoins the Pilgrim Way; turn left along it, heading broadly west.

5.22 - Fork; turn right, west.

5.27 - Hilltop; the N120 is visible below.

5.31 - A shed and then a house, both on the left.

5.40 - Cross the old and new tracks of the N120 at a bend, climb over the safety barrier, and go down, bearing left; here you will come upon sections of the CAMINO running parallel with the road; do not stray away from the road.

6.00 - Turn north-west from the N120 on a track which is tarmac for about 100 metres.

6.08 - Ignore a fork to the left and continue west-north-west.

6.16 - Hut on the left. Continue north-west.

6.23 - Veer to the west.

6.25 - Col, with a view to the west over Nájera.

6.30 - Vast plateau, with construction work on the right. Follow a gravel path going west.

6.42 - Road leading to Huércaos; follow it for two minutes to the right, north-west.

6.44 - Take a gravel path bearing left, west.

6.45 - Bridge and gravel path on the right, north-west, beside a river flowing north.

6.53 - Cross the river by a concreted ford. Take a good track straight ahead, west, along beside the Najerilla canal.

7.00 - Ignore the first bridge on the left.

7.10 - Factory on the left. Turn right, west, onto another track.

7.20 - Cross the new track of the N120, which now detours to the

ACCOMMODATION

Navarrete:
- Fonda La Carioca, tel.44.00.06
- Pensión Marín, tel. 40.00.10.

Nájera:
- H** San Fernando, tel. 36.07.00.
- Fonda El Moro, tel. 36.00.52

FREE ACCOMMODATION

Navarrete: See Los Padres Camilos, north of the village, tel. 44.00.87.

Nájera: See Los Padres Franciscanos de Santa María la Real, tel. 36.01.06.

north round Nájera, 20 metres north of the 'Logroño 25' sign, and take a path towards the outskirts of Nájera.

7.30 - Municipal housing on your right. Take the avenue - which in February 1985 had a poor dirt surface.

7.35 - Outskirts of Nájera. Continue right, south-west, along the old route of the N120 on its way into Nájera from the east.

8.00 - Bridge over the River Najerilla. Just before this bridge there is a square on the left, south, with bus-stop, hotel, restaurant, and public telephone. Prosperous pilgrims can look for accommodation here; across the bridge there are restaurants and rooms at much lower prices.

THE GASTRONOMIC PILGRIM IN RIOJA

This is a border area, gastronomically as well as historically, between Navarre and Castile. The distinctive and full-bodied wines of Rioja are amongst those most frequently exported from Spain.

A few specialities:
- 'Sopa cana' ('white soup', with garlic);
- Dishes 'à la Riojana' for 'callos' (tripe), or 'caracoles' (snails);
- 'Perdiz estofada' (partridge braised with onions and oil);
- Locally produced vegetables, particularly asparagus.

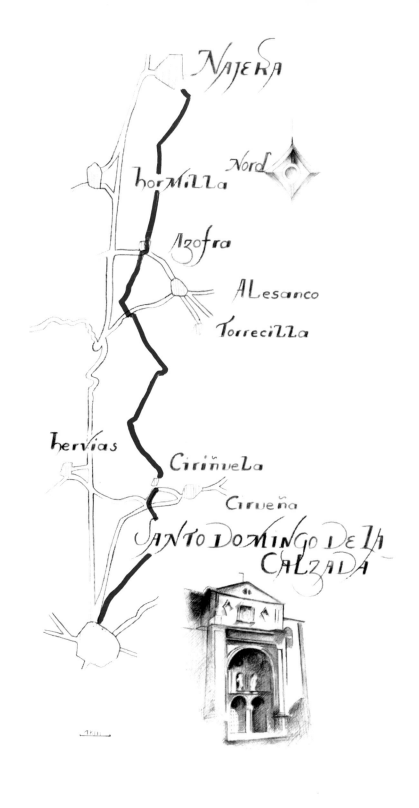

NAJERA

Nord

horMilLa

Azofra

ALesanco

TorreciLLa

hervias

CiriñueLa

Cirueña

SANTO DOMINGO DE LA
CALZADA

1 KM

Stage 9 - 24 kilometres - 6 hours

NAJERA TO SANTO DOMINGO DE LA CALZADA

B*ecause much of the Old Road has been obliterated by tarmac or changes in land usage, we established in spring 1985 a route which remains faithful to the spirit of the Pilgrim Way if not to its precise itinerary. Almost entirely avoiding tarmac roads, it follows gravel roads or tracks to Azofra and Cirñuela, thus keeping to the south of the N120.*

Azofra has a few reminders of the pilgrimage, but the San Millán monastery is of much greater artistic interest. For walkers, however, it is perhaps rather far from the Road. This stage ends at an outstanding site - Santo Domingo de la Calzada, known both for the legendary cock and hen still living in the cathedral, and for the historic memory of its founder, the 'builder of the Road'.

OFF THE ROUTE:
SAN MILLAN DE LA COGOLLA AND CAÑAS

Although at some distance from the Road to Santiago, about a dozen kilometres south of Azofra in the Cardenas valley, San Millán de la Cogolla is worth a detour for those who can manage it. There are two monasteries: the older, Suso, meaning the higher, has some Visigoth remains including its chapel cut into the rock containing the tomb of San Millán, a Berceo shepherd who died in AD 574. The effigy dates from the 12th century. The other monastery, Yuso, meaning lower, is a Renaissance and neo-classical building with fine ivory reliquary panels.

IVORY - IGNORED BY THE LOOTERS
OF THE EMPIRE

There are two reliquaries of San Millán. That of the saint himself originally consisted of 24 ivory plaques mounted in gold set with precious stones. In 1809, during the Napoleonic wars, looters took the gold and the jewels but ignored most of the ivories which in 1944 were reset in a new chest. They represent scenes from San Millán's life as a 6th-century hermit, as it was imagined in the

0.00 - Nájera. From the western end of the bridge over the River Najerilla, take the street to the north-west, the old route of the N120, passing three minor 90-degree turnings to the left.

0.02 - Plaza de Queipo de Llano. Go through the gateway, into the third of the streets mentioned above, Calle de Esteban M. d. Villegas, and turn right along it.

0.04 - Turn left into a street heading south.

0.05 - On the left, a square and church - Parroquia de la Santa Cruz.

0.06 - Triangular open space. On the right, the Monastery of Santa María la Real, which you skirt, ignoring the Calle de las Viudas, to the south.

0.08 - Next, turn right along another street which broadens as it goes up to the west.

0.15 - Turn off this into a track to the right, west-south-west, up through pine-trees.

83

Romanesque period. The other reliquary, containing the remains of San Felices, depicts the Last Supper, also in ivory.

CERAMICIST NUNS AT CAÑAS

Five kilometres south along the little road from Azofra to San Millán lies the village of Cañas, birthplace of Santo Domingo de Silos, who died in 1073 after founding the fine monastery of the same name some 50 kilometres south-east of Burgos. In the Gothic convent here, the Cistercian nuns create artistic ceramic ware which is sold by the Portress-Sister. The simple Gothic church is full of light, particularly since removal of the monumental reredos. The Chapter House contains a museum of religious art, notably the 14th-century sarcophagus of the Abbess, Doña Urraca Lopez de Haró, who lived from 1170-1262. She is shown here with her crook, between two angels. Doll-sized novices pray at her feet. The side panels show the history of her life: as kneeling novice, as abbess with her book, being greeted by St Peter in Paradise at her death, and on the opposite side, her burial with three bishops, mourners tearing their clothes, and a funeral procession of nuns.

AZOFRA:
THE PILGRIM'S SPRING

In Azofra, where the parish church perched in the middle of the village has two statues, St Martin of Tours and St James the Pilgrim, the ancient 'hospital' founded in Azofra in 1168 has disappeared. At the edge of the village, however, there is still the *fuente de los romeros*, the pilgrims' spring. Two old houses close by have Latin inscriptions on their escutcheons: *Hoc opus ist lavor* and *Auspice Deo*.

0.22 - Col cut through the rocks. The track descends to the west, leaving on the right a large breeze-block sheep-pen.

0.26 - Another small col.

0.32 - 50 metres before reaching a large building on the left of the track, the waymarking indicates a right turn, north, along a small side turning.

0.34 - Cross a track, go over a small bridge, and continue north-west. This takes you across an undulating plateau of fields and vineyards.

0.45 - Tarmac road, running roughly east-west and apparently following the original Pilgrim Way. Turn left along it.

1.26 - Coming into Azofra, fork left.

1.30 - Azofra church on the right. Continue down streets heading north-west.

1.35 - Crossroads, with fountain on the left. Take the bridge over the River Tuerto, and follow the small tarmac road to the north-west for about 200 metres.

1.38 - Turn off the tarmac road where it bends right, north-east, and turn left, west, along a track.

1.42 - Ignore a left, south-west, turn.

1.53 - A large stone column on the right. Continue along the track between the vines, ignoring waymarking.

1.58 - Small col.

1.59 - Fork: ignore the right turn waymarked in yellow, which leads to the N120, and turn left, west.

2.01 - Take the first right turn, down to the north then north-west.

2.05 - Fork left, south-west.

2.15 - Take the small tarmac road running south from the N120 to Alesanco, which lies about 2 kilometres to the south, for about 200 metres.

2.18 - Arches of a small aqueduct;

DOMINGO DE LA CALZADA AND JUAN DE ORTEGA, CIVIL ENGINEERS FOR THE SANTIAGO PILGRIMS

Santo Domingo de la Calzada - Saint Dominic of the Highway - is named after a Benedictine monk born nearby in 1019, who died at the age of 90 in 1109, and who has become the patron saint of public works. Turned away from the Monastery at San Millán, Domingo entered the service of St Gregory, Bishop of Ostia - and when the Bishop died, returned to his native land to establish a hermitage on the banks of the River Oja. Moved by the sufferings of the pilgrims, he undertook the construction of a bridge in 1044, followed by a hostel and a road, work which was continued by his disciple Juan de Ortega.

Domingo's 16th-century tomb is in the right aisle of the cathedral transept.

WHERE THE ROASTED COCK AND HEN BEGAN TO SING

The thoroughly heterogeneous cathedral of Santo Domingo de la Calzada has preserved two Romanesque apses, traces of the construction work undertaken by the saint. Generally speaking, however, its style is Gothic.

But its greatest fame is derived from the white hen and cock which can be seen, alive (changed twice a month), behind a metal grille which prevents modern pilgrims from pulling out their feathers as relics. They commemorate a surprising miracle which several ballads locate here (only Aymeric Picaud places it in Toulouse). A young Frenchman had been unjustly hanged for theft, wronged by a jealous servant; but as his parents were returning from Compostela they heard him announce from the gibbet that he was alive, for St James protected him. The judge to whom they immediately applied, and who was in the middle of eating roast chicken, replied sarcastically, 'If he's alive, then this cock and hen are going to start crowing'. And - miracle of miracles - the cock immediately crowed and the hen cackled. The judge was overwhelmed and the young man cut down from the gallows.

go either left, south, or right, north, around this, in either case crossing a small bridge over the feeder canal. Go up the slope, north-west. Beyond the bridge, ignore the path running along the canal bank.

2.30 - At the top of the slope continue south-west.

2.35 - Shelter on your right; fork left, south-west, 100 metres beyond it.

2.50 - At the junction turn west-south-west along the gravel road.

3.00 - Turn right, north-west, along the gravel road.

3.10 - Junction of tracks; rejoin the yellow waymarking and continue north-north-west.

3.15 - Crossing of paths. The waymarking leads left, westwards, along a path heading up to the ridge and towards Cirñuela, a full kilometre south of the old Pilgrim Way which has suffered from changes in land use.

4.00 - Go towards the cemetery between Cirueñela, which you leave on your right, and Cirueña. At the Stop sign turn right for 200 metres along the Santo Domingo road, then left, north-west, on a footpath beside quarries for 200 metres. At the fork turn right, north-west, towards the hilltop.

4.45 - A high point provides a view of Santo Domingo de la Calzada to the north-west.

5.10 - Crossing of paths; continue straight ahead, north-west.

5.16 - Pelota court on your right. Carry on along the gravel path, west-north-west.

5.20 - Municipal sports-ground, El Rollo, to the right of the tarmac road LOV810l which we abandoned at 4.00.

5.25 - Junction of our road, the Avenida de Torrecilla en caminos,

THE 'HOSPITAL' TURNED PARADOR

Opposite the cathedral, the 'hospital' built by the saint and rebuilt in the 16th century, is today a national Parador, or tourist hotel, where visitors can have coffee beneath the ancient vaults.

At the other end of the town, near the bridge, is the Renaissance *monastery of San Francisco* and, facing it, the 1969 *monument to Santo Domingo* with bas reliefs depicting the miracle of the cock.

There are also traces of old walls, and ancient doorways.

stamp here

NOTES

0.32 - We recommend that you continue along the path to the west and wait as long as possible before bearing right, north-west, to join the gravel track, which is likely soon to be tarmac-surfaced, in view of its importance. The track, however, is undoubtedly the ancient Pilgrim Way and can be used while it awaits the tarmac.

1.53 - What should we call this great stone column? Abbé Bernés calls it the 'Cruz de los Valientes'; others, the 'Cruz de los Peregrinos'. All that is certain is that there is no cross on the column.

with the N120; cross the N120 and continue west-north-west along the Calle de los Martires de la Tradición.

5.30 - Cross a tarmac road, LO 750, and continue straight on, past a Parador Nacional sign, to the west, along the Calle de Zumalacarregui. Pass the front of the Cistercian Convent on your left.

5.35 - Square with the cathedral on the right, north, and the Parador Nacional to the west. Today's stage stops here, and tomorrow's route begins at the bridge over the River Oja, 15 minutes away and unmistakable since it is the only bridge.

5.50 - Bridge over the River Oja.

ACCOMMODATION

Santo Domingo de la Calzada:
- H*** Parador Nacional, tel. 34.03.00.
- H* Santa Teresita, tel. 32.07.00.
- HR* Rio, tel. 64.00.85
- Mesón El Peregrino, tel. 34.02.02
- Fondas

FREE ACCOMMODATION

Azofra: Enquire at the parish church, tel. 37.90.63.

Santo Domingo de la Calzada: Enquire at the Cofradía del Santo (the Brotherhood of the Saint)

Santo Domingo de la Calzada

Nord

Corporales

Morales

Greñon

Villarta Quintana

Redecilla Del Camino

Ibrillos

Castildelgado

Quintanar De Rioja

Viloria

Quintanilla

Villamayor Del Rio

fresneña

Belorado

1 Km

Stage 10 - 28 kilometres - 7 hours

SANTO DOMINGO DE LA CALZADA TO BELORADO

Still travelling through rich agricultural land, shortly beyond Grañón we leave the province of Rioja and enter Burgos, cradle of Old Castile.

As with yesterday's stage, and for almost the whole of this one, the old Pilgrim Way has been swallowed under the tarmac of the N120 main road, or obliterated by changes in land use or ownership. Luckily it is quite easy to avoid the tarmac and the heavy lorries by taking the tracks and gravel paths to Grañón, Redecilla del Camino, Bascunama, Viloria Rioja - birthplace of Santo Domingo - and Fresneña, so that we still pass through places rich in pilgrim memories. Belorado, however, where the stage ends, is the most interesting of all.

OFF THE ROUTE:
THE CROSS OF THE BRAVE

The 'Cruz de los Valientes', near kilometre marker 9 on the N120 road between Santo Domingo de la Calzada and Grañón, commemorates a battle between the two towns to win the 'Judgement of God' for possession of a pasture. The Lord granted victory to Grañón. Until recently, the parishioners of Grañón recited a *pater noster* during the service each Sunday to give thanks for the soul of Martin Gracia, their brave champion.

ANCIENT REMAINS IN GRAÑON

Grañón the Victorious (see above) no longer has its 'hospitals' and ancient walls, but still has a few relics of the past along its Calle Mayor, and a 14th-century church with classical altar-piece.

0.00 - Santo Domingo de la Calzada. West of the town, take the only bridge over the River Oja. Once on the west bank, leave the N120 and turn left, south, on a track along the river bank. At 150 metres from the N120 this track forks: turn right, south-west, cross a gravel road, and go up the path skirting round to the right of the water-tower. This path then crosses a plateau heading west-south-west.

0.45 - Fork: bear right, west, on the path down towards Corporales, across the valley-bottom and up to the village.

1.00 - Corporales. Pass a brick transformer building on your left, and turn right along a lane, north

La Ermita de los Judios - the Hermitage or Chapel of the Jews - is a 16th-century Calvary.

DEATH OF THE PILGRIM JEAN AT REDICILLA

First village in the province of Burgos, Redecilla-del-Camino retains a former hospital, emblazoned houses, a 14th-century church with a Virgin over its door watching the passing pilgrims, and, on a 12th-century holy water stoup, a carved picture of the Holy City of Jerusalem.

The village archives also tell of a penniless French pilgrim, Jean, who died here in the 16th century; it cost the community four hundred maravedis (one maravedi was equal to about one-third of a farthing) to bury him - thus the Road still remembers its humblest pilgrims. *Off the route*, about 4 kilometres to the south, the chapel of Our Lady of Ayago owes its name to a shepherd's vision of the Virgin in a beech-tree (haya).

VILORIA, BIRTHPLACE OF SANTO DOMINGO

Viloria, the village where Santo Domingo de la Calzada's was born, still has the Romanesque font in which he was baptised. His feast-day is 12 May.

OFF THE ROUTE: CASTILDELGADO AND THE THREE LIES OF VILLAMAYOR

Our route skirts round and avoids two riverside villages on the N120 which once formed part of the pilgrimage:
- *Castildelgado*, where the church has a Romanesque baptismal font; the village owes its name to Bishop Delgado, whose tomb was discovered in this church. There is a former 'hospital' beside the church.
- *Villamayor del Rio*, nicknamed 'town of the three lies'; for one thing, the name means 'The chief town on the River', but in reality it is a 'A tiny village on a stream'.

THE SNAKE OF BELORADO

Belorado, Aymeric Picaud's 'Belforatus' - meaning well cut - no doubt owes its name to the gorges of the Rio

then west, leading quickly to the road into the village from the N120. Follow the tarmac road for 200 metres to the left, towards Morales, and turn down a path to the right, north-west.

1.12 - Junction of paths: continue straight ahead, north, for 200 metres.

1.15 - Another crossing of paths: go straight ahead, up to the north-north-east.

1.30 - Up on the level, take a 90-degree turn to the right on a path, north-east, for 200 metres.

1.33 - Bear left, north-west, on a straight but undulating track over small hillocks.

1.40 - Grañón is visible to the north-west. Go down the track which bends first to the left and then to the right.

1.45 - Paths cross: continue straight ahead, north-west.

2.00 - Another crossing: turn left, west, past the cemetery, leaving it on your left.

2.10 - Guardia Civil police - post on the left; crossroads. Head towards Grañón church.

2.15 - Grañón. Skirt round the church to the right, north-east, pass the porch and go through the village, as the pilgrims did, following a street going west.

2.20 - On the western edge of Grañón aim for a T - junction of tracks 250 metres to the north-west. You reach this by taking a track down to the north-east and then a footpath back to the south-west.

2.25 - At the junction take the path to the north-west.

2.27 - Cross a bridge.

2.29 - Crossing of paths. Continue another 10 metres to the north-west.

2.31 - Take a turning to the left, south-west. After 400 metres, rejoin the old Pilgrim Way,, heading up to a high point from where Redecilla

Tirón, where, beside the bridge on the N120, the remains of the pillars of the original bridge and two arches of the intervening one built by Peter the Cruel still exist.

In 1116 this town was peopled by Franks, by the clemency of Alfonso the Quarrelsome, and became 'head of Castile' during Navarre's greatest days. Here you can see, one after the other:
- On the way into the village, the 'ermita' of Santa María de Belén (Bethlehem) on the site of a former 'hospital';
- In the centre, an arcaded Plaza Mayor with shade and flowers, and the large church of San Pedro;
- Behind that church, in the shadow of the mountain which is topped by a castle and riddled with hermits' caves, the old church of Santa María lies beside the river, rich in pilgrim souvenirs;
- On the way out of the village the 'Hospital' of San Lazaro, with a 14th-century Gothic figure of Christ in its chapel, surrounded by votive offerings in gratitude for favours granted. The strangest of these is the skin of a large snake, from which a pilgrim was protected by the intercession of San Lazaro;
- Until 1923 the inhabitants performed each year, on Easter Saturday, a Mystery play of the Trial of Judas. The tradition has now died out.

THE SEVEN CAVES

The anchorites' caves in the mountain are known in the village of Cerezo del rio Tirón as the Seven Windows. One is called the Cave of San Caprasio, who is supposed to have lived there, and whose statue used to stand in the cave, but was later moved to the church of San Nicolás. A near-by site also bears his name in a distorted form, the 'San Cabrás'.

SANTIAGO PILGRIM MEMORIES OF SANTA MARIA

In the church of Santa María de Belorado, the carved stone Renaissance altar-piece has a figure of St James the Pilgrim and, above, a bas-relief of St James-Matamoros. Two more bas-reliefs depict his martyrdom and one of his miracles. The main altar has a 12th-century seated Virgin. There is a Holy Family on the side altar, and a figure of Christ between the two robbers, a fine work in ivory.

del Camino is visible.

3.10 - Cross the N120 beside a column on the way into Redecilla and aim for the village church.

3.15 - Church of Redecilla del Camino. Rejoin the N120 on the south-western edge of the village, and turn along it for 200 metres to cross the River Belachigo.

3.30 - Almost at the top of the hill 200 metres beyond the bridge and about 500 metres beyond Redecilla, turn left, south-west, onto a path.

3.45 - Turn left, south, on the access road to Bascuñana.

3.50 - Bascuñana. 300 metres before the church, by a drinking trough on your left, turn right, north-west, on a track which soon veers to the right then left, before going up to the west.

4.00 - Viloria de Rioja can be seen from the ridge; head towards it.

4.10 - Bridge. The path climbs up to the village.

4.15 - Viloria de Rioja. Cross through it to the south-west.

4.20 - 200 metres beyond the church take a track to the west between two tarmac roads. This leads to a wood and crosses it south-south-westwards, with the edge a few metres on your left. This track was fairly overgrown in March 1985.

4.40 - Cross a track and then a large uncultivated plateau, south-west, aiming for a football pitch. Pass this on your left.

4.47 - Take a track up to the right, west.

4.52 - The village of Fresneda is visible to the west. Go down into the valley.

5.00 - Cross a path running north-south, and continue straight ahead, west, on the track as it leads up onto a plateau.

5.20 - Fresneña. Leave the village

BELORADO DID NOT WISH TO PAY

The municipal archives of Belorado contain a parchment over a metre long, recording a court-case which the municipality brought when it wished to avoid paying 'St James's Tribute'; it considered that it did not come under the jurisdiction of the king who introduced it after the victory of Clavijo: it is possible to be devout and still look after one's own interests! The case continued until 1408, the date of the document which bears the signature of King Juan II.

ALTERNATIVE ROUTE

In bad weather, and particularly when visibility is poor, you avoid the plateau and the football pitch, as follows:
4.40 - Take a path to the right.
4.50 - Junction of paths at the bottom of the valley; continue straight ahead, west, on the path which then bends to the left to Fresneda.

ACCOMMODATION

Redecilla Del Camino: - Bars and a restaurant which sometimes have rooms to let.

Castildelgado:
- H El Chocolatero, tel. 58.00.63
- Pension-bar-restaurant El Caserio, tel. 58.01.01.

Belorado:
- HR Beldorado, tel. 58.06.84
- Fonda Martinez
- Fonda Alaska

FREE ACCOMMODATION

Redecilla: Enquire at the parish church

Belorado: Enquire at the parish church, tel. 58.00.85.

on a small tarmac access-road, south-west.
5.27 - Pass on your left, south, the road to Eterna. Continue along the tarmac road to the north-west.
5.32 - 200 metres farther on, turn left along a gravel path which initially runs parallel to the road and then continues to the north-west.
6.00 - Cross the N120 and take a gravel path opposite, leading to the large Comarcal co-operative; pass this on your left. Cross a path and continue north-west along the track, which bears left and north round the 898m hilltop just to the east of Belorado.
6.30 - After a col the path goes west, down to Belorado, which you enter from the north-east. On reaching the first houses bear left, south-west, leaving on your right the road coming in from Tormantos.
7.00 - Belorado, 760m. Rejoin the N120, which we have managed to avoid for much of the day, although this has meant missing the genuine Pilgrim Way through Castildelgado.

BELORADO

San Miguel

Rras De
Villafranca

Tosantos

Villambista

Espinosa

Nord

Villafranca
Montes de Oca

San Juan de
Ortega

1 Km

Stage 11 - 25 kilometres - 6 hours 15 minutes

BELORADO TO SAN JUAN DE ORTEGA

oday we have the pleasure of keeping very faithfully to the Pilgrim Way, almost always avoiding tarmac, and ending the stage at one of the most moving sites of the Camino, San Juan de Ortega, which takes its name from Santo Domingo's disciple, like him a 'Builder of the Road'. Before that we pass through Villafranca, the 'Frankish town', and across the Montes de Oca. These formerly redoubtable heights are now merely picturesque: but walkers should realise that they will have to climb about 400m during the day.

THE THREE BRIDGES ON THE RIVER TIRON

The bridge taking the N120 road over the River Tirón on the way out of Belorado is the third to cross the river down the centuries. Of the oldest bridge only the foundations remain, of the second, built by Peter the Cruel, parts of two arches are still visible here and there.

A FEW TRACES ALONG THE WAY

At *Tosantos* (All Saints) the walls of the sanctuary of the Virgin de la Peña can be seen on the right, hollowed

0.00 - Belorado, 770m. Leave the Plaza Mayor and its central bandstand by the west corner. Take the Calle Jose Antonio Primo de Rivera, then another street, to the left, west-south-west. 0.04 - Cross the Calle de la Cerca (the Haro road), and continue straight on, south-west, along a path parallel with the N120, a few dozen metres to your left. 0.08 - Triple fork: take the centre track, west. Pass the monastery 100 metres on your right. 0.14 - Rejoin the N120 40 metres

out of the mountainside: the statuette of this 'Virgin of the Peak' dates from the 12th century.

- At Villambistia the chapel is dedicated to St Roch, worshipped by pilgrims, showing him with the dog which he cured of rabies and which collected bread for him.

- *Espinosa-del-Camino* has a Romanesque polychrome statue of San Indalecio, who was believed to have evangelised the area. Leaving the village between walls and rows of elm trees, the Road to Santiago still retains its age-old character.

- The site known as *San Felices*, in the middle of cornfields, still has the ruined apse of the old Monastery of San Felix de Oca - 9th century, with a Mozarabic arch, currently being restored.

VILLAFRANCA DE OCA, THE FRANKISH TOWN AT THE FOOT OF THE MOUNTAINS

Villafranca-Montes de Oca was originally the Roman town of Auca. Its first bishop is said to have been San Indalecio, appointed by St James himself. Situated as it is on the Road, Villafranca should be translated as the Town of the Franks rather than, as is it in French, Villefranche or Free Town, even though the two went together, for the name indicates that like Los Arcos it was repopulated by the French, at the same time as it received its franchise. This may have been from Count Diego Porcelos *repoblador de Burgos*, who may be buried here.

The Montes de Oca are the mountains near-by, which have also inherited the Roman name.

The 'hospital' which stood here from AD 884 has disappeared. The present *'Hospital' de la Reina*, dedicated to San Antonio Abad, was founded in 1380 by Juana Manuel, wife of Enrique II, and transformed under Ferdinand and Isabella (*Los Reyes Católicos*, 'The Catholic Sovereigns'), whose coat of arms appears on an arcade. Now abandoned, it still provided 36 beds in the 18th century - though perhaps not very clean ones, since tradition has it that 'Villafranca has more beds than sheets'.

In the 18th-century *parish church of Santiago* the holy water stoup is an enormous scallop-shell from the Philippines, there is an *Ecce homo* attributed to Juan de Mena, and one of the two statues of St James has a reliquary set in its chest.

before the River Tirón; take this road first to the north-west then the south-west, once across the bridge.

0.24 - At the junction of the N120 with the San Miguel road, take the old Pilgrim Way to the south-west.

0.25 - Ignore a turning up to the left and continue along the Way, which remains roughly parallel to the N120 on the other side of the River Retorto.

0.35 - Junction of tracks: continue straight on, westwards.

0.40 - Go straight past a turning to the right and then another to the left, 20 metres farther on.

0.53 - The Old Road joins a path coming in from the left and merges with it; continue towards Tosantos, still parallel with the N120.

1.05 - Just before the crossroads to the south of Tosantos and the N120, cross a small bridge over the River Palomar.

1.08 - By a transformer on your right turn left, south-west, along a dirt track.

1.09 - Ignore a track to your left and continue straight along the path.

1.13 - Villambistia comes into view. The track broadens out into a road (not surfaced at the time of writing).

1.35 - Church of Villambistia on the right. Go down, over a bridge, across a small square with a fountain on the right, and take a broad track west-north-west.

1.40 - The track broadens into a road (but not surfaced at the time of writing). Continue west towards Espinosa.

1.55 - Cross the N120 and turn left along it, south-west, for 40 metres, then take an old track to the right, west-north-west, to the edge of Espinosa.

2.00 - Espinosa del Camino. Head north-east towards the church, pass

OFF THE ROUTE: THE VIRGIN AND THE MARTYR'S WELL

The chapel known as the Ermita de la Virgen de Oca at the bottom of the romantic gorge of La Hoz, to the right of Villafranca, has a 12th-century statue. There is a pilgrimage each year on 11 June to the the well beside it, edged with red stones where they say that when San Indalecio was martyred here, the water gushed out over the blood-stained stones. The pilgrimage includes a dance with staves to the sound of a drum.

THE MONTES DE OCA: THIEVES AND WOLVES IN OLDEN TIMES

In the Montes de Oca forests there are still a few wolves, which keep away from humans. In the Middle Ages the passage through these mountains was very hazardous; however, for Aymeric Picaud it was the most difficult stretch between 'wild Navarre' and welcoming Castile. Plunging deep into the woods, which could only be crossed in day light, he stopped for a bite of food at the spring called 'Mojapan', meaning 'moisten-your-bread'.

Now replanted, and crossed by the road which is never more than 200 metres from the footpath, the forest is very different from what it was in the 15th century, when the Italian traveller Laffi got lost here and only survived by eating mushrooms. There is also a legend that a young French pilgrim who died in this forest was resuscitated by St James, and went on to complete his pilgrimage.

The Puerto de Pedreja col (1163m) is snow-covered in winter, and the wind is fierce. It dominates the 'Valle de Robles gordos' - the valley of great oaks - which used to be infested with bandits. *Si quieres robar, véte a los Montes de Oca*, as the proverb still proclaims: 'If you want to be a thief, go to Oca'.

VAL DE FUENTES, VALLEY OF SPRINGS

The Fuente del Carnero (Sheep Spring) lies on the way to the Ermita de Val de Fuentes, a green valley with plenty of springs of drinking water. The road runs past the place now, but for the medieval pilgrim on his way down from the mountain it was a real oasis.

In 1187 Alfonso VII granted a 'fuero', or charter, to

it on your right, and turn left into a concreted street heading west, on the edge of the village.
2.08 - Fork at the end of the village: follow the concrete to the left and after 20 metres turn right, south-west, onto a path.
2.25 - Ignore a turning off to the right. Continue west-south-west, parallel with the N120.
2.30 - Top of the hill: ignore a fork to the right, and go on down the path.
2.35 - 50 metres beyond the ruin of San Felices on the right, the path veers left towards the N120.
2.45 - You rejoin the N120 300 metres before kilometre marker 77. Turn south-west along the road.
3.00 - The north-eastern edge of Villafranca-Montes de Oca, at the junction of the N120 and a road from the north. Bakery on the left of the N120 and bar-restaurant 'El Pájaro' on the right; just to the left of this bar climb up a short tarmac lane to the west, then a stony track.
3.06 - Beyond a high-tension pylon the track bears left, south-west.
3.13 - Join a gravel track on a bend, and follow it westwards.
3.20 - Ignore an almost parallel right turn and continue west-south-west.
3.24 - Deep cleft below and to the left, with a farm 200 metres away in the valley.
3.26 - Spring on the left. The undulating track climbs gently through a wood of young oak trees.
3.45 - Ignore a turn to the right and continue south-west across a plateau of heather and bushes.
3.47 - Beyond a barbed-wire fence the track runs through a plantation of conifers.
4.00 - Col, 1163m. The N120 is 50 metres to your left, and a monument 30 metres to the right.

a 'hospital' here, and one end of the chapel still remains, with crossed ogives and a human-head corbel, which was partly restored as a hermitage in the 19th century.

SAN JUAN DE ORTEGA, BUILDER OF HIS OWN CHURCH

An inn and a few houses around a church designated as a National Monument, constitute this village, which bears the name of its builder in about 1150. The nave and transept with paired windows are Romanesque in origin, as are the crypt and the saint's very simple memorial.

Born in about 1080 at Quintaortuño, near Vivar-del-Cid, he was fourteen when his bold compatriot conquered Valencia. Juan himself made the pilgrimage to Jerusalem and on his return, in fulfilment of a vow, built the sanctuary here, in a field of nettles (*ortegas* = nettles, from the Latin *'urtica'*).

Architect and builder of bridges and churches, he became assistant to Santo Domingo de la Calzada. After his death in 1162 and burial in his own church, numerous miracles were attributed to him, notably births to apparently barren women, and the cure of a dumb child of Irish pilgrims.

ACCOMMODATION

Villafranca Montes de Oca:
- Fonda-restaurant El Pájaro, tel. 58.01.29
- Enquire at the parish church and the Town Hall to see if there are rooms available.

FREE ACCOMMODATION

Villafranca-Montes de Oca: Enquire at the parish church, tel. 58.02.01.

San Juan de Ortega: See the final lines of the walking instructions.

Cross a path. The track goes downhill, across a stream, and up again through a wood.
4.25 - It peters out into a broad cleared strip (marker MP57): follow this fire-break to the right, west.
4.32 - Marker MP58. Continue west along the fire-break.
4.43 - Cross one track.
4.50 - Then another track (marker P61)
5.00 - Join a path coming in from the chapel of Valdefuentes, the remains of a Cistercian monastery 1 kilometre to the left beside the N120. Carry on along this track, which is suitable for vehicles, heading west. Lined with crosses, it is known as the Path of the Crosses of San Juan de Ortega.
5.20 - Fork: bear right.
6.15 - Monastery of San Juan de Ortega, 1000m and a few scattered houses. Magnificent architectural grouping of the Romanesque church with hospital and cloisters. The priest, Father José Maria Alonso, Arroco, San Juan de Ortega, Provincia de Burgos, offers lodging to pilgrims in dormitories with washing facilities. Leave a sum of money for each person's stay, corresponding to the current charges of the French Randonnées Pyrénéennes.

SAN JUAN DE ORTEGA

Barrios De Colina

Santovenia De Oca

Ages

zalduendo

Atapuerca

Ibeas de
Juarros

Villalval

Cardenuela Riopico

Quintanilla

Rubena

Orbaneja

Villafria

Villayerno

Morquillas

Villimar

BURGOS

Nord

1 km

Stage 12 - 28 kilometres - 7 hours

SAN JUAN DE ORTEGA TO BURGOS

T his is a fairly long stage: as well as the actual distance covered, we must take into account the climb up to a plateau at an altitude of more than 1,000m. There is a long stretch across this mountain, which is occupied by a military zone, and means skirting round an enormous quarry and an airfield, and avoiding two main roads, a motorway and a railway - but nonetheless it takes us through beautiful countryside.

First capital city of old Castile and bridgehead of the Reconquest, Burgos has a treasury of monuments and in particular one of Spain's finest Gothic cathedrals.

FROM CARDEÑUELA TO THE GATES OF BURGOS

Cardeñuela-de-Riopico derives its noble name from a stream which, as the name indicates, is modest; at the top of the village is a church with carved Renaissance porch and a bell-tower with two large bells.

- *Villafría*, which now forms part of Burgos, also has a Renaissance church with two towers and bell-tower.

0.00 - Monastery of San Juan de Ortega. Take the small tarmac road to the west.

0.05 - Fork: bear left for 20 metres, then right onto a track up through the wood, west-south-west.

0.25 - Beyond a barbed-wire fence the track leaves the wood and crosses a plateau.

- *Gamonal*, today a suburb of Burgos, has a Gothic church with carved porch, a painting of the Virgin, and ancient baptismal font. But above all, you will see in the adjoining cemetery a Calvary with carvings illustrating themes related to the pilgrimage, which once stood beside the Pilgrim Way. Gamonal was then a bishopric, a former bishop of Villafranca-Montes de Oca, the successor to San Indalecio, having moved his see there from 1075 on.

- *Capiscol*, finally, an outlying district of Burgos and now without any great attraction, once had a 'hospital'. This was in effect the junction of the *Camino Frances* with two secondary routes to Santiago, including the Road from Bayonne via the Basque coast and Vitoria.

BURGOS, CITY OF EL CID

The name Burgos (Burg = castle) would seem to indicate a fortress from the days of the Germanic invasions. Legend, more picturesque, attributes the name to a German pilgrim, Belchides, son-in-law of Count Diego Parceos who in 844 organised a fast-growing repopulation.

Another instance of history merging with legend came about in the following century: the great locally-born captain Rodrigo de Bivar, otherwise known as El Cid Campeador, with his horse Babieca and his sword Tizona, was a descendant of a Burgos alderman. His contemporary Fernán González sought to make the area an independent county. And in 1035 Burgos became capital of the new Kingdom of Castile, its first king being Fernando I, son of the King of Navarre, Sancho The Great.

THE QUEEN OF GOTHIC CATHEDRALS

Burgos is too rich in monuments for us to give a full guide here, so we shall restrict comment to those which pilgrims will see on their way through the town, and the history of which is relevant to St James.

- On the edge of the town, outside the walls, the 'Hospital' de San Juan Evangelista was placed under the protection of the Benedictines of La Chaise-Dieu by Alfonso VI in 1091; their prior was San Lesmes-St Adelesme of Loudun. His tomb was in the Gothic church until 1968 when his remains, which appeared to be complete, were exhumed and the tomb moved to the choir during major restoration

0.30 - The track runs along an earth embankment with strange-looking gullies dug out on both sides.

0.40 - Fence and path (under construction at the time of writing); follow this new track.

0.50 - Agés, 970m. Take the small road to Atapuerca.

1.30 - Atapuerca. In front of the bakery (Panadería), i.e. below and to the west of the church, set off heading due west across the grass and after 100 metres pick up a broad track.

1.40 - You come to a military zone, where the path and yellow waymarking evidently no longer apply now that the camp has been established. Do not enter the military zone, but at the first pyramidal marker, P.M., take a track to the right westwards.

1.45 - Second marker, P.M., 10 metres to the left. Continue heading west up the track.

1.50 - Third marker, P.M., on the left. Continue west along the track, which becomes less clear. Next continue gently uphill along a wider track with short grass and gravel.

1.55 - Fourth marker, P.M. Continue gently up to the west.

2.00 - Fifth marker P.M. Carry on up to the west.

2.05 - Sixth marker P.M. You reach a limestone plateau at an altitude of about 1070m. Two large radar antennae can be clearly seen, 1,500 metres to the west, but the large quarries below to the left are not yet visible. Head towards the antennae, or better, slightly to the left, west-south-west.

2.10 - Now the quarries are visible to the west, and to the south-west the hamlet of Villalval, which we shall pass through. Head downhill, south-south-west, leaving the

and inaugurated the following year in the presence of pilgrims from Loudun. The 'Hospital' is now used as an Arts Centre.

- In the centre of the town, the *Gothic cathedral* is one of the finest in Europe, and of amazing architectural richness. Building started in 1221, and the German-born bishop Johann of Cologne completed the tower in the 15th century. In particular, note the carved 13th-century porch, the 'Santo Cristo' of the same period from the Augustinian monastery, the chapel of St James, a pilgrim head on a cloister capital, a statue of St James in the Museum and, in the choir, a seat panel depicting the appearance of the Virgin of Pilar to the Apostle.

- Across the Maltos Bridge and beyond the military hospital, (on tomorrow's route out of Burgos but slightly to the south of it), a large group of buildings providing hospitality was established by the *Monastery of Huelgas Reales* and the *'Hospital' del Rey*, where poor pilgrims were cared for and even clothed. This complex dates from the 12th and 16th centuries, with a Romanesque cloister and Moorish infirmary. Its chapel of San Amaro is dedicated to the French Saint Amer who, returning from Compostela, settled here until he died, helping poor and sick pilgrims whom he sought out along the roads.

- Among many other monuments, palaces, and churches, the castle dominating the town should also be visited.

OFF THE ROUTE:
LA CARTUJA DE MIRAFLORES AND THE TOMB OF EL CID

- *La Cartuja de Miraflores*, a Carthusian monastery 5 kilometres east of the town, is a jewel of flamboyant Gothic architecture from about 1453, and has among its tombs that of the parents of Isabella the Catholic.

- The more modest *Monastery of San Pedro de Cardeña*, 20 kilometres to the south-east, and dating from the 11th and 12th centuries, was the final resting place of El Cid and his wife Chimene.

quarries 400 metres to your right.

2.15 - *It is possible to continue westward on the track leading to the quarry access path, and go 1 kilometre down it to Villalval, but it is more direct and pleasanter to go steeply south-west down the middle of the valley to reach the hamlet.*

2.45 - *Villalval. Go on down the small access road.*

3.15 - *Cardeñuela-Riopico: a bar here will provide meals - check the prices. Continue west along the small access road.*

4.30 - *Villafría de Burgos, 880m, with the N1 road running about 500 metres to the west of the town centre. Cross the N1, leaving on your left a coach-stop for Burgos (line No.8) and a bar/hotel/restaurant. Continue along a track heading north.*

4.34 - *Small bridge over the River Vena, with football ground opposite. Take the gravel track left, west, then turn off it, passing the sports changing-rooms on your left, and continue to the north.*

4.39 - Small bridge and track aiming north-west.

4.42 - *Go under the high-tension wires and take a track westwards, which may be the original CAMINO.*

4.45 - *The direct road to Villimar has disappeared; take another to the right, north-west.*

4.55 - *Join a small road to the left, south.*

5.20 - Villimar church on the right. Carry on along the small road (Calle de Pozo).

5.25 - Bridge south of Villimar. Stay on the road, which bears right, south-west, with a bicycle track running along its right side.

5.43 - Crossroads. Continue almost straight ahead, west-south-west on the main road to Pozo.

5.47 - Church 100 metres to the left. Take the Calle de Las Cardelas to the west.

5.50 - Bus-stop and crossroads. You can take the Calle de las Escuelas, south-west, but bear back to the left as soon as possible to join the main avenue, part of the N120.

5.55 - Calle de Vitoria: follow this to the south-west.

6.15 - Triple junction (Madrid to the left, Santander to the right). Take the middle road, west, the Calle de Vitoria, to the town centre.

6.30 - Just before reaching a canal turn right into the Calle de San Lesmes.

6.33 - On the left a bridge, a gateway, and the Calle San Juan.

6.36 - Cross the Calle de Santander.

6.40 - Continue on along the Calle de Los Avellanos, heading west.

6.42 - Then along the Calle Fernan Gonzalez.

6.47 - Cathedral on the left.

6.50 - Church of San Nicolás on the right. Facing away from it, go down the steps to the south, to the square in front of the Cathedral, which deserves a lengthy visit.

ACCOMMODATION

Villafria de Burgos:
- HS** Iruñao, tel. 21.41.25.
- H** Vitoria, tel. 22.51.00.
- HSR** Buenos Aires, tel. 22.41.15.
- HSR** Las Vegas, tel. 22.41.00

Burgos: Numerous hotels, restaurants, fondas. Enquire at the Tourist Office (Oficina de Información de Turismo).

FREE ACCOMMODATION

Enquire at the Archbishopric, 18 Martinez del Campo, tel. 22.74.00

Stage 13 - 40 kilometres - 10 hours

BURGOS TO CASTROJERIZ

I*n the course of this very long stage we shall discover the immense landscapes of the Meseta, the limestone and clay plateau at an altitude of over 900m, sun-scorched by day but cool at night, even in summer. We shall follow long paths alternating between the high semi-desert and the fields which even in Aymery Picaud's day were famous for their fertility. Because of the great distance it is important to start the day very early, to avoid, if possible, walking during the hottest part of the day. Some may prefer to divide the stage into two, and stay overnight at, for example, Hornillos del Camino, which has some rare relics of pilgrim times. Castrojeriz, at the end of the stage, is considerably more interesting.*

'DE TARDAJOS A RABÉ, LIBERA NOS DOMINE'

The bridge into Tardajos on the main road is called 'del Arzobispo', for the Archbishop had his palace here in the town which also had a 'hospital'. A few ruins and heraldic stones remain from those days of its importance.

The spates of the River Alanzón were notorious. Alfonso VI fell from his horse when chasing thieves and was only saved from drowning by his prayers to the figure of Christ of Benavel, and St Teresa of Avila herself, on her way to found the Carmelite convent at Burgos, also fell into the Alanzón with her carriage. Hence no doubt the pilgrims' saying:

'De Rabé a Tardajos
Note faltaran trabajos
De Tardajos a Rabé,
Libera-nos Domine!'

(From Rabé to Tardajos, perils galore, but from Tardajos to Rabé, deliver us Good Lord!)

The two places are in reality very close to each other, but separated by a marshy expanse which was often flooded. The Romans used both as halting-places, under

0.00 - Burgos. From the Paseo de las Fuentecillas cross the Malatos bridge. Once on the south bank of the River Arlanzón, follow the avenue to the right, north-west.

0.07 - Leave on your right the Veterinaria bridge over the Arlanzón, and continue along the avenue for more than 500 metres to the west-north-west, passing the stadium on your right and the 'Hospital' del Rey on your left.

0.15 - This avenue, departure point for Valladolid and León, goes under the Burgos-Santander railway line. Carry on along the avenue for another 600 metres.

0.23 - 50 metres before a left-hand, south-westward, bend in the road, turn right, north-west, into a small road. Continue along the tarmac to the west, leaving a church on your right and a factory on your left. After

the names of Augustobriga and Alterdalia.

The name of Rabé de las Calzadas is a reminder of the pilgrim 'highway', which passed through the town. There is a hermitage on the edge of the town, and a Romanesque crucifixion in the church.

HORNILLOS DEL CAMINO, AFFILIATE OF ROCAMADOUR

Vicus under the Romans, Hornillos later became a Visigoth town - a tombstone from this period has been found recently in a house wall. Next it became an important staging post along the Camino, preparatory to the arduous crossing of the Meseta. From the 12th to the 14th centuries the Kings of Castile favoured the 'hospitals' here, which were run by the Benedictine monks of St Denis, Paris and later affiliated to Rocamadour, in south-west France. Very little remains. The single long street lies along the Pilgrim Way with:
- On the way into the town, a watermill on the River Hornazuelas and old bridges.
- On the first house on the right, a former presbytery which was previously the 'Hospital' de Sancti-Spiriti, a cross of St James with a chalice and two keys.
- In the town centre, a large Gothic church with three aisles.

THE SICK PILGRIM DEVOURED BY LOCUSTS

The harsh Meseta, the high plain between Hornillos and Hontanas, is split by the green valley of the Sambol stream with, to the south, its spring of drinkable water. Only ruins of the sheep-pens remain, but the name of Sambol still bears witness to the existence until the 15th century of the monastery of St Boal, or Baudilla.

The Bolognese priest Laffi recounts that in 1673, travelling through a dense cloud of locusts, he discovered a dying pilgrim, half devoured by the grasshoppers. He arrived in time to hear the man's confession and promptly bury him.

the entrance to a nursery-garden on your right, take a path to the west-north-west. This leads to a poplar plantation, passing under high-tension cables.

1.15 - Villalbilla de Burgos, 837m; cross the railway line which leads to the flour-mill on the right, but leave on your left the Madrid-Irun line, the church, and the village. Continue straight on, west, along a path leading to the N120.

1.25 - Join the N120 which you reach 400 metres before marker 122. Turn west along it for about 2.5 kilometres.

2.00 - Tardajos, 828m. From the outskirts follow a series of streets slightly to the left of the N120 to go through the village, heading broadly west. Next take the small tarmac road leading south-west to Rabé.

2.30 - Rabé de las Calzadas, 831m. Go through the village heading north-west, then turn west on a track, leaving a chapel and cemetery on your left. Suitable for vehicles for the first kilometre, the track heads generally west across the Meseta. The yellow waymarking and signs at the crossings keep you on the right route.

4.00 - Cross the road linking Villanueva (5 kilometres to the north) with Estepar (8 kilometres to the south) and go straight ahead, west, on the road to Hornillos.

4.10 - Cross Hornillos del Camino, 825m, heading west, leaving the church on your right. Beyond the municipal weighbridge take a path to the west-north-west.

4.25 - Take a track south-west to the left of the path.

4.35 - Fork: go straight ahead, west.

4.45 - After crossing a stream, take a track to the left, south-west, beside the stream; carry straight on, west, at each intersection across the

THE ANTONINES OF HONTANAS
WHO CURED ST ANTHONY'S FIRE

Hontanas (the Fountains) was described in the 17th century as a handful of shepherds' huts surrounded by a palisade as a defence against wolves. The church, however, retains the traces of an older construction, and the sunken track is not without charm. But the genuine pilgrim relic is a bit farther on, at the roadside beyond the Garbanzuelo ('little chick-pea') stream: this is the Convento de San Antón, St Antony's Monastery, where the road ran through the gateway and the monks distributed food to the pilgrims.

Alfonso VI handed it over the Antonines in 1146, the regular Canons of St Antony, of French allegiance. Their order had been founded in Dauphiné (in eastern France) to care for those suffering from 'St Anthony's Fire', or erysipelas, a sort of painful gangrene which appeared in 10th-century Europe. Many sufferers came here seeking a cure, no doubt helped by the climate. Flute-playing monks walked ahead of the sick, who had to wear the 'Tau', a T-shaped cross, over their habits. This T appears on some of the windows and in the rose-window of the church. The present building dates from the 14th century, with the apse and a section of the wall used as a hayloft remaining from that time.

stamp here

ALTERNATIVE

0.00 - After crossing the bridge over the River Arlanzón, there is a small irrigation canal about 10 metres above the road, near a ruined house; the footpath running beside the canal leads to Tardajos (2.00).

undulating plain.
5.20 - Cross a gravel path.
5.25 - The path goes down to the south-west.
5.32 - Bridge
5.35 - Cross a gravel road and continue to the west. The track leads up on to the Meseta again.
6.00 - Road linking Ollos (8 kilometres to the north) with Iglesias (4 kilometres to the south): cross the road a few hundred metres to the south of the turning, by a wayside Calvary, to Castrojeriz (13 kilometres away). Continue straight on, west, between cornfields, along the track across the Meseta at an altitude of 920m.
6.12 - Cross a farm track.
6.30 - Hontanas is visible below.
6.45 - Hontanas, 870m. Cross the village and follow its access road, heading west.
7.00 - Cross the road leading to Castrojeriz (9 kilometres away to the west-south-west) and take a track running at first beside the road then moving farther away but remaining roughly parallel, about 200-300 metres from the road.
7.25 - Large ruin on your right. The track goes down and joins another, more clearly marked, heading west-south-west.
7.30 - Continue straight ahead, on a grassy track.
7.50 - Rejoin the quiet and shady road to Castrojeriz; it is possible to remain on this road, but we shall leave it from time to time.
8.15 - Just before the ruins of the monastery of San Antón turn left, south, on a track to Villaquirán de la Puebla.
8.35 - At the church, which you pass on your right, turn westward, leaving the public weighbridge on your right, cross the village's small

CASTROJERIZ AND LA VIRGEN DEL MANZANO

Still crowned by the ruins of an old fortress, Castrojeriz is the 'Castum Sigerici' founded in AD 760 by Sigeric the Goth, brother of a Count of Castile. Pilgrims following the high street will find:

- On entering the town, *Nuestra Señora del Manzano* (Our Lady of the Apple Tree), a national monument named after the polychrome stone Virgin whose miracles were celebrated by Alfonso X the Wise in his *Cantigas.* Founded in 1214 by Doña Berenguera la Grande, this transitional Romanesque-Gothic church contains among other items a 'Santiago Peregrino' painted by Brunzino, and the tombs of various famous people including Doña Léonor, Queen of Aragon.

- In the town centre, the 16th-century parish *church of Santo Domingo* and the museum beside it share the treasures from other churches, including tapestries after Rubens.

- Beneath the paving in the *Plaza Mayor,* the skeleton of a pilgrim was found, surrounded by scallop-shells and French and English 14th-century coins.

- Near the last crossroads, the vast early Gothic church of San Juan was attached to one of the many 'hospitals'.

access road, and go north-west on a path leading to Castrojeriz which curls round the foot of a 919m hill dominated by castle ruins.

9.05 - On the left, church and surrounding wall: take a 90-degree turn onto a wide track to the right, north.

9.12 - Rejoin the road near the 'Castrojeriz' sign. Although the town centre lies one kilometre to your left, head right, north-east, towards the church of Santa María del Manzano. Beyond the monument to the Road to Santiago (which you pass on your left) follow in the pilgrims' footsteps and go through the town, heading first to the south-west, with the church of Santo Domingo on your right and the church of San Juan on your left.

10.00 - Centre of Castrojeriz, 800m.

ACCOMMODATION

Villabilla de Burgos:
   - Hostal San Roque, tel. 20.44.49
Tardajos:
   - Fondas Ruiz, tel. 45.11.25
Castrojeriz:
   - Fonda Casa Carlos (restaurant Anton), tel. 37.70.12
   - Casa El Chato
   - Bar-restaurant

FREE ACCOMMODATION

Tardajos: Enquire at 'Los Padres Paules', tel. 45.10.03.k
Hornillos del Camino: Enquire at the Town Hall.
Hontanas: Enquire at the Town Hall
Castrojeriz: Enquire at the parish church.

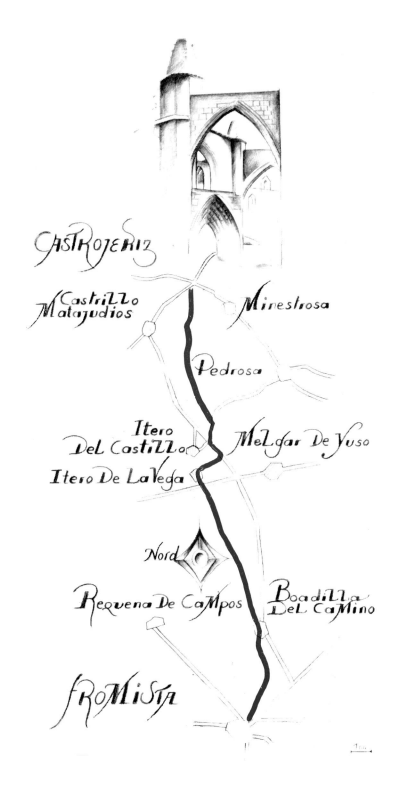

CASTROJERIZ

Castrillo Matajudios

Minestrosa

Pedrosa

Itero Del Castillo

Melgar De Yuso

Itero De La Vega

Nord

Requena De Campos

Boadilla Del Camino

FROMISTA

Stage 14 - 24 kilometres - 6 hours

CASTROJERIZ TO FRÓMISTA

More *treeless plateaux, and the great high arable plains, green in spring and endlessly yellow later in the season. But no main roads, no tarmac; at the half-way point the Fitero bridge crosses the river which divides Itero, one half in Castile and the other in León - for this frontier between the provinces of Burgos and Palencia also marks the division between two former kingdoms. This easier stage offers some genuine archaeological treats, at Itero and Boadilla, but the high point is the magnificent church of San Martín de Frómista.*

THE PUENTE FITERO, FRONTIER BETWEEN CASTILE AND LEON

Dividing the two parts of Itero, 'del Castillo' and 'de la Vega', the River Pisuerga marks the frontier between the kingdoms of Castile and León. The 'Puente Fitero' bridge with its eleven Romanesque arches was built, or rebuilt, by Alfonso VI in the 12th century.

On the left bank before the bridge, Itero-del-Castillo, the last hamlet in Castile, is dominated by the 13th-century castle of the dukes of Frias; the ruins of the San Nicolás hermitage lie at its foot.

On the right bank the first village in León, Itero-de-la-Vega, is slightly larger. The 13th-century Piedad hermitage has a statue of St James the Pilgrim at its door, and the 16th-century church of San Pedro still has a 13th-century porch.

0.00 Castrojeriz, 800m. From the church of San Juan head down to the west; cross the Hinestrosa-Villasilos road (running south-west-north-east), and the Castrillo road (running south-east-north-west).

0.05 - Continue west along a motor road.

0.25 - After a bridge across the River Odrilla, at 765m, take a track heading north-west.

0.30 - Fork; bear left, west, along a path for 20 metres, then take the facing track, west, climbing up and across the bare hillside. Note the many fragments of gypsum on the ground.

0.50 - You reach the edge of the

THE ORDER OF CALATRAVA

The substantial 'Hospital' of St John, founded in 1174, was also close to the bridge. Sixteen years earlier its Navarrese abbot, Raymond de Fitero, had led 2,000 men in defence of the fortress of Calatrava in La Mancha against the Moors; subsequently he and Diego Velásquez founded the order of chivalry named after Calatrava.

BOADILLA'S PILLORY AND ROMAN HEATING

Besides the 15th- and 16th-century Gothic church of Santa María, with its wealth of statues and paintings and its Romanesque baptismal font, Boadilla also has a *rollo gótico*, a column or carved pillory.

There are houses throughout the region with air-duct heating; known as a 'gloria', this system is the direct descendant of the Roman hypocaust.

FROMISTA-DEL-CAMINO, A ROMANESQUE JEWEL

Frómista, whose name in Roman times may have been derived from *frumentum*, meaning corn, was destroyed and then rebuilt in the 10th century.

At the entrance to the town you pass near the *Hermitage of Nuestra Señora de Otero*, with Gothic remains, and containing a seated polychromatic 13th-century Virgin which is widely venerated.

Entering the town along the *Calle de los Franceses*, street of the French, and passing through the suburbs, you will find the old bastide-style town on your right, with its wealth of ancient monuments.

The three-aisled Romanesque *church of San Martín*, the purged branch of the church at Jaca, with which its capitals form a visible link, is the only remaining trace of a Benedictine monastery founded in 1066 by Doña Mayor de Navarra. Although the vigorous restoration of 1896 unfortunately removed various carvings which were considered improper, it did nonetheless restore due importance to this jewel of Romanesque architecture reminiscent of the brick buildings of Toulouse both in design and in the precision of its ochre-pink stone construction.

Other monuments include the baroque church of

plateau, 914m; head approximately west across it, guided by waymarked cairns which mark a detour round the right-hand side of a field.

1.00 - Take a footpath down to the west through the scrubland.

1.06 - Continue west along a track through the fields; at intersections, keep going straight ahead.

1.20 - Turn off a motor track onto a grassy track going down to the left, west.

1.26 - Go straight ahead on another more heavily used track

1.50 - Fuente del Piojo and drinking trough on your right, a few metres from a small road to the right; turn onto this for a full kilometre, heading west-north-west.

2.10 - Crossroads: turn left, south-west, on the road to Boadilla-del-Camino, BU403.

2.20 - After passing on your left all that remains of the Hermitage of San Nicolás, cross the bridge over the River Pisuerga at kilometre marker 34 and just beyond, turn right, north, on a motor track.

2.50 - Itero de la Vega, 77m. Go through the village, heading west, and continue on a small road, still westward.

2.55 - Cross the Osorno to Astudillo road and take the gravel path opposite, west. After one kilometre this passes a hamlet of 'bodegas', 400 metres away to the left.

3.15 - Bridge over the Canal del Pisuerga, then the track climbs westward.

3.45 - From the top of a rise, 840m, it drops down again, west-south-west.

4.40 - Boadilla del Camino; make a detour of 200 metres to the left of the waymarked route to visit the impressive 15th/16th-century church. Go through the village heading north-west; there is a bar

Santa María del Castillo, built on 14th-century foundations and containing a 29-picture reredos; San Pedro, dating from the 15th century, with paintings by Ribera and Meng and a silver custodial; and in the Plaza Mayor the 'Hospital' de los Palmeros, with 16th-century arcading, has been restored and converted to gastronomic purposes.

ST ELMO'S FIRE

A statue surrounded by water in the Plaza Major at Frómista recalls Pedros Gonzalez Telmo, who was born here in 1190. A Dominican and Dean of Palencia, Confessor to Fernando III the Saint, he devoted himself to the seamen of Pontevedra in Galicia and of northern Portugal. His name has been attached to 'San Telmo's fire', the discharge of natural electricity down ships' masts. His feast-day falls on 5 April and is celebrated, sometimes on another date because of Holy Week, with a civic procession accompanied by castanets, joke sermons, and fireworks.

The phenomenon is known in English as 'St Elmo's fire', and it seems that the name of this seafarers' patron has been confused with a St Elme (or St Erasmus), martyred in Italy under the rule of Diocletian by disembowelling with the aid of a winch.

on the left.
4.45 - Continue along a track to the north-west, then another to the left, west-south-west.
5.00 - The Canal de Castile; take the path along the south bank, heading west.
5.40 - Cross the lock, go down path to the north, and follow a short track to the west.
5.43 - Then a road to the north-west.
5.46 - Cross under the Palencia-Santander railway into Frómista.
5.50 - Halt and major crossroads.
5.55 - Church of San Martin
6.00 - Frómista town centre, 787m.

ACCOMMODATION

Boadilla del Camino:
  - Fondas, bar Dori (sandwiches), tel. 81.03.71. Groceries

Frómista:
  - HSR* San Telmo, tel.81.01.02
  - Fonda Marisa, tel. 81.00.23
  - Bar-restaurant Los Palmeros, tel. 81.00.67
  - Bar-mesón Poli, tel. 81.10.43

FREE ACCOMMODATION

Frómista: Enquire at the parish church, tel.81.01.44 (shelter at the end of a garden near the railway).

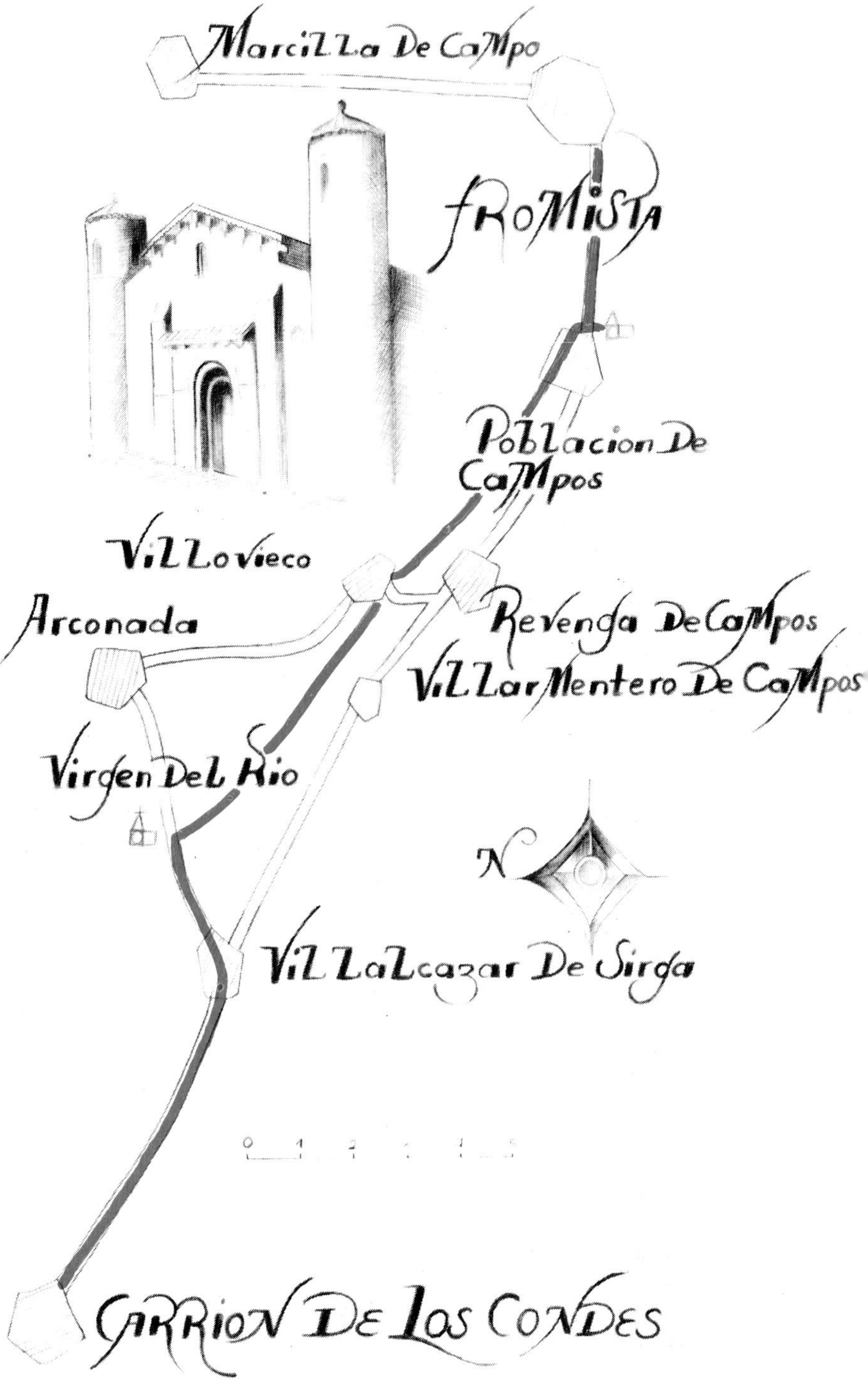

Marcilla De Campo

Fromista

Poblacion De Campos

Villovieco

Arconada

Revenga De Campos

Villar Mentero De Campos

Virgen Del Rio

N

Villalcazar De Sirga

Carrion De Los Condes

Stage 15 - 22 kilometres - 6 hours

FRÓMISTA TO CARRIÓN DE LOS CONDES

T*his is a fairly short stage, of lesser interest from the walking point of view; it includes long stretches along roads - fortunately quite quiet roads - and straight tracks leading directly to Carrión de los Condes. Historically and architecturally, however, it is a very interesting stage. The church of Villalcazar de Sirga, a Templar monument with rich furnishings, merits a lengthy visit; and if you are late sitting down to a meal at the 'Mesón' next door, don't worry; they are accustomed here to seeing modern pilgrims camping beneath the church porch. Two Romanesque porches at Carrión de los Condes are classified as national monuments.*

FROM POBLACION DE CAMPOS TO LA VIRGEN DEL RIO

- At *Población de Campos,* ancient fief of Malta, the baroque 17th-century parish church of Santa Magdalena has three aisles, and there is a 13th-century polychrome statue of the Virgin at the late Romanesque Ermita del Socorro on the way into the village. Traces of a former 'hospital' lie beneath one of the houses.
- *Villovieco* has the Renaissance church of Santa María with an altar-piece of St James.

0.00 - Frómista. Take the Carrión de los Condes road west out of the town, and follow it for 4 kilometres.
1.00 - after kilometre marker 16, with the Ermita de San Miguel on your left, take a 90-degree turn due north off the road, along the edge of a field for 300 metres, to a path and the first houses of Población de Campos, at 790m. Go through the village, heading north-west, and

- *Revenga de Campos,* on the main road to the south of Villovieco has the baroque church of San Lorenzo, and heraldic carvings on the houses.

- Pilgrims following the River Ucieza often made a detour to the north to visit the two hermitages, *del Cristo de la Salud* and the *Virgen del Rio,* which has an alabaster statue of St James the Pilgrim.

THE TEMPLARS' CHURCH AT VILLALCAZAR DE SIRGA

For a long period Villalcazar de Sirga was simply Villasirga, 'sirga' being another word for 'calzada', roadway, which is still used locally. There is a striking contrast between the small size of the sun-baked village, rich in 'hospitals' and devoted to gastronomy, and the enormous Templars' church of Santa Maria la Blanca.

Begun in the 12th century, the church is Romanesque in its Cistercian ground-plan and Gothic in its completion during the following century, as witness the great glowing rose-window. Serving as both cathedral and fortress, with a well for times of siege, it has more treasures in its three aisles and two transepts - tombs, statues, paintings - than we can list here.

DON FELIPE, THE TWICE-MARRIED ARCHBISHOP

The most remarkable of the tombs in the church at Villalcazar is that of Don Felipe and Doña Léonor. Fifth son of San Fernando, who won back Seville from the Moors, Prince Felipe was a brother of King Alfonso X the Wise of Castile. A cleric and fellow-disciple in Paris of St Thomas Aquinas and St Bonaventure, he became Archbishop of Seville. But in 1258 when Alfonso repudiated his fiancée, Christine of Norway, Felipe became her champion and then left the church to marry her. However, she died of melancholia, and her tomb at Covarrubias is a place of pilgrimage for lovers. Eleven years later Felipe married again, this time Leonor de Castro, who lies in the tomb next to his; they are shown side by side in effigy. The bas-reliefs on Felipe's tomb depict his burial with great realism. The prince's body was exhumed in 1897 and found to measure almost two metres.

passing close by the church.

1.15 - 300 metres west-north-west of the church take a track north-west for 4 kilometres.

2.15 - Villovieco, 790m: pass the village on your right and follow the access road across the bridge over the River Ucieza. Take a track north-west, along the bank of the river, to your right.

2.45 - Pass Villarmentero de Campos, 790m, 400 metres away on your left. Continue north-west along the track by the river.

3.30 - A small road at the foot of the Virgen del Rio leads to Villalcazar de Sirga, a full kilometre away to the south-west; tracks lead on to Carrión, avoiding considerable stretches of tarmac surface and skirting round the north of Villalcazar; but we shall continue along the road to see Villalcazar, which is well worth a visit.

3.45 - Beyond kilometre marker 10 turn right, west, along a street through Villalcazar de Sirga, 810m.

3.55 - Pick up the Carrión road again, and follow it for 5 kilometres.

5.15 - Signpost: 'Carrión de los Condes': turn left along a minor road (sign, '0.8 Camping') and after 100 metres go right, north-west, on a track. The waymarked route passes the Monastery of Santa Clara and then San Francisco on your left.

5.30 - At the crossroads in Carrión town centre continue straight on, down the Calle Santa María, with the church of Santa María del Camino on the right; bear right and go past the front of the church of Santiago, to the north-west edge of the town.

THE FOURTEEN MIRACLES
OF MARIA LA BLANCA

The *Cantigas* of Alfonso the Wise contain an extensive celebration of the merits of the Virgen Blanca. Some authors identify her with the Virgen del Rio, others with the statues of the Virgin in the Templars' church, one on the altar-piece and the other beside a pillar facing the chapel of St James. The latter, a seated Virgin with the now headless Child on her knees, would seem the more likely.

Whatever the truth, Alfonso the Wise attributed fourteen miracles to her, including:
- A Toulouse pilgrim walking with an iron staff saw it break, marking the completion of his penance.
- a blind French lady, sheltering in the church from the rain , recovered her sight; and another, brought in paralysed on a stretcher, recovered the use of her limbs.
- a peasant who was reluctant to deliver an ox as promised saw it removed from him.
- seafarers were saved from storms, etc.

THE GASTRONOMIC PILGRIM
IN OLD CASTILE

Here we are firmly in the zone of 'asados', roast and grilled meat. Among the wines of southern Castile, Valdepeñas is particularly well known.

Specialities include:
- 'Cochinillo asado': sucking pig grilled in the baker's oven;
- 'Lechazo': baby lamb cooked either in the oven or under the grill;
- 'Sopa al cuarto de hora', fifteen-minute soup, with garlic;
- 'Morcilla Burgalesa' - a Burgos version of black pudding made with pork for frying or with beef for boiling in the 'cocido';
- 'Olla podrida' - a mixture, a variation on 'Cocido', a thick soup or stew with chick peas and any kind of meat;
- fresh sheep's-milk cheese.

THE BULLS AND CARRION'S
HUNDRED VIRGINS

Carrión played an important role in the Romancero
(old ballads). 'The Song of Pamplona' says of
Charlemagne:
  'E viren Carrión
  'E la tour noire e bise'
Tomorrow we shall visit the 'Princes of Carrión'. Today
our concern is with two legends about the struggle against
the Moorish overlords:
- Carts of coal were used as a Trojan horse to seize the
castle, since destroyed, which used to dominate the
heights.

- Every year, it was said, the town was required to deliver
a tribute of virgins - either four or a hundred, depending
on which version you follow - to add to the royal harem.
On one occasion wild bulls burst in, attacked the Moors,
spared the young girls, and brought an end to the tribute.
There are claims that this scene is evoked in the somewhat
time-worn carvings on the porch of Santa María del
Camino, but in fact the carvings show horses and their
riders. However, the episode is depicted in an 18th-century
picture.

PILGRIMS AT CARRION DE LOS
CONDES

Crossing Carrión we shall see in succession:
- The 13th-century *convent of Santa Clara,* with several
carvings;
- The *church of Santa María del Camino,* a 12th-century
national monument with a Romanesque porch, richly
decorated with scenes of the Nativity, not to speak of
the famous 'bulls'.

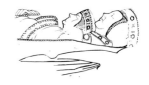

- The *church of Santiago,* burnt down in 1809, of which
only the impressive 1160 porch remains - also a national
monument, showing Chist in majesty, biblical characters,
and daily activities.
- Beyond the bridge, on the next stage, the *Monastery
of San Zoilo,* now a seminary and heavily restored; with
a few Romanesque arches, a silver reliquary of the Roman
martyr, and most notably the Renaissance cloisters and
the princes' tomb.

OFF THE ROUTE: To the north of the village, the patronal
church of Our Lady of Belén, high up above the River

Carrión, is Gothic with a baroque 'Plateresque' altar-piece.

NOTE

The historic Road itself runs through Revenga de Campos and Villarmentero, but we have already spent too much of this stage on tarmac roads.

ALTERNATIVE ROUTES

From the Virgen del Rio a number of tracks lead on generally westwards, then west-north-west, to Carrión de los Condes. Likewise from Villalcazar de Sirga you can take a track to the north-west, followed by another to the west, also leading to Carrión de los Condes.

ACCOMMODATION

Poblacion de Campos: - Fondas
Revenga de Campos: - Fondas
Villalcazar de Sirga: - Fondas and Posadas

Carrión de los Condes:
  - H La Cortés
  - Mesón Pisarrosas
  - Fonda Casa Estefania
  - Pensión-Restaurant Rasbalón, tel. 88.04.33
  - Campsite near the River Carrión, with reduced prices for pilgrims.

FREE ACCOMMODATION

Carrión de los Condes:
  A hostel for pilgrims is planned at the Real Covento des Clarisses, with places for 20 (beds, water): contribution to expenses.

Villalcazar
  - Enquire at the Town Hall about a hostel with 20 places, with showers and kitchen.
  - A hostel is planned on the road from Frómista, with 20 places.

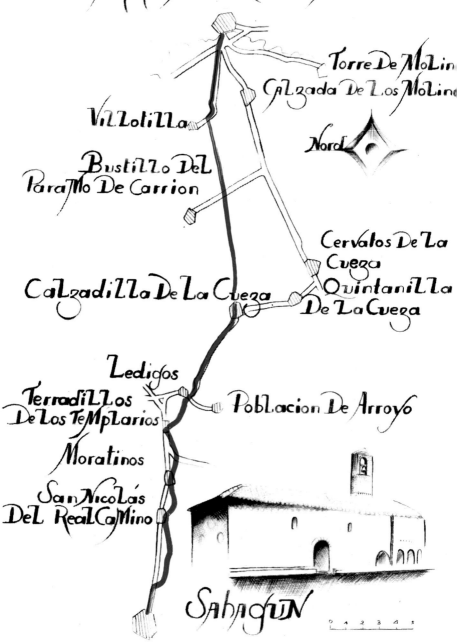

CARRION DE LOS CONDES

Torre De Molin

Calzada De Los Molino

Villotilla

Nord

Bustillo Del
Paramo De Carrion

Cervatos De La
Cueza

Calzadilla De La Cueza

Quintanilla
De La Cueza

Ledigos

Terradillos
De Los Templarios

Poblacion De Arroyo

Moratinos

San Nicolas
Del Real Camino

Sahagun

0 1 2 3 4 5

Stage 16 - 40 kilometres - 10 hours

CARRIÓN DE LOS CONDES TO SAHAGÚN

T his is an extremely long stage, which would benefit from being divided in two if the appropriate facilities were available; however, these endless tracks take you only across a great plateau of cornfields. At harvest time, in addition to modern combine-harvesters, you will certainly come across a peasant or his family sitting on their 'trillo', a harrow with flint teeth drawn by a mule, circling round and round the threshing area; or perhaps some old person winnowing the grain with a sieve, as in former times. At other seasons these broad horizons encourage calm and meditation. Set out early in the day, to avoid risks of sun-stroke. Four kilometres before reaching Sahagún you will cross from the province of Palencia into León, both within the ancient kingdom of León itself. At the end of this stage the brick-built 'Romanesque-Moorish' churches of Sahagún are a fine reward for the long walk.

THE CID AND THE 'PRINCES DE CARRION'

The San Zoilo monastery, on the way out of Carrión, is the site of the tomb of the 'Infantes de Carrión' mentioned in the previous stage.

The Counts of Carrión, the Beni Gomez, were rivals of the Cid; and legend relates that the Cid, who was lord of Valencia, granted his daughters to the Beni Gomez sons, the Infantes - who, as soon as they had left the town, abandoned their brides, stripped and tied to a tree. The Cid's vengeance was prompt, and his daughters subsequently married the princes of Navarre and of Aragon.

FROM BENEVIVERE TO SAN NICOLAS DEL REAL CAMINO

- Benevívere, a little to the north of the Pilgrim Way, owes its Latin name of 'good living' to an Augustine monastery, of which only a few stones still remain.

0.00 Carrión de los Condes 840m. Leave the town, heading north-west, across the bridge over the River Carrión. Leave the monastery of San Zoilo to your left.

0.15 - Major crossroads: turn west along the N120.

0.20 - Turn off the N120 as soon as it begins to bend to the left; go straight ahead, west-north-west, on the small road to Villotilla, for 4 kilometres.

1.20 - At kilometre marker 2 leave the tarmac, which bears right to Villotilla, 2 kilometres away, and take the stony track running straight ahead, westwards. Follow this straightforward track for 12 kilometres.

4.20 - Go through Calzadilla de la Cueza and then take the N120 north-west, for 5 kilometres.

- *Calzadilla de la Cueza* has a Renaissance altar-piece in the San Martín church.
- The only remaining traces of the former *monastery of Santa María de las Tiendas* now form the walls of a large farm, on the N120 road.
- The church at *Ledigos* has a statue of St James.
- *Moratinos* still bears the name of a 'Calle Real', or 'Calzada Francesa' - the road of the French.
- In 1198 *San Nicolás del Real Camino* had a 'hospital' for lepers run by the Augustinian Canons. This is the final village in the province of Palencia, before reaching León.

SAHAGUN, THE CLUNY OF SPAIN

The name Sahagún is a corruption of San Facundo, a martyr of Roman times. By 904 there was a monastery here which provided a refuge for the monks of Córdoba who escaped the Muslim domination. After 1080 Sahagún became the equivalent of Cluny in France, with similar traditions of cultural influence and 'imperialism': French was spoken a great deal, and the Abbot Bernard, future Archbishop of Toulouse, caused a revolt of the local population by seeking to impose a code of laws which, far from offering new freedoms, introduced Burgundian feudalism.

The monastery had accommodation for 60 pilgrims. Although it has now vanished completely apart from a few remains scattered among various museums, there is still much to see in the town:
- On the way in, the great brick hermitage of the *Virgen del Puente* beside the old bridge across the River Valderaduey has great symbolic importance: it has its own pilgrimage each year, on April 25.
- Two 'national monuments', *San Tirso* (12th century) and *San Lorenzo* (13th century) are the oldest and purest examples of Romano-Moorish brick construction with blind arcading - one with semicircular arches, the other horseshoe shaped.
- Another 'national monument', on a hill to the south, is the former Franciscan *monastery of the Peregrina*, with Romanesque remains in a neo-classical building. It owes its name to a 17th-century statue, of Seville origin, showing the Virgin in pilgrim dress which is now in the care of the Benedictines.
- Among various other monuments the *Museum of Religious Art*, set up by the Benedictines, is worth seeing.

5.35 - Before reaching Ledigos, 883m, turn left, south-west, on the road to Población del Arroyo, across a bridge.

5.40 - 150 metres beyond the bridge and just before reaching a dovecot, turn right, north-north-west, onto a footpath.

5.45 - The path bears left, west-north-west, passing a turning to the right.

6.15 - At a crossways south of Terradillos, 885m, turn right towards the village but do not go through it; at the electricity transformer on the outskirts take a footpath bearing west, with a copse on your left.

6.35 - On reaching a small road, turn left, south-west, along it for 400 metres.

6.40 - 20 metres before reaching kilometre marker 1, turn right, down a track; cross two streams, and continue uphill again.

7.05 - Moratinos. Leave the church on your right and take the concrete road to the north-west then, after 40 metres, a footpath to the left, south.

7.07 - Reach a fork and bear right, west, on a track which initially crosses undulating ground as it heads west and then north-west.

7.45 - San Nicolás del Real Camino, 840m. Continue west from the church, ford the River Sequillo, and take a footpath to the right.

7.55 - At a crossing of paths go straight ahead, west.

8.10 - Fork: bear right, north-west, then west.

8.50 - Turn right, north.

8.55 - Join the N120 and turn west-north-west along it.

9.00 - Just beyond the bridge, turn right on a footpath to Virgen del Puente. 9.05 - Take a grassy track leading west-south-west out of Virgen del Puente towards the N120.

BROTHER BERNARDIN, PRECURSOR OF AZTEC ETHNOLOGISTS

Sahagún was the cradle of some important clerics: San Juan de Sahagún, patron of Salamanca; Fray Pedro Ponce de León, 16th-century pioneer in the teaching of deaf-mutes; and above all, Fray Bernadino de Sahagún, the precursor of modern ethnology.

In 1530, at a time when Spanish colonialism was wiping out pre-Colombian civilisations, he took the opposite course and sought to preserve what was left of them, by calling together groups of Mexican nationals in order to gather and record relevant information. He was the author of a uniquely valuable manuscript, now conserved in the Madrid National Library, with parallel texts in Aztec, Spanish and Latin and illustrations showing the flora, fauna, and ancient gods of 'New Spain'.

ACCOMMODATION

Ledigos:
- A free hostel was due to open in August 1989, with places for 20; enquire at the Town Hall, tel. 78.00.01

Sahagún:
- Hotel La Codorníz, tel. 78.02.76.
- Fonda La Asturiana, tel. 78.00.73.
- Mesón Aranzazu. - Mesó Covagonda.
- Camping Pedro Ponce (with restaurant), tel. 78.11.12
- Restaurants: Camino de Santiago, tel. 78.01.77; Pacho, tel. 78.07.75

FREE ACCOMMODATION

Calzadilla de la Cueza:
- Free hostel, planned for opening in summer 1989, with showers and kitchen; enquire at the town hall.
San Nicolás del Real Camino:
- Enquire at the Town Hall about the possibility of using one of the school buildings.
Sahagún:
- the Brothers of Charity, Hogar de San José, tel. 78.00.89
- The Benedictine convent, tel. 78.00.78
- Free hostel with 40 places, planned for 1990, in the former Trinity church.

9.15 - You come to a crossways, with the N120 200 metres away on your left. Continue straight ahead.
9.35 - Sahagún. Cross a road and carry on, westwards, along the small street opposite, with a silo on your left. On reaching the railway, with the station to your left, turn along beside the line and cross the bridge over it.
9.45 - Leave the church of La Trinidad on your right and turn down right, north-west, along José Antonio street.
9.50 - Fork, with a bar/tea-shop in the angle; drop down to the right.
9.55 - Plaza Mayor. If you want to rest your legs after the long walk, only 5 minutes away there are
10.00 - San Tirso and Arc San Benito

NOTES

- Between Calzadilla and Ledigos you can avoid the tarmac of the N120 by following the parallel course of the River Cueza. You then cross a stretch of heathland to pick up the road again a few dozen metres before marker 223.
- Close to this 223 marker you take a path to the right of the N120, to reach Ledigos; water-source before reaching the village.
- Between Ledigos and Terradillos, one of our authors was unable to find the official route as indicated by another!

Sahagún

Calzada

Bercianos Del
Real Camino

Gordaliza
Del Pino

El Burdo Ranero

Vallecillo

Graneras

Castrotierra

N

Villa Moratiel
De Las Matas

Villamarco

Matallana

Reliegos

Grajalejo

Valdearcos

Mansilla De Las Mulas

0 1 2 3 4

Stage 17 - 40 kilometres - 10 hours

SAHAGÚN TO MANSILLA DE LAS MULAS

P*ilgrim, prepare to suffer: if you are to gain merit from your pilgrimage, this is the place for it! But Yan L. Crispel's opinion may alleviate your fears: 'One of the finest stages of the whole route, one of the most captivating'. Forty kilometres of straight paths stretching endlessly across a vast plain. You will reach an understanding of the infinite, the curve of the Earth, and the grandeur of deliberate effort. In the furnace of a summer afternoon you may see in the distance the mirage of a tree or a shadow, or dream of a babbling spring ... Take care all the same to drink plenty of water before setting out, and do not forget your hat. In summer you may almost need to undertake this stage by night; in any case, avoid being on the move between mid-day and about 4 p.m. A system of waymarking is under consideration, with a new emblem for the route - a stylised scallop-shell, the nearest place-name, the distance still to be covered, and the name of the province. Some stretches are going to be asphalted. At the end of the stage, the fragmentary ramparts of Mansilla de las Mulas retain only slight traces of their past splendour.*

CHARLEMAGNE'S FLOWERING LANCES

The Carolingian epic credits Charlemagne with the founding of Sahagún, in memory of his battle on the 'Vega del Cea', the plain of the River Cea. Archbishop Turpin recounts the miracle in the *Codex:* 'The spears of the Christians were planted in the earth and flourished; cut down to the ground, they sprouted again from the roots'.

... Perhaps the story relates to the planting of poplars along the river's edge.

THE WALLS OF MANSILLA DE LAS MURAS

Aymeric Picaud described 'Manxilla' as surrounded by walls. The eastern gate, the 'Arco de la Concepción' still exists, as well as two complete towers, two more in

0.00 - Sahagún, 816m. From the Plaza Mayor take the avenue Primo de Rivera. Pass San Tirso on your left, and go under the San Benito Arch. A hundred metres farther on turn right, west, along a street which bends to the left.

0.15 - Bridge over the River Cea; take the León road north-west for 4 kilometres.

1.15 - Ignore the road to the right (north) leading to Calzada de Coto, and 100 metres farther on turn right off the León road onto a footpath bearing west-north-west.

2.23 - Church 100 metres to the left: Ermita de Perales.

2.30 - Top of a hill, farm to the

ruins, and a short stretch of wall.

Attractive features include a square with wooden arcading, houses with columns, and in the parish church of Santa María, a 13th-century stone statue.

The church of San Martín, however, also 13th century, has been turned into a shop, and the ruins of the Augustinian monastery, dating from about 1500, are used partly as a pelota court, partly an abattoir.

Mansilla is supposed to be the home of the heroine of a picaresque 18th-century novel, 'La Picara Justina', an earthy tale of her less than orthodox 'pilgrimages'.

CROSSING LA CAÑADA DE LAS MERINAS

- At Bercianos del Real Camino the church of San Salvador has a Renaissance statue of St John the Baptist, and a 16th-century painting of the Crucifixion.

- Between Bercianos and Burgo Ranero, Laffi in 1681 saw two wolves devouring the corpse of a pilgrim and took the remains for proper burial.

- Coming out of Burgo Ranero the path crosses the 'Cañada de las Merinas' - the 'Sheep Track', similar to drovers' roads in Great Britain, the 'drailles' in the Cevennes, or the seasonal 'transhumance' trails of flocks in the Alps or the Pyrenees. In these areas the sheep pens alternate with the pools and little water-courses of Buensolana, Valdeasnero, Tutielga, names which reveal the nature of the countryside: a somewhat free translation would give us Little Town of Frogs, the Streams of the Sunny Side of the Mountain and the Valley of the Donkeys.

- The church at Reliegos, now in ruins, had a square tower. It was the site of the Roman town of Palentia, at the junction of three great roads.

ALTERNATIVE:
LA CALZADA DE LOS PEREGRINOS

There are two pilgrim routes from Sahagún to Mansilla de las Mulas:

- The REAL CAMINO FRANCES - the French Royal Road, described here;

- And the CALZADA DE LOS PEREGRINOS - the Pilgrim Way, lying to the north of the railway, and even longer and more arid. This coincides with the old 'Via Trajana' of the Romans, running through the thickets on Mount Valdelocajos which in earlier days were feared for their

right: San Esteban

2.33 - Bridge over the Arroyo Coso

2.45 - Bercianos del Camino, 855m. Go through the village, with a detour to the left to take a photograph south-west of the church; continue on a footpath heading north-west, for 8 kilometres.

4.45 - Go through El Burgo Ranero, 880m; fonda and bar serving snacks. Continue along the footpath.

6.55 - Paths cross, with Villamarco 800 metres away to the left; continue straight on, north-west.

7.20 - Cross the León-Palencia railway, and carry on in the same general direction. The terrain becomes a little less flat, and there are even a few trees!

124

wild animals, and then the village of Calzadilla de los Hermanillos - Little Road of the Little Brothers - lined with cob-walled houses.

ACCOMMODATION

El Burgo Ranero:
- Fonda Lozano, tel. 33.00.60

Mansilla de las Mulas:
- HR* La Estrella, tel. 31.02.18
- Fonda Las Delicias
- Fonda Las Faroles
- Fonda Casa Marcelo
- Fonda Los Asturianos

7.50 - Building on the right, then the plain again, with a few vines.
8.00 - Down to Reliegos.
8.07 - Reliegos, with a bar serving sandwiches: cross through the village, following the yellow waymarking, then continue on a path heading north-west.
9.20 - The track becomes tarmac (in 1985).
9.35 - Bridge over the canal. Cross a road, with a crossroads 50 metres to the left, and take the lane opposite, against the one-way traffic system.
10.00 - Centre of MANSILLA DE LAS MULAS.

FREE ACCOMMODATION

El Burgo Ranero:
- Free hostel planned for summer 1989, with beds, showers, and kitchen.

Mansilla de las Mulas:
- Possibility of shelter in the school-room; enquire at the Town Hall, tel. 31.09.41

NOTES

There used to be two routes from the outskirts of Calzada del Coto to Mansilla de las Mulas:
- EL CAMINO REAL FRANCÉS, the route which is described here but which may one day be tarmac surfaced;
- LA CALZADA DE LOS PEREGRINOS, further to the north, and even more desert-like than the CAMINO. It crosses Calzada del Coto, heads towards the railway 2 kilometres away, and continues for 7 kilometres to Calzadilla de Los Hermanillos. A footpath 4 kilometres along the road draws steadily closer to the railway and reaches it at Villamarco station. Continue north-west, passing one kilometre to the north of Reliegos.

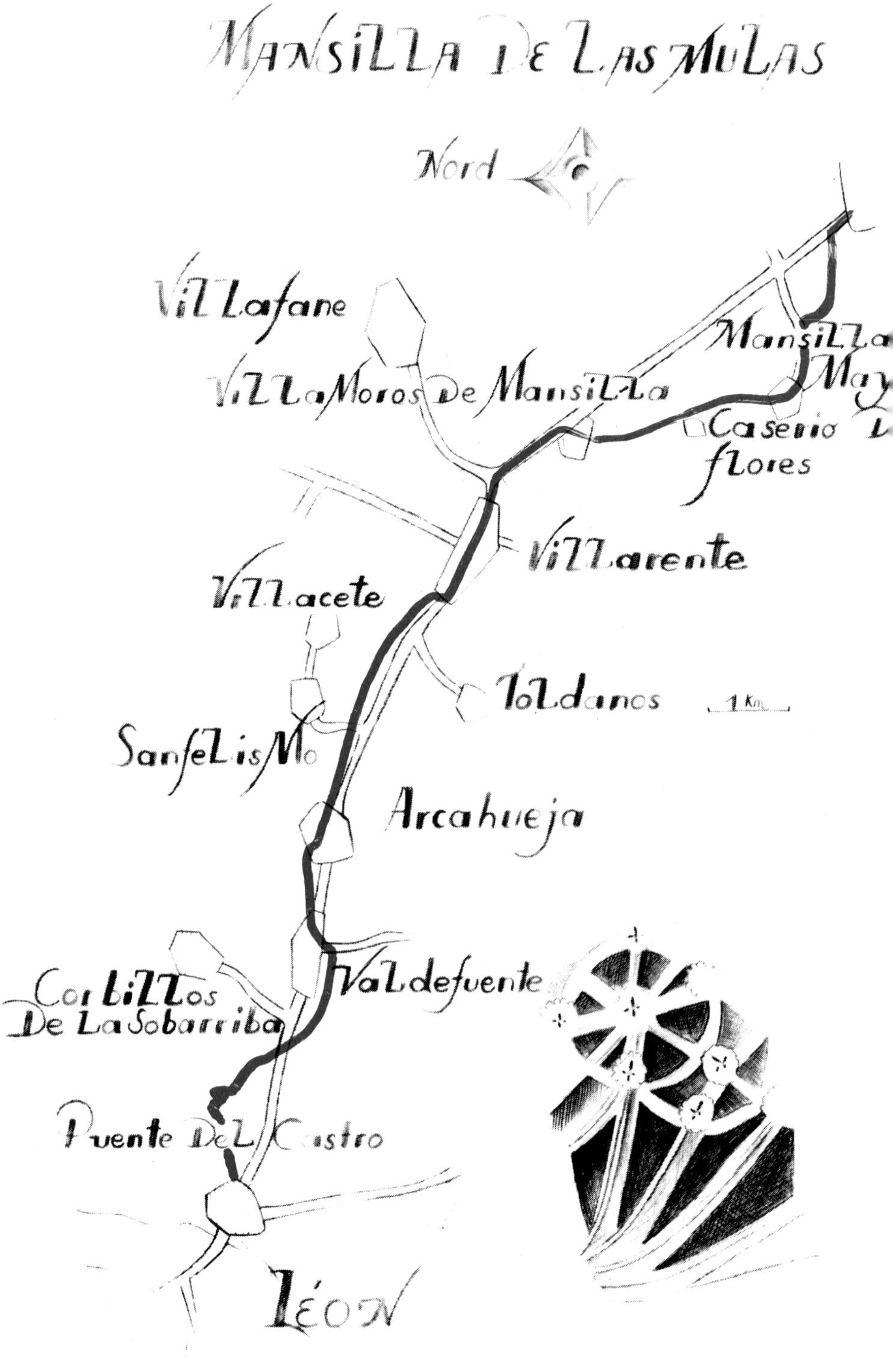

MANSILLA DE LAS MULAS

Nord

VilLafane

ViLLaMoros De MansiLLa

MansiLLa May

Caserio L flores

VilLarente

ViLLacete

ToLdanos

1 Km

SanfeLisMo

Arcahueja

CorbiLLos
De LaSobarriba

VaLdefuente

Puente DeL Castro

LéoN

Stage 18 - 22 kilometres - 5 hours 30 minutes

MANSILLA DE LA MULAS TO LEÓN

Τ his short stage leaves sufficient time to explore the town of León as it deserves; it is a former capital city and a historic preserved site, with its Romanesque pantheon, its Gothic cathedral, and its ornate early Renaissance 'hospital'. On leaving Mansilla it would be agreeable to be able to visit the rare Mozarabic sanctuary of San Miguel de la Escalada: however, since it lies isolated some 12 kilometres off the Road, it is not easily accessible unless you can secure some means of transport. For the Mansilla to León stretch we have tried as far as possible to avoid the tarmac of the N601. A footpath has been established alongside the highway, on the route of an old track, but we suggest a different itinerary in this guide.

OFF THE ROUTE: SANDOVAL, LA ESCALADA, GRADEFES

A crossroads a few hundred metres beyond the bridge over the River Esla, on the way out of Mansilla, is the starting point for two possible detours:
- The road to the left leads to *Santa-María de Villaverde de Sandoval*, 4 kilometres away, where the 12th-century Cistercian church is a national monument. The church has an unusual origin: Count Ponce de Minerva, captured by the Moors and then released, was making the pilgrimage to Compostela when his wife, who was working in the Orbigo hospital, washed his feet, and recognised him by his ring. In thanksgiving for this, they founded Sandoval.
- The road to the right leads north-east to another national monument, 12 kilometres away: *San Miguel de la Escalada*, a pure jewel in the Mozarabic style, with its double windows and horseshoe arches of an astonishing lightness and delicacy - particularly in the cloisters. It was consecrated in the year 913.
- A few kilometres beyond La Escalada the 12th-century *monastery of Gradefes*, still inhabited by Cistercians, offers shelter to the public.

0.00 - Mansilla de las Mulas, 800m. Go north out of the town on the N601, which crosses the River Esla.
0.05 - 200 metres beyond the bridge turn left, west, onto a track.
0.07 - Ignore a turning to the left.
0.09 - Cross a broad track and continue along the path, north-west.
0.14 - Cross a bridge.
0.17 - Turn left along a wide path for 40 metres.
0.18 - At a crossways, turn right, north.
0.19 - Take a track to the left, north-west.
0.22 - Cross a path, stepping over an irrigation conduit.
0.27 - Turn left, west-north-west, along a tarmac road.
0.33 - Go through Mansilla Mayor, on a street heading west-north-west and then bending to the right, north.
0.40 - Outside the village take a path going north.

FROM VILLARENTE TO PUENTE CASTRO

- On the left at the far side of the great bridge at *Villarente,* the *'Hospital' de los Peregrinos,* established in the 16th century, received an unusual endowment: a donkey to carry sick pilgrims on to León.

- Between Valdefuentes and Puente Castro, at the 'Alto del Portillo', the top of the small col, a modern stone cross to the left of the main road marks the site of a medieval cross, later moved to the Hostal de San Marcos square in León.

- *Puente Castro* - Bridge of the Fortified Camp - owes its name to an *Aljama,* a Jewish community on the neighbouring hillside which was suppressed in the 12th century. The present bridge dates from the 18th century, but when the water is low it is still possible to see the foundations of the old Romanesque bridge, 50 metres downstream.

LEON, THE LEGIONARIES' TOWN

From the year AD 70, the site of León was the new camp of the 7th Gemina Legion, one of whose centurions, San Marcelo, was martyred in the third century, together with his wife and their sons. Abandoned during the Moorish occupation, it retained the name of *Legionis,* hence León.

In 510 it became the capital city of the new kingdom of Ordoño II. This primacy was lost in the 13th century when it merged with the more recently established Kingdom of Castile, but León remained a wealthy city.

In recent years there have been efforts to revive in either August or June the old tradition of the *Cantaderas,* a sort of religious ballet based on the theme of the hundred virgins yielded by the Christians to the Moorish kings.

THE PILGRIMS' ARCHAEOLOGICAL JOURNEY

Once past the Puente Castro over the River Torio, traces of the Pilgrim Way through León can be seen in the following places:
- The *church of Santa Ana,* originally dedicated to the Holy Sepulchre, but then given over to the Order of St

0.45 - Cross an irrigation conduit and aim for a hamlet 600 metres to the north-north-west with a clump of pine trees, passing them on your left after ten minutes. Make use of temporary tracks as available; there has been clearing and irrigation work here in recent years.

0.55 - Leave the hamlet, Caserio, on your left and continue along a path, north-west, and then veering to the north.

1.05 - Junction of paths; continue straight ahead, north-north-west.

1.13 - Take the shady but sometimes muddy track facing you, heading north.

1.27 - Villamoros de Mansilla. As a result of the work being undertaken around the village, the simplest way at the time of writing is to rejoin the N601 by the Calle de la Carretera, north-east of the church.

1.30 - Take the León road, which is shady and has verges.

1.40 - Restaurant on the left.

1.45 - Bridge over the River Porma; follow the main road through Villarente.

2.10 - 200 metres beyond kilometre marker 315, turn right towards a bar-restaurant (Los Pirineos), and after 40 metres turn left, north-west, along a grassy path parallel to the

John of Jerusalem, whose Maltese cross appears on the west door.

- The *church of Santa María del Mercado* (St Mary of the Market, previously of the Road): 12th century, Romanesque, but damaged. There is a neo-classical fountain behind the church, in the Plaza del Grano.
- On the other side of the street, tightly hemmed in by houses, the *Monastery of the Conception,* founded in 1518 within 14th century walls.
- The street known as *La Rúa,* lined with old houses.
- In the *Plaza de San Marcelo,* the Town Hall, old houses, and the 16th-century church of San Marcelo, alongside the 'Casa de Botines' designed by the great Catalan architect of today, Gaudi.

At this point, passing through the town walls by the gate which was once the 'left hand' of the Roman settlement, you come to the town's principal sacred sites.

main road. Cross a damp area, and pass a public rubbish tip.

2.25 - Bridge over a canal, then continue along a good track.

2.40 - Cross a tarmac road and take the broad track opposite, heading north-west.

2.55 - Arcahueja: go through the hamlet and carry on along a footpath, west-north-west.

3.05 - At a fork, bear left, west-south-west.

3.15 - Valdelafuente: cross the León road and take the Villaturiel road, facing you, for 300 metres.

3.20 - Turn right, north-west, along a footpath parallel to the main road.

SAN ISIDORO, ROMANESQUE; THE CATHEDRAL, GOTHIC; SAN MARCOS, EARLY RENAISSANCE.

These three monuments are essential viewing for all visitors to León:

- *San Isidoro,* the pantheon with its 23 royal tombs, was built on the ruins of a Roman temple of Mercury, near a pre-Romanesque church razed to the ground by Almanzor. San Isidoro was built in the 11th century to receive the relics of Saint Isidore, brought from Seville in 1063. The saint, a theologian, who died in 635, had resisted the Arian heresy which was the Visigoth religion. Note the Romanesque paintings on the vaulting, and in the Museum, among other items, the Visigothic bible dating from AD 960. This remains a collegiate church, the monks saying an evening office at 9 p.m.

- The *Cathedral,* begun two centuries later in 1203, is a marvel of Gothic art, with light pouring in through its 125 windows, its 25 roundels, its 1,800 square metres of stained glass. The cloister was rebuilt in the 16th century by Juan de Badajoz, and the museum's 11th-century 'Mozarabic antiphonary' contains pre-Romanesque canticles.

- The *Hostal de San Marcos* is the successor to a very plain 'hospital', of which one building still remains beside the church, constructed in the 12th century by Doña Sancha *ad recipiendum pauperes Christi* - to shelter the Christian poor. In 1513 Ferdinand the Catholic commanded the building of the present Hostal, with its ornate early Renaissance façade and its church decorated with scallop-shells. Inside is the cloister of Juan de Badajoz and the Museum. In the Plaza de San Marcos can be seen the 15th-century cross l'Alto del Portillo; its Gothic shaft, 2.50m (over 8ft) tall, has scenes from the Gospels and Saint Raphael dressed as a pilgrim.

THE VISIGOTHS

Although León's oldest extant monument is

Romanesque, there are reminders of the city's importance in the days of the Visigoths. The Bible of AD 960 has already been mentioned, and also the relics of Saint Isidore, who died in 635, brought from Seville. A palimpsest (a parchment scraped and re-used) still exists with a Latin version of the Bible transcribed in the 7th century, overlaying the *lex Romana Visigothorum,* a 6th-century code of laws.

The Cathedral, as aforementioned, also contains a Mozarabic antiphonary preserving early liturgical chants of the ancient Visigoth ritual, later replaced by those of the Gregorian reform.

NOTES

From the Plaza de San Marcelo, if you take the Calle del Cid you can visit the church of San Isidoro on your way to the cathedral.

ACCOMMODATION

Villarente:
- HR** La Montaña, tel. 31.08.61
- HR* Delfin Verde, tel. 31.09.15

León:
Many hotels, restaurants, fondas
- H***** San Marcos, tel. 23.73.00
- H**** Conde Luna, tel. 20.65.12
- H** Riosol, tel. 22.38.50
- HR** Quindos, tel. 23.62.00
- HR* Reina, tel. 20.52.12
- HR* Paris, tel. 23.86.00
- HR** Don Suero, tel. 23.06.00
- HR** Reino de León, tel. 20.32.51 etc.

FREE ACCOMMODATION

San Marcos: There are plans for a free hostel in a small building by the Parador. No date given. Enquire at the Town Hall, tel. 25.31.12

Mansilla Mayor de las Mulas: From 1989 shelter is available in an unfurnished room in the school (with water supply); for 6 people. Enquire at the Town Hall.

3.30 - Junction of paths: carry on straight ahead for about 200 metres.
3.33 - Take the right turn towards the main road.
3.38 - Road to León, kilometre marker 321; turn left along it briefly, then take a small tarmac road up towards some television antennae.
4.10 - Beyond the antennae and before reaching a large electrical installation turn left down a path across rolling ground, which turns into a rough track suitable for cross-country vehicles.
4.30 - Back to the tarmac; cross the bridge, left, over the motorway, and go through the Puente del Castro district.
4.35 - Church of San Pedro in Puente del Castro. Take the main road crossing the River Torío by the Castro bridge.
5.00 - León, altitude 840m. Head towards the town centre, passing the front of the church of Santa Ana and then along the Calle Barahoma and the Calle Puertamoneda towards the church of Santa María del Mercado.
5.15 - Next, continue to the right, north, along the Calle La Rúa towards the Plaza and church of San Marcelo. Take the Calle del Generalísimo to the cathedral.
5.30 - León Cathedral.

Stage 19 - 35 kilometres - 8 hours 30 minutes

LEÓN TO HOSPITAL DE ORBIGO

*A**nother very long stage; it can be halved by using, for example, one of the two hotels before reaching Villadangos del Páramo-where there are two representations of Santiago-Matamoros. The 'Páramo' is the harsh and seemingly endless flat landscape, somewhat softened today by the Orbigo irrigation channels. At the end of the stage, though the 'Hospital' has gone, the 20-arch bridge over the Orbigo still exists.*

LEON:
FROM THE WALLS TO THE BRIDGE

Pilgrims used to leave the walls of León behind the church of San Isidoro, where traces of the town's defences still exist.

The name of the Calle de Renueva recalls its creation as the 'New Street' of the 12th century.

After San Marcos pilgrims would cross the River Bernesga; the present bridge dates from the 16th century.

VIRGEN DEL CAMINO:
FROM EARLY LEGEND TO MODERN
CHURCH CENTRE

La Virgen del Camino - The Virgin of the Road - is now a village, but around 1505 there was nothing here but

0.00 - Go north-west from the Plaza Santo Domingo in León to the Plaza de Calvo Sotelo, and carry on in the same direction.
0.10 - Enjoy the view of San Marcos on the right.
0.15 - Cross the bridge over the River Bernesga and head west-south-west on the Astorga road, the N120, for about 1.3 kilometres.
0.35 - 200 metres before reaching the railway, leave the N120 as it bends up and to the right to cross the railway bridge; keep straight on instead and cross the railway by a footbridge.
0.40 - Trobajo del Camino: cross the N120 and turn left along the

a simple hermitage when the Virgin appeared to a shepherd, Alvar Simon, asking him to build a sanctuary. When he asked for 'a sign', she took her sling and threw a small stone 600 paces away, where it turned into a large rock. A chapel was then built, where miracles multiplied, giving rise to pilgrimages which still continue on September 15 and 29, and October 15.

Legend tells the miraculous history of a León man, enslaved by the Moors, who prayed each evening to the Virgin of the Road for release on his birthday. On that day his master, though sceptical, had him chained inside a great chest, and then sat on it, but went to sleep. When he awoke, it was to the sound of bells and canticles: the chest and its passenger had been miraculously transported to Christian territory. The liberated prisoner donated his chains as a votive offering.

A boldly modernistic church was built here in 1961 by the Portuguese architect F. Coello, with thirteen giant statues and four bronze doors by J. M. de Schirach, part of a religious, social and cultural centre run by Dominican fathers.

THE SAINT JAMES WITH THE TRICORNE AT VILLADANGOS DEL PARAMO

In most places along the Pilgrim Way the connection with Saint James appears only in their names - *del Camino* or 'of the Virgin': nothing now remains of the former 'hospital' of San Miguel del Camino, and its 16th-century statue of Saint James the Pilgrim is now in León Museum.
- *Villadangos del Páramo,* on the other hand, still has its church of St James: its 18th-century altar-piece of Santiago-Matamoros pictures the saint on horseback, wearing a tricorne hat. The polychrome wooden church door evokes the battle of Clavijo.
- In the year 1111 Villadangos was the site of a battle between the two armies of Alfonso of Aragon and his wife Urraca of León.

THE LOST 'HOSPITAL' OF SAN MARTIN DEL CAMINO

Our route through San Martin del Camino follows the Calle Ancha and half-way along it passes the site of a former 'hospital' near the church.

Calle de los Pelegrinos, parallel with the N120, westward.

0.45 - Rejoin the N120 as it goes through Trobajo, passing in front of the chapel of Santiago, on your right.

0.50 - 40 metres beyond the traffic lights turn left, south, down a street, then promptly right, west; pass a bar on your left, then a restaurant, El Abuelo.

1.00 - At the N120 cross over and go left along it for a few dozen metres, then take a tarmac footpath up to the right.

1.05 - Leaving the picturesque bodegas on your right, continue west-south-west, parallel to the N120 along a succession of footpaths and tracks waymarked in yellow. In due course the immense shaft of the cross of La Virgen del Camino becomes visible to the south-west.

1.45 - La Virgen del Camino, 905m. At the modern building, join the N120 for about 100 metres south-west.

1.47 - Pass to the left of the safety barrier.

1.49 - Go down the verge of the main road, with care.

1.50 - Cross a small bridge and take the track facing you.

1.51 - Take a footpath heading west-south-west.

1.53 - Cemetery on the left. The track comes closer to the N120.

1.55 - Cross the road to Fresno and take a gravel path parallel with the main road, which runs about a dozen metres to your right.

2.00 - Continue along a track, also parallel with the highway.

2.03 - The path comes up to the main road just before an intersection; if preferred, in dry weather, you can ignore the waymarking (which follows the tarmac) and keep to the

THE PARAMO: A DESERT NO LONGER

At an average altitude of 800m above sea-level, the Páramo forms a plateau to the south of León between the Rivers Orbigo and Esla. Like Villadangos, seven other villages add the generic term 'del Páramo' to their names. The dictionary definition of the word is 'desert' - a term also applied to the North Pole! However, this definition is no longer true here, for the area has benefited considerably from the economic development of the 1960s: irrigation channels bring in water from the reservoir on the River Luna, and high-yield commercial crops are now widely grown here. There is a striking contrast between the description of the pilgrim Domenico Laffi, who in 1670 wrote of a wretched and beggarly population living in hovels, and the feverish atmosphere of recent construction.

One of the most important villages of the Páramo - though at some distance from the Pilgrim Way- is Laguna de Negrillos, with the ruins of a medieval castle built by Alfonso IX to protect the Via de la Plata. Its picturesque festival on the day of Corpus Christi combines pageantry, drama, and folk-dance; it moves from one church to another, and two statues are carried in procession, preceded by a costumed cortège. In the lead is a live St Sebastian as grave and dignified as the Pope, recognisable by the large arrow he carries, and wearing a Napoleonic bicorne hat. Next come the saints and apostles, each with their identifying 'props' such as St John the Baptist's girdle of skins. All around are the dancers, dressed in white lace.

THE DON QUIXOTE OF THE BRIDGE OVER THE ORBIGO

The famous Romanesque bridge over the Orbigo, with 20 arches and 205 metres long, has two monolithic columns at its centre with an inscription commemorating the famous knightly combat of the *Paso Honroso de armas*, the grand tournament. Here in 1534, in honour of a lady, Don Suero de Quinones, with nine companions from León, challenged all the knights of Europe who dared to cross the bridge. The tournament lasted for a month, with 300 broken lances and one death. The victors travelled to Compostela to offer up a gold necklace, which is still worn in the procession by a figure of Saint James the Less.

left of the fence.

2.08 - Pass close by two huge irrigation channels on your right and head for an underpass, due south, beneath the motorway.

2.13 - Cross under the motorway and then, off the path but without difficulty, bear west down a grassy valley, heading for a clump of about a dozen young oak-trees.

2.20 - From the north-west corner of a small field continue north-west, beside untended vines.

2.23 - Pass near a brick-built house, leaving it on your right, and go westward down its gravelled access drive.

2.25 - Cross a small tarmac road and take the facing track, west.

2.33 - Rejoin the N120 shortly before Valverde de la Virgen, 778m.

2.37 - Cross the N120 and continue on below it.

2.42 - Valverde church; shortly after, turn right down a lane, then left along a 'street' parallel with the N120, which we will leave for about half an hour. Beyond the village take a path to the west.

2.52 - Fork: go straight ahead, north-west.

2.54 - Go down to the west between the bodegas.

3.00 - Crossing of tracks; turn left, south-south-west, along a broad track.

3.08 - Church of San Miguel del Camino on the right. Continue along the road to the south-west.

3.13 - Rejoin the N120 where the Robledo road leaves it, follow this to the right for 150 metres.

3.15 - Turn left, south-west, onto a track.

3.25 - White buildings on the right. The track comes back to the road again.

3.30 - The track runs beside the road,

Twenty-four years later Don Suero was killed in a tournament by a knight he had previously vanquished, Don Quijana - who perhaps was one of the models for Don Quixote. The combat is evoked in a poem by the Duke de Rivas.

Two earlier battles took place on the banks of the Orbigo: in AD 456 the Visigoths drove back the Suevians, and it was here that Alfonso III defeated the Moors.

A stone Calvary stands on the ruins of the Orbigo 'Hospital', and the church of Santa María has a Maltese cross.

ACCOMMODATION

La Virgen del Camino:
- HR** Soto, tel. 23.01.15
- H* El Central, tel. 30.00.11
- HR* Julio Cesar, tel. 30.01.29
- Fonda la Cuesta

On the way to Viladangos:
- 4.30 Cafe-bar-restaurant (Avenida)
- 4.35 HR Montico, with swimming pool, tel. 39.00.11
- Fondas and posadas

Viladangos del Páramo:
- Fondas and posadas

San Miguel del Camino:
- Restaurant, Las Chuletes

Hospital de Orbigo:
- HR** Paso Honroso, tel. 37.49.75
- H Suero de Quinones, tel. 37.47.38
- H Canguro
- Pensión Rosa
- Restaurants

FREE ACCOMMODATION

La Virgen del Camino:
The Dominican Fathers offer free shelter, with 30 places, foam mattresses, showers, water. Preferably book in advance, tel. 30.00.01.

a few metres from it, for several kilometres. Some reference points are:
4.17 - Cross a tarmac road.
4.20 - Another tarmac road.
4.30 - Cross the road linking the N120 with Villadangos station. Pass a cafe-bar-restaurant (Avenida) on your left.
4.35 - Note the Hostal-Restaurante (Montico) on the other side of the N120.
4.40 - Cross the Santa María del Páramo road and continue along the broad path facing you, still parallel with the N120, for about 20 metres.
4.50 - The path becomes tarmac as it approaches Villadangos.
4.55 - Cross the N120 at kilometre marker 19, and take a road west-south-west for Villadangos del Páramo, 890m. At a crossways on the way out of the village take the path facing you, cross a bridge, then a path, and continue on the track straight ahead.
5.15 - Rejoin the N120, 100 metres before reaching the sign 'Hospital de Orbigo 11'; there are tracks running along both sides of the N120 that you can use.
5.30 - Beyond kilometre marker 21 the track on the left is generally better.
5.35 - From the Celadilla track (1.7), onward, however, at the time of writing these grassy tracks provided less easy walking .
6.00 - To go into San Martín del Camino, take a street to the right of the N120 and follow the waymarking.
6.15 - Reach the N120 again, cross it, and take a path southward, running parallel with the canal for the first 500 metres.
6.23 - After passing a bridge on your left the path leaves the canal and heads generally south-west.

Hospital de Orbigo
- Municipal campsite with Olympic-sized swimming pool, free for pilgrims, tel. 38.84.48
- Hostel for 30-40 people (bedding, showers, water), no charge, due to open 1989
- Ayuntamiento, tel. 38.82.06
- Parroquia, tel. 38.84.44.

THE GASTRONOMIC PILGRIM IN LEON

In general terms the León cuisine is similar to that of Castile, with rather more local dishes between Astorga and the Cantabrian Mountains.

A few specialities:
- 'Chafoina en cazuela' (giblet stew);
- 'Ancas de ranas de Astorga' (frogs' legs)
- Meat or fish 'Al-Ajoarriero' (with garlic)
- 'Alubias con callos' (tripe and beans)
- Pimientos (sweet peppers) del Bierzo;
- Sweets: Astorga 'Mantecadas' (buttered toast and sugar) and - 'Maragate' chocolate.

6.45 - Cross the railway, with the station on your right, and take a path south-west running parallel with the line.
7.15 - Continue south-south-west along a tarmac road.
7.25 - Villavante church. Carry on southward to the edge of the village, and take a path heading west.
7.40 - Cross a canal, and then the railway 60 metres further on. Continue west along the path for about 1,500 metres.
8.03 - Turn right, north-west, along a tarmac road.
8.10 - Cross the N120 and take a path facing you, north-west.
8.20 - Take a bridge over a canal.
8.25 - Halt; church 100 metres away on your right. Aim for the famous bridge.
8.27 - The magnificent Orbigo bridge, over the River Orbigo.
8.30 - Into Hospital de Orbigo.
8.35 - Hospital de Orbigo; church on your right, and a little farther on, halt and crossroads.

HOSPITAL DE ORBIGO

Villarejo De Orbigo

Villares De Orbigo

Estebanez De La Calzada

Santibanez De Valdeiglesias

Nord

Nistal

San Justa De La Vega

rio Tuerto

San Roman de La Vega

ASTORGA

Stage 20 - 17 kilometres - 4 hours

HOSPITAL DE ORBIGO TO ASTORGA

A *short stage that leaves time at the end of the day, to explore Astorga with its Roman bridge and ramparts, Gothic cathedral, and its museums, including Gaudí's romantic Bishop's Palace.*

Since most of the CAMINO lies beneath the bitumen of the N120, the suggested route runs further to the north, in the open countryside, an interesting stretch though not waymarked. Walkers must therefore take care and be observant. The route includes the only place along this stage with a historic feature, San Justo de la Vega.

THE FLIGHT OF SANTO TORIBIO

San Justo de la Vega, near the River Tuerto, retains in its renovated church a 16th-century statue of Saint Just and a 17th-century altar-piece.

Off the route described here and nearer to the N120, about one kilometre farther up the hill, there is a Calvary, itself a place of pilgrimage, set on a fine viewpoint over Astorga, its plains, and the surrounding mountains. This is the 'Crucero de Santo Toribio', which commemorates the flight of a 5th-century Christian bishop, expelled from Astorga. When he reached this point, Toribio shook the dust off his sandals over the ungrateful town.

THE ASTURES, MARAGATES, AND VIA DE LA PLATA

Astorga, the ancient capital of the Astures and the Amacos, was the 'Asturica Augusta' of Roman times; a substantial

0.00 - Hospital de Orbigo, 820m. From the crossroads west-south-west of the church (halt) take the street going west-south-west. Coming out of the village take the path facing you, leading to the N120.

0.20 - At a junction of paths created in 1985, 300 metres before the N120 (which can be reached to the south-west, at kilometre 31.4), turn right, west-north-west.

0.40 - Junction with a path running north-south linking Villares, 1 kilometre to the north, with the N120, 800 metres to the south, and parallel with an irrigation canal. Cross the path, then take a small bridge over the canal and go up a clearly marked track to the west.

0.50 - Reach the top of a hill between

fragment of the Roman wall still exists, behind the Cathedral and Gaudi's palace.

The town marks the junction between two Pilgrim Ways, the *Camino Francés* which is described here and the *Via de la Plata* - the Silver Route - from Andalucia via Salamanca and Zamora. This is no doubt the reason for the record number of 'hospitals' - 22 in the Middle Ages.

Astorga is also the capital of the Maragates, muleteer families living in a dozen local villages on the way to the Teleno mountains. Mysterious origins have been suggested for them, such as a Berber or Egyptian background; the ethnologist Julio-Carlos Barojo, however, sees them as simply a little knot of Asturians who have remained faithful to their traditions in a land taken over by the Castilians. They are an enterprising minority, highly successful at trade, artisan crafts, and transport.

Their magnificent costumes are brought out for the dances held on the last Sunday in August; they can also be seen in the Museum and on the figures on the Town Hall clock.

FROM CATHEDRAL GOTHIC TO THE GOTHIC OF GAUDI

- On the way in to Astorga a three-arched Roman bridge crosses a canal.
- Immediately beyond the former Puertasol, or southern gate, *las Cinco Llagas* - the Five Wounds - is a group of 'hospital' buildings of which the oldest dates back to the 11th century. The Franciscan monastery has Gothic traces.
- The picturesque *Plaza Mayor*, with its porticos and balconies, has a baroque Town Hall with two square towers, famous for its 'animated' clock. It also contains a fragment of the banner from the battle of Clavijo. Recent expert tests prove that the fabric does indeed date from the high Middle Ages.
- The *Cathedral*, built in 1471, is Gothic inside and baroque outside, with a statue of Pero Mato, the hero of Clavijo, in the apse. Sculpture round the main door represents Christ sending his apostles forth to preach, with Saint James kneeling, in his pilgrim's clothing. The choir-stalls, cloisters, and diocesan museum - with reliquaries, a fragment of the True Cross, paintings, and medieval manuscripts - should also be seen.
- The *Episcopal palace* is dizzily romantic - even the lift is

the Hospital plain and the Santibanez valley; continue down to the village, which is clearly visible.

1.00 - Church of Santibanez; go through to the north of the village and take a footpath heading northwest.

1.20 - Hilltop: continue along the path, now more accurately described as a track.

1.23 - Ignore a track up to the left, west, and two more to the right, east; keep to the path past a quarry on your left, through undulating fields, heading generally west.

1.33 - Fork: bear right, west-north-west.

1.42 - Ignore what looks like a grassy track to the left, on the edge of an oak wood, and a turning to the left, west; a minute later, turn left up a not very clearly marked track through the middle of the oaks.

1.50 - Plateau, and fields to the right. The track goes west-south-west down through bushes.

1.55 - Carry on up again in the same direction.

2.00 - And then down again; go under a high-tension cable.

2.05 - There is a clump of poplar trees on the left, in the valley bottom. The track climbs once more.

2.13 - Large sheep-pen on the right.

2.20 - At a junction of footpaths, continue straight ahead, west.

2.23 - The path goes downhill, with the cathedral of Astorga visible in the distance.

2.30 - Go under a high-tension cable.

2.35 - Fork: bear right, west.

2.50 - Rejoin the León road beside the church of San Justo de la Vega (hotel, restaurant): go along the road for 400 metres to cross the bridge over the River Tuerto.

2.57 - 60 metres beyond the bridge turn down a track to the right, and

neo-Gothic - designed in 1889 by the Catalan architect Gaudi. It has a 'Museum of the Caminos', including Roman pillars and documents concerning St James.

THE WOMEN WALLED UP ALIVE

Next to the Cathedral is the 'Hospital' of St John and also the somewhat disturbing house of the *Empedradas*, meaning 'caged in stone', where the only opening is a barred window through which the walled-in women received their food from compassionate pilgrims anxious to share their provisions.

Were the women condemned, or were they voluntary penitents? A Latin inscription tends to indicate the latter: it can be translated: 'Remember me and what I am: as I was yesterday, so are you today.'

ACCOMMODATION

San Justo de la Vega:
   - HR* Ideal, tel. 61.66.81

Astorga:
   - H*** Gaudi
   - HR** Gallego, tel. 61.54.50
   - HR** La Peseta, tel. 61.53.00
   - H* Norte, tel. 61.66.66
   - HR* Coruña, tel. 61.50.09
   - HR* Delfin, tel. 61.62.10
   - P* La Concha, tel. 61.61.59
   - P* Garcia, tel. 61.60.46
   - HS La Paz, tel. 61.52.77
   - HS Alya, tel. 61.62.35

FREE ACCOMMODATION

Astorga: Enquire at the Netherlands Brothers monastery; unequipped sports hall, tel. 61.59.76

shortly afterwards another track heading west-north-west, parallel with the Astorga road. (In summer there is no need to use the road between San Justo and this track beside the road: on the right of the highway, and below it, a track leads to the river, which can easily be crossed at a ford.)

3.30 - After crossing a small and attractive bridge, turn off to the left to rejoin the N120 near kilometre marker 45.

3.35 - Use the N120 to cross the León-Coruña railway.

3.38 - 20 metres before another level crossing, on the Plasencia-Astorga line, take a lane to the left, cross the railway, and continue straight on beside a small irrigation canal for 50 metres.

3.41 - Take a path heading west (Traversia Minerva).

3.44 - Take the Calle Perpetuo Socorro to the left, south-west.

3.45 - Take the Calle Puerto del Sol up to the right, north-west, and go through Astorga as follows: Plaza de San Francisco - Calle del General Sanjurjo (going north-east) - Plaza de España: continue northward - Plaza del General Santocildes - Calle de Lorenzo Segura - Plaza del Obispo Alcolea and then to the north-west, Calle de los Sitios.

4.00 - Gaudi's palace will be on your right, and the cathedral straight in front.

ASTORGA

Murias
Castrillo
Braguelo Santa Valdespino
Catalina Val
EL ganso Pedredo Laguna De
SoMoza
Viforcos Santa Zuyega
Colomba
Habanal Del Camino
Santa Marina
foncebadon

Manjarin
Montes De Léon

EL ACEBO

0   5

Nord

Stage 21 - 37 kilometres - 9 hours

ASTORGA TO ACEBO

T his stage will seem extra long since it involves climbing over 600m. This is the end of the Meseta, the sea of wheat, the interminable dusty paths. A small, picturesque and peaceful road takes us across the mountains - the Montes de León - which are 1,500m high.

If you do not feel confident of covering the whole stage at once, you may be able to find accommodation in an empty house at Foncebadón, a ghost village of dry-stone walled houses with thatched roofs. Ask the last remaining inhabitants - two shepherds, the Viuda (widow) Maria and her son Angel.

CROSSING THE MARAGATERIA

Many of the 'Maragata' villages of this stretch of the route have a 'Calle Real', relating them to the Santiago road -

- Between Murias and Santa-Catalina we shall pass *Castrillo de Polvazares,* which once had a 'hospital'; this was the source of the 14th-century altar-piece in the Astorga museum. The village name is derived from the Roman camp which lies beside the road and dominates it.

- In *El Ganso* - the Goose - also the site of a former 'hospital', the church has a chapel of 'Christ of the Pilgrim'.

- *Rabanal del Camino* has two hermitages side by side, a house which was once a 'hospital', fountains, and an 11th-century Romanesque Templar church dedicated to Santa María.

THE IRON CROSS ON ITS CAIRN

- The tower at Foncebadón indicates the possible site of a 'hospital' comparable with that at Roncesvalles; it was here that Ramiro II called a council in the 10th century.

- Further on and higher up, at 1,490m, is the 'Cruz de Ferro', the iron cross mentioned in the walking instructions. A metre and a half high, it stands on a long shaft set in a cairn to which every Spanish pilgrim adds

0.00 - Astorga, 878m. From the cathedral square set off south-west down the Calle de Poeta Leopoldo Panero - a one-way street.

0.04 - Turn right, north-west, into the Calle de Puerta Obispo.

0.06 - In the same direction, the Calle de San Pedro.

0.09 - Church of San Pedro on the right.

0.10 - Traffic lights and crossroads; take the Castrillo road, LE142, facing you. 0.20 - 150 metres beyond the Residencia San Francisco de Asís turn right, north-west, along a track to Valdeviejas, 866m.

0.30 - From Valdeviejas church a footpath leads back to the road.

0.40 - On the left of the road, the Ermita del Ecce Homo; 100 metres farther on bear right, west-north-west, along a track which at first runs parallel with the road.

1.10 - Once you are north of Murias de Rechivaldo, bear left, south, between walls. Leave a large electric pylon on your right and take the footbridge across the River Jerga to

a stone.

Is this a Christianised pagan ritual, as might appear from the name of 'Monte Mercurio', Mountain of Mercury? Whatever the truth, it is a place that moves one to meditation, with the summit of El Teleno to the south, the Castilian Maragateria behind and the Galician Bierzo ahead.

ACEBO, AN ANCIENT VILLAGE

Acebo (Holly) has the charm of an old but still lively village community: external stairs, tiled roofs, covered passage-ways. The 'hospital' no longer exists, but the church has a Romanesque statue regarded as representing St James, though it is more likely to be St John the Evangelist.

OFF THE ROUTE:
THE COMPLUDO IRON-WORKS

A track south-west out of Acebo leads on the right to La Herrería de Compludo, beside the stream of Carrecedo de Prada, and on the left to the village of Compludo.

La Herrería is an ironworks which was working, at least intermittently, until 1971, of a type which was both very old and very ingenious. The water of the little river also drove the power-hammer, consisting of a heavy beam, and the bellows. The installation is evidence of the local mineral wealth. Further to the south, the Romans exploited the gold mines at Médulas and left behind them a bare lunar landscape. To the north the roads of the Asturian mountains still give access to active coalmines. The iron mines are further away towards the coast.

The village of Compludo itself retains only the memory of the monastery founded in the 7th century by San Fructuoso - a Visigoth noble related to the kings of Toledo - which has now disappeared.

stamp here

the church and the Plaza Mayor, 882m, in Murias de Rechivaldo; or bear right round the village.

1.18 - Cross the LE142 road and 100 metres farther to the south take the waymarked track leading generally west-south-west.

1.55 - Cross the LE142 to take the minor road opposite, to Santa Catalina.

2.15 - 30 metres beyond the Santa Catalina sign, take a track to the right of the road, leading to the church, 971m and continuing in the same direction. There is a bar-restaurant in Santa Catalina.

2.25 - Rejoin the quiet minor road, where it is often possible to walk along the verges on either side of the tarmac. Continue to El Ganso, 3 kilometres ahead.

3.10 - 30 metres beyond the El Ganso sign take the old track to the right of the highway, through the picturesque village with its thatched roofs, 1,013m.

3.15 - Rejoin the road near the church, and continue along it for 6 kilometres.

4.40 - Ermita del Santo Cristo on your left; 50 metres beyond, at the junction, take the track to the right, north-west.

4.50 - Rabanal del Camino, 1,149m. From the church continue along the lane, and once outside the village continue westward along the track which is more or less clear though at first rather marshy and at the time of writing, not well waymarked.

5.10 - Rejoin the road, and continue along it for 4 kilometres.

6.10 - Foncebadón, 1,430m. Just beyond the sign turn left off the road along the track through the village which is partly ruined and almost completely abandoned. It may be

144

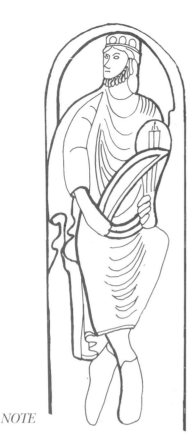

NOTE

In 1985 Georges Veron was unable to check the short detour via Valdeviejas, and took the Astorga route to the Ecce Homo hermitage. In 1986 Yan L. Crispel considered this additional mileage 'not worthwhile'.

possible to shelter overnight in an empty house. Continue next along a footpath beside a wall to the ruins of a chapel on your left. Ignore a sunken path bearing downhill and take another path to the right, more clearly marked, which climbs slightly. After five minutes turn off it to take a footpath up a gully to the right.
6.40 - Rejoin the road, 1,480m.
6.50 - Iron cross on a shaft set in a cairn of stones, with the small, modern Ermita de Santiago a little to the right. Continue along the road for about 6 kilometres.
8.20 - Turn right onto a footpath, up to the north-west over a small hilltop, and down to the road again.
8.30 - Follow the road for 100 metres; to avoid some tarmac, use a somewhat scrubby and uninteresting footpath to the left of the road and below it.
8.40 - Col: take a footpath to the west on the hilltop, which continues in the same direction down to Acebo.
8.55 - Rejoin the road, with Fuente de la Trucha 20 metres to your right. Take the main street (unsurfaced) through the village.
9.00 - Acebo, 1,145m.

ACCOMMODATION

Murias de Rechivaldo:
- Three restaurants, book ahead, tel. 61.60.21
El Ganso:
- School converted into shelter, free
- a bar open in summer
Rabanal del Camino:
- Restaurant mesón Chonina, tel. 72.94.68
- The former presbytery is being converted into a hostel with places for 12 (beds, kitchen); with free stabling for horses.
Foncebadón:
- a simple refuge under construction, with open fire and running water, free.

EL ACEBO

Riego De AMbros

Nord

MoLinaseca

LoMbiLLo

SaLas
V.ZZ.

rio Boeza

CaMpo

San Lorenzo

PonferRada

rio Sil

Stage 22 - 18 kilometres - 4 hours 20 minutes

ACEBO TO PONFERRADA

A short and attractive stage down to Ponferrada, allowing plenty of time to explore the village. The name is derived from the iron bridge, an almost unheard-of luxury in the Middle Ages, only possible in a rich mining area such as from here to Oviedo. The Templar castle is open to visitors, and in one of the suburbs is the Mozarabic church of Santo Tomás de las Ollas.

MOLINASECA BRIDGE

- Outside Molinaseca, the chapel of the *Virgen de las Angustias* (Our Lady of Sorrows), is in very poor condition.
- Entering the village, a *Romanesque bridge* crosses the River Meruelo.
- Near the church you can be shown round the *house of Doña Urraca*, Queen of Castile, who lived her turbulent life around 1100.
- In the village square where there was once a 'hospital' stands a Calvary, often with flowers round it, and a miniature chapel.

THE IRON BRIDGE AT PONFERRADA

Ponferrada lies at the confluence of the Rivers Boeza and Sil. The *medieval bridge* over the Boeza has Romanesque arches.

The Sil, as you leave the town, is crossed by the eponymous *iron bridge*. It was built in the 12th century by Osmond, Bishop of Astorga, and at a time when all bridges were built of wood or stone it aroused great admiration.

Another nationally classified monument is the 13th-century *Templar castle*. Fernando II of León had granted the town to the Knights Templar in 1185; they were expelled in 1312. Each August there are performances of the play 'Señor de Bembibre' (Bembibre is a town some 20 kilometres away) in the castle.

0.00 - Acebo, 1,145m. Follow the main street through the village (no tarmac in 1985); this leads you on to the Ponferrada road.

0.30 - Col, 980m. Take a track left, north-west, which runs on below the road.

0.38 - After a high point the track goes through a cutting to reach the first houses of Riego de Ambros. Take a picturesque lane, then a footpath to the right, north, leaving the church on your left.

0.44 - Fork: bear left, along a lane leading north-west.

0.45 - Plaza de la Paz.

0.46 - Beyond the village take a track down to the right, north-west. It is cut through the rock, but may be overgrown in places, and muddy along the lower stretches.

0.52 - Take a footpath heading north-west.

0.54 - Junction of paths; bear west-north-west to a clump of enormous chestnut-trees, and to the south of them, take a broad track to the west-north-west.

0.58 - Ignore a turning to the left.

1.00 - With an electricity line on

In addition you can see the 16th-century *church of Nuestra Señora de la Encina*, commemorating the appearance of the Virgin on an oak tree in the days of the Templars; *San Andrés*, a baroque 17th-century church with its 14th-century Christ; the *Monastery of the Conceptionists*, 1542; the 16th-century *Clock Tower;* and the baroque 17th-century *Town Hall.*

OFF THE ROUTE: MOZARABIC AND ROMANESQUE CHURCHES

Even more than the relatively minor monuments listed above, the local sanctuaries testifying to the powerful expansion of faith from the 10th century onwards merit a visit, if time allows.

- *Santo Tomás de las Ollas* - a 10th-century Mozarabic church with horseshoe arches - lies in a suburb to the north of the town.

- To the south, in the quiet seclusion of the 'Valle del Silencio', the 12th-century *San Pedro de Montes* is partly Romanesque; and from there a footpath leads on to *Santiago de Peñalba*, where the lacy Mozarabic marble dates from 937.

- Rather nearer, at Otero on the south bank of the Boeza, the 11th-century church of *Santa María de Vizcayo* is transitional Mozarabic-Romanesque.

CAMPO: THE FOUNTAIN AND THE WELL

The pretty village of Campo retains as its sole running water supply the medieval fountain in a half-buried niche.

Its access path still bears the name of 'Los Gallegos' (The Galicians), and the street which links it to the medieval bridge is called 'la Francesa', the French way. Its central square has several dressed stone buildings - a chapel, a parish house converted to an inn, the well.

THE ALTERNATIVE ROAD

As it approached Ponferrada the Road to Santiago divided. The southern branch is described here; the northern branch is no longer of interest, except from a historical point of view, since it has now been overwhelmed by the main road. It crossed the River Boeza at the Paso de la Barca, where a 19th-century

your left, a telephone line on your right and another on your left, continue along the footpath, through clumps of broom, to the north-west.

1.03 - Go under the telephone wires.

1.05 - Pass on your left a gateway (two cart-wheels) and a small polygonal house; rejoin the road above, and go down it for about 100 metres northwards then north-north-west, then west.

1.08 - Turn right onto a track.

1.12 - Col. Leave a large electricity pylon 20 metres to your right, and go north-west down a track, almost beneath the high-tension wires.

1.15 - Drop down into the hollow of the valley below, right.

1.18 - Take a footpath heading west on the opposite flank, generally running parallel with the axis of the valley on your left.

1.23 - The footpath follows a telephone line.

1.26 - The path forks, but the two branches meet again. Next, follow a track heading north.

1.35 - Valley bottom; the road is below, about 100 metres to your left.

1.36 - Leave the track as it drops down to the road, and take a footpath to the right, climbing gently up, west-south-west.

1.38 - It passes through a modest col, with veins of quartz in the rock.

1.43 - Rejoin the road at kilometre marker 7, and follow it.

1.45 - On the right, Ermita de las Angustias. About 100 metres down the road turn left across the picturesque medieval bridge over the River Meruelo.

1.50 - Molinaseca, 603m. Go through the village and rejoin the Ponferrada road for 3 kilometres. The various detours indicated by the waymarking are not very interesting.

bridge has taken the place of the old ferry; from there it goes directly to the middle of the town, and the castle.

ACCOMMODATION

Ponferrada:
- HR*** El Temple, tel. 41.09.31
- HR** Conde Silva, tel. 41.04.07
- H** Madrid, tel. 41.15.50
- H** Libos, tel. 41.13.50
- H** La Madrileña, tel. 41.28.57
- HR* Fonteboa, tel. 41.10.91
- H Cornatel, tel. 41.09.12
- P* María Encina, tel. 41.12.37

FREE ACCOMMODATION

Molinaseca: Planned development of an inn on the edge of the town, near the St Roque hermitage.

Ponferrada: Enquire at the parish house of the church of N.S. de la Encina, tel. 41.19.78 and 41.00.59.

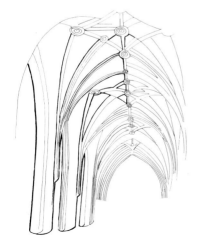

2.30 - *100 metres beyond a high point, 610m, with a view over Ponferrada, turn left off the road onto a gravel track beside a telephone cable, heading west-south-west.*

2.35 - *Fork: take the track down to the left, south-west.*

2.40 - *Valley bottom; the track climbs, south-west.*

2.45 - *Then descends, in the same direction.*

2.50 - *Go through Campo, heading generally westward.*

3.00 - *Minor road: go west along it, past some public rubbish tips.*

3.15 - *Abattoirs on the right.*

3.20 - *Small bridge over a tributary of the River Boeza.*

3.35 - *Medieval bridge over the Boeza. Next, take a street to the left heading north-west.*

3.45 - *Go under the railway line and up a lane to the north (Camino bajo de San Andrés).*

3.50 - *Turn right, north, along the Calle de l'Hospital.*

3.55 - *Church of San Andrés on your right, north, and the Templars' castle in front: turn right, north-east, along the Calle Gil y Carrasco.*

4.00 - *Fork: bear right to the Plaza de la Virgen de la Encina, and from there go left, north-north-west, down the steps of the Calle El Ranadero.*

4.10 - *Cross, left, the bridge over the River Sil, and follow the Avenida de la Puebla, west-north-westwards.*

4.20 - *Plaza de Lazurtegui, town centre.*

PONFERRADA

Cortiguera

fuentes Nuevas

Camponaraya

Nord

DNaroyala

Cacabelos

Valtuille
De Abajo

Valtuille De
Arriba

Toral de Los
Valdos

Villafranca
DEL Bierzo

1Km

Stage 23 - 22 kilometres - 5 hours 15 minutes

PONFERRADA TO VILLAFRANCA DEL BIERZO

This short stage linking two 'mountain' stretches allows you the time to explore Villafranca del Bierzo. This is another 'Frankish Town', with 12th- and 13th-century churches, a 15th-century castle, a 16th-century monastery, and armorial carvings. Six kilometres of the Old Road were to be cleared and restored in 1989-90, with redevelopment of the unusable stretch from just above kilometre 403 as far as the village of Valtuille de Arriba, continuing along an existing road to join the current track 1,200 metres before Villafranca de Bierzo.

VILLAGES IN THE HEART OF THE BIERZO REGION

- At the intersection of the NVI and the Villablino road at Compostilla, the modern neo-Romanesque church occupies the site of the former hermitage of Nuestra Señora del Refugio; the statue of the Virgin has been moved to Orense museum.

- *Columbrianos,* which is skirted round by the Pilgrim Way, is dominated on the left by a Roman camp; the church with its triple aisles has a baroque altar-piece.

- *Camponaraya* formerly had two 'hospitals'.

- *Fuentes Nuevas* has a 'calle real' where the Santiago Road runs past its chapel of the Divine Christ.

- *Cacabelos* has a fountain in the Plaza San Lazaro where there was once a chapel. The 16th-century church of Santa María has some 12th-century remains, and a statue

0.00 - Ponferrada, 525m. From the Plaza Lazurtegui take the Avenue del General Gómez Nuñez (the Villablino road) to the north, for two full kilometres.

0.35 - 100 metres beyond the Montecastro service station and 200 metres before a road bridge taking the NVI over the Villablino road, turn left, north-west, along a gravel path.

0.40 - Go under the NVI and continue to the left, north-west, along a gravel track.

0.50 - The track crosses a small metric gauge railway (the mine track from Ponferrada to Villablino which,

of the Virgin dating from the 13th century. There is also the 18th-century neoclassical sanctuary of Quinta Angustia, flanked by a 'hospital'; and a museum of local archaeology.

- Off the route: The Benedictine monastery of La Bega de Espinareda lies to the north as you leave Cacabelos;
- to the south, traces of the Cistercian monastery of Carracedo, and a Romanesque church.
- *Pieros*, on the N6 road, has a carved stone from 1086 in its church. The village is overlooked by the site of a Roman camp, Castrum Bergidum - probably a Celtic name, with the same etymology as the surrounding district of Bierzo.

VILLAFRANCA, THE FRANKISH TOWN WITH TWO MAYORS

As its name indicates, Villafranca del Bierzo was a 'Frankish town' born out of the Road to Compostela in 1070 and ruled by the Cluniacs. It had two mayors, one for the Franks and the other for the Spanish. Villafranca became a marquisate in 1486, and capital of the short-lived province of Bierzo from 1822-1833.

Along the Pilgrim Way through the town we find:
- On the way in, the main door of the *church of Santiago* is 12th-century Romanesque, decorated. At the Perdón door a plenary indulgence was granted to sick pilgrims unable to continue along the Road: a French pilgrim made use of the door once more in 1965.
- Slightly to the right and near the Plaza Mayor, the church of *San Francisco* has a 13th-century Romanesque main door and a 14th-century Gothic apse.
- The *Marquises' castle*, 1490, lost its towers during the War of Independence against Napoleon.
- On its left is the Franciscan sisters' *Convent of the Annunciation*, 1606, with an Italianate main door. It was the mausoleum of the ruling Marquises and contains the tomb of San Lorenzo of Brindisi.
- The former *Calle del Agua* with carved armorial stones is famous for the palaces of Torquemada and Alvarez de Toledo; and a chapel.
- On its right the collegiate church of *Santa María de Cluniaco*, 16th century with a fine altar-screen, retains its original Cluniac 13th-century tower.
- To the north of the Plaza Mayor lies the baroque 17th-century monastery of San Nicolás, with cloister and altar-piece.

until 1984, was the last remaining steam train in Spain); continue in the same direction, north-west.

1.10 - Join a gravel path, and turn left, west, along it through the northern part of Fuentes Nuevas.

1.40 - Join the road from Ponferrada to Villafranca del Bierzo via Cacabelos, and follow it north-westwards through Camponaraya.

2.05 - Beyond Camponaraya and the bridge over the River Cargalón, leave the road temporarily as it bears right; continue instead straight ahead, north-north-west, up a track with a wine co-operative on your left at the junction.

2.15 - At the top of the slope ignore a left fork; continue straight on, north-west.

2.20 - The track crosses a small concrete bridge over an irrigation canal, then goes down between vineyards.

2.25 - Leave the track where it goes down to the right, north, to the village, and turn west-north-west instead onto a track with deeper tractor ruts.

2.30 - Ignore a left fork 20 metres before a small bridge over the River Magaz, and keep heading north-westwards even where the main track takes a 90-degree turn to the right. Shortly afterwards cross a more clearly-marked track, and continue north-west along a grassy track. After going up through the vines pass a breeze-block building on your left, and rejoin the road 100 metres farther on.

2.50 - 2 kilometres south-east of Cacabelos cross the road from Ponferrada and take a broad path heading north-west. After 1 kilometre it bears left, west, and reaches Cacabelos, with the village centre another kilometre ahead.

OFF THE ROUTE

Excursions to the south of the town:
- The Romanesque church of *San Fiz de Visonia*, successor to the third monastery founded in the 7th century by San Fructuoso.
- Two Romanesque churches and a 14th-century castle at Corullón.

ACCOMMODATION

Camponaraya: fondas

Cacabelos: fondas

Villafranca del Bierzo:
- H*** Parador Nacional, tel.54.01.75
- H* Comercio, tel. 54.00.08
- H* El Cruce, tel. 54.01.85
- HR* La Charola, tel. 54.02.00
- HR* Ponterrey, tel. 54.00.85
- Fonda El Carmen, tel. 54.00.30

FREE ACCOMMODATION

A hostel is planned on land beside the church of San Francisco, with 20-30 places, free; apply to the Guardia Municipal (Police Station).

3.30 - *Cacabelos, 483m. The simplest thing now is to follow the road towards Villafranca for 4 kilometres.*

4.30 - A full kilometre beyond the marker 405 (at the time of writing marker 406 was untraceable), turn right, north-west, on a track going uphill and then bearing right, north.

4.45 - Concrete building on your left, and junction of tracks: turn left, west, for Villafranca.

5.15 - Villafranca del Bierzo, 524m.

NOTE

It would be preferable, and no doubt possible, to avoid several kilometres of tarmac after Cacabelos. Having only old maps and inaccurate route-plans we were unable to check this out thoroughly in the time available before publication. It should be possible, however, to go via Valtuille de Arriba, from where a good track leads to the junction indicated at 4.45 above.

We would be grateful for your comments.

stamp here

VILLAFRANCA DEL BIERZO

Nord

1 Km

Dragonte

Moral de Valcarce

Villar

Sanfiz do Seo

Vega de Valcarce

Serviz

Villasinde

Las herrerías

Barjas

Lindoso

La faba

La Laguna

CEBRERO

Stage 24 - 40 kilometres - 10 hours

VILLAFRANCA DEL BIERZO TO EL CEBREIRO

B *eyond Villafranca, the Pilgrim Way merges with the NVI for 18 kilometres. There are notes below on the places along the way.*

Many walkers, however, will, like us, feel little enthusiasm for the notion of a four or five hour climb on a congested motor road, no matter how historic the route. We therefore offer two possible solutions:

- Those in a hurry and who are more impatient and pragmatic can hitch-hike, at least as far as the Vega de Valcarce fork, perhaps as far as the Herrerías turning.

- Truly dedicated walkers - the purists - will certainly enjoy the detour we suggest through ancient villages. Although it does not actually follow the course of the Pilgrim Way, it does offer the advantage of exploring a landscape which is still more or less as the original pilgrims saw it.

And of course we shall rejoin the true Road before it reaches the very fine climb up from Herrerías to Cebreiro. All the same, our suggested route is appreciably longer and somewhat mountainous, and therefore tiring; so be prepared to camp overnight, since accommodation along the way is uncertain on the detour. However, a hostel awaits walkers at Cebreiro, on the frontier between Castile and Galicia on the crest of the Cantabrian cordillera - a high point in every sense of the word: altitude 1,300m and date 11th century.

IF YOU FOLLOW THE NVI

Once through Villafranca, whichever route you take, and though we are still in the province of León, the language, traditions and history are those of Galicia; many place-names have spellings from both.

Places on the Old Road that we pass by using the NVI are the following:

- *Pereje* still retains its medieval atmosphere, although it no longer has the 'hospital' which was so important to pilgrims when the mountains were blocked with snow. Attached to Cebreiro but coveted in vain by Villafranca, it was the object of an enduring feud between their mother-houses of Aurillac and Cluny.

- *Trabadelo* was the Roman 'Utaris' mentioned in the Antonine itinerary, a name long perpetuated in the former Castillo de Auctares. This vanished castle was the seat of pillaging overlords who seized pilgrims for ransom, but who were persuaded to reason by Alfonso VI.

- *Vega de Valcarce* is the main village in this enclosed valley, hence no doubt its name, meaning 'Valley prison'. It still has its two castles, Vega and Sarracín; the latter, visible from afar like an eyrie, dates from the 14th century. Charles V stayed there in 1520.

- the chapel at *Ruitelán* is dedicated to San Froilán, who lived there as a hermit before becoming Bishop of León.

ON THE BORDERS
OF CASTILE AND GALICIA

Timeless, and unrecorded in the history books - perhaps because happy peoples have no history - Da Dragonte, Moral and Villar de Corrales have few historians.

- *Herrería*, at the junction of the two routes, owes its name to the ironworks of former days: Laffi was highly impressed by the size of the hammers driven by the river.

- *La Faba* and *Lagune de Castillo* are the last two mountain villages under the administration of Castile.

0.00 - Villafranca del Bierzo, 524m.
Take the Calle del Agua northward, then a lane up to the left for 100 metres to rejoin the old Lugo road. Turn north-west along this road and cross the bridge over the River Burbia. Leave the old N6 and turn left along the Calle de la Concepción. Cross a bridge (10 tons) over the River Valcarce, then take a street which was tarmac at the time of writing.
0.20 - At a main crossroads to the west of the town, cross the modern NVI, leaving the tunnel 30 metres to your right, and take the small tarmac road opposite, south-west, to Corullón. Turn right off this after 50 metres, up a steep track, and rejoin the tarmac which has taken a more gentle Z bend; turn right along it. Shortly before Dragonte ignore a tarmac turning to your left.
1.30 - Dragonte, 900m. Go through this picturesque hamlet, actually the upper part of the village, heading west-north-west on a dirt track. Continue next on a track which climbs slightly, descends a little along the hillside, then goes up again; on the opposite flank, to the right, is the peak of La Corona, 1,121m.
2.00 - As you reach the crest where the route becomes almost level, turn right, north-west, up another less well-marked track leading to a further ridge about 100 metres away. From this crest, 1,090m, a good track descends steeply on the far side, roughly north-west.
2.20 - Join a path (road apparently under construction at the time of writing) at an altitude of about 980m, and turn left, south-west, along it. After 500 metres it crosses a small ridge, 990m, and continues in the same direction down to the outlying

CEBREIRO:
FROM THE 9TH CENTURY ONWARDS

Cebrero in Castilian, Cebreiro in Galician, this town of nine forges is in all senses a high point: situated on the 1,300m pass between two kingdoms, it has inherited spiritual, historical and prehistorical riches.

Pilgrims are known to have found shelter here from as early as the 9th century, but no further details survive. In 1072 Alfonso VI handed the place over to the Aurillac abbey of Saint Gérard, later annexed to Cluny. In 1487 the bad behaviour of the French monks brought about the transfer of Cebrero to Valladolid, though still within the Benedictine fold, which continued until the law of expropriation in 1854.

- *Santa María la Real* dates from the 11th century, on 9th-century foundations. You should not miss the statue of the Virgin, the miraculous chalice, and the tombs with human figures.

- The former monastery-cum-'hospital' has been restored and converted into a hotel, *El Mesón de Europa*.

- The village of *pallozas*, celtic dwellings with thatched roofs, houses a museum of ethnology and a pilgrim halt.

houses of a village.
2.30 - Moral de Valcarce: go through the village, following the waymarked path. The waymarking leads generally north-west, down the hairpin bends of a fairly steep track.
3.00 - In the valley bottom cross a small stream, then a larger one. Continue up a waymarked footpath which becomes gradually wider.
3.35 - The track reaches the edge of Villar de Corrales; continue to the top of the village.
3.40 - Leave the waymarking, which takes a northward track and which at the time of writing had vanished completely at the end of the first kilometre, and take instead an old track up to the col a few hundred metres to the west of the village.
3.50 - From this col, 1,050m, a good dirt track heads downhill and then twists through hairpin bends to the footpath from Serviz to San Fiz. This track disappears near the bottom: cross a meadow and a bridge over a small brook to reach the path on the opposite flank.
4.45 - Turn right along this path for two full kilometres, heading generally north-east. 5.15 - San Fiz, 650m; bar, groceries, snacks. Since this stage from Villafranca to El Cebreiro is very long and includes many uphill sections, it is sensible to divide it in two and to stay overnight either at San Fiz or at Herrería. Leave the village on a roughly cemented track which is waymarked, heading roughly west and almost flat.
5.30 - Fork: the waymarking leads to the left, south-west, branch, a gentle descent. At a second fork a few hundred metres further on, turn right. The track runs close to the River Pojsadela, below and on your left. The clearly marked track follows

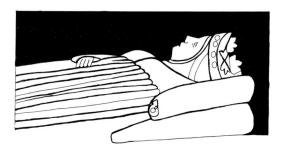

THE MONK OF LITTLE FAITH, AND THE MIRACLE OF THE HOLY ELEMENTS

Tradition tells that around the year 1200, on a winter's morning when storms piled the snow up to the roof-tops, a shepherd of the village of Barxamayor came, as he did every day, to attend Mass. The monk of little faith who hastened through the service thought to himself, 'He must be a fool to travel in such weather, just for a little bread and wine'.

Immediately the communion bread was transformed into real flesh and the wine into real blood which filled the chalice. The chalice and paten, which date from the 12th century, are still on display. The divine elements were carefully preserved - when the 'Catholic Monarchs', King Ferdinand and Queen Isabella, passed through the village in 1486, they had the flesh and wine put into a reliquary and flask which can still be seen.

Local people add to the narrative: Queen Isabella, they say, wanted to take the relics away with her, but the mule refused to leave, which was taken as a divine message. And two of the tombs with human figures are attributed to the monk and the shepherd.

Wagner too passed through Barxamayor: 'Parsifal' is said to refer to it.

158

the hillside.

5.50 - The village of Moldes is visible 1,500 metres away to the south-west. The track forks - take the right turn, north-west, steadily uphill.

6.00 - Junction with the small tarmac road from Barjas to Vega de Valcarce, just below Villasinde; cross the road and climb up a short track to Villasinde. Go through the hamlet, using the gravel lanes heading north-west. Next continue slightly downhill to the north-west on a good track.

6.16 - Ignore a small turning up to your right.

6.20 - Fork; bear right, up to the north-west.

6.30 - Crest, 1,010m. Ignore a turning, head up to the left and continue straight ahead and slightly downhill along the track which loops down into the valley bottom.

6.40 - Next it climbs up to the north-east, slightly overgrown by broom and bracken.

6.50 - Col. A footpath leads down to the north, heavily overgrown and often damp, fortunately followed by a track of increasing breadth.

7.20 - Herrerías, 680m. Continue north-west through the village along the minor tarmac road on the right bank of the river, i.e. the southern bank of the River Valcarce.

7.35 - After a kilometre leave the tarmac as it climbs left to Lindose; turn right onto the footpath to La Faba, across to the left bank of the river and up, generally north-west, for 3 kilometres, then bending to the left, south, and up again for a kilometre.

8.40 - La Faba, 917m. From the hamlet the stony track leads up northward.

8.50 - Fork: bear right, north-east.

8.55 - Ignore a turning to the right and continue up to the north-west.

ACCOMMODATION

Vega de Valcarce:
- HSR** Valcarce, Madrid-Coruña road, km.424, tel. 54.04.98.
- P* Fernandez, tel. 54.04.27

El Cebrero:
- P** Hospedería de San Giraldo de Aurillac, tel. 36.90.25.
- Refuge Las Pallozas, tel. 36.90.25

9.15 - Laguna de Castilla, 1,098m. Go through the hamlet.
9.20 - Fork: take the track to the left, north-west.
9.25 - Turn left onto a track bending uphill through clumps of broom to Cebreiro.
10.00 - El Cebreiro, 1,298m. High point of the Road to Santiago, on the crest of the Cantabrian Mountains, the boundary of Galicia. Inn.

NOTES

- As the Villafranca to San Fiz section was reconnoitred on light motor-bikes (all-terrain!), the times indicated for walkers are approximate.

- Recent Spanish maps indicate a road from Moral-de-Valcarce, but in August 1985 we saw no trace of it. The waymarking led down to the valley bottom mentioned at '3.00', which seems reasonable; there is probably a track higher up which keeps more closely to the contour line.

- At the fork mentioned at '5.30' we would have been inclined to go to the right, had it not been for the waymarking; the route shown perhaps needs to be studied more closely.

- The stretch leading up to San Fiz can be avoided: 500 metres before the village the path crosses the River Posjadela. From here it should be possible to go directly up to the left, north-west, to join the waymarked route.

- The route to the north of Vilar seems correct, but at the time of writing the waymarking was not clear, and after trying three tracks though scrubland, the search for the route had to be abandoned.

We would welcome any comments on these points.

CEBREÑO

1km

Linares

hospital

Padornelo

Void

fonfria

Biduelo

LaMas

Vilar   fiLLoval

RaMiL Pasantes
TRiaCasTeLa

Stage 25 - 23 kilometres - 5 hours 40 minutes

CEBREIRO TO TRIACASTELA

T his is an attractive shorter mountain stage, where walkers play hide-and-seek with the L634 road, constantly making use of footpaths and tracks on each side of the road, which in parts is fairly quiet. There are no striking monuments along the way, but a few modest reminders of the Santiago pilgrimage. Triacastela has some Romanesque apses - and some rather more modern hotels.

FROM LINARES TO BIDUEDO

- The churches at *Linares* (meaning flax fields) and Hospital Da Condesa have scallop-shells over their doors, similar to the Cebreiro church; likewise at Veiga de Forgas, slightly off to the left of the route.
- On the way into *San Juan de Padornelo*, the chapel of the former Hospitallers' Priory has been converted into a place of burial.
- At the summit of *Alto del Poyo*, the Santa María chapel is dedicated to St Mary Magdalene.
- At *Fonfría* (cold spring), nothing remains of the Sancti Spiritus monastery, which disappeared over a century ago; it offered pilgrims a free light, salt, water, and a bed with two blankets, and sick pilgrims were also entitled to an egg, bread, and bacon.

TRIACASTELA:
THE FRENCH PRISONERS' CARVINGS

According to some, the name of Triacastela comes from the three local castles which figure on its coat of arms; but it may simply

0.00 Cebreiro, 1,298m. Leaving the tarmac road to Rubiales on your left, cross the village heading west to the road from the Col de Pedrafita to Triacastela, LU634; turn southwest along it.

0.20 - 500 metres beyond kilometre 34, turn right down a broad gravel path.

0.30 - 10 metres before a hairpin bend, turn left onto a track heading up to the south-west. At the first fork bear right, south, and continue parallel with the road.

0.50 - Return to the Triacastela road on the edge of the hamlet of Linares; turn right along it for 100 metres, then left on the old track which goes close to the church. Next rejoin the tarmac and follow the road.

1.10 - Col, Alto de San Roque, 1,264m. Panoramic viewpoint. Take the track to the right of the road; it goes over a hilltop while the road

be a distant derivation of the Roman 'Telamina Sextrorum'.

Count Gaton founded a monastery here in the 9th century, and in the 13th century King Alfonso IX intended to develop it into a city, a project which was never realised.

- The church, which was rebuilt in 1790, still retains two Romanesque apses. The high altar and processional cross bear the image of St James.

- In the former prison, French prisoners cut pictures of cocks in the wood of the heavy beams.

- The Pedreira, Aira and Dos Ponte houses used to offer hospitality.

A STONE FROM EACH PILGRIM

On the way out of the village is a pyramid of stones with a small statue of a pilgrim on top.

According to tradition, each pilgrim would take a heavy stone from the local quarry, carrying it all the next day to the kilns of Castañeda five leagues away. There the stones were converted into lime, used to build the church at Compostela.

curves round to the left.

1.20 - Rejoin the road 200 metres beyond kilometre marker 30 and continue along it.

1.45 - Hospital de la Condesa, 1,260m. At kilometre 29 go into the hamlet along the track to the right of the road, passing the church on your left, and rejoin the road 200 metres farther on; continue along the road.

2.00 - 150 metres beyond kilometre 28 take the footpath to the right, leading to Sabugos.

2.05 - Next, take the track to the left, north, winding along the hillside well below the road.

2.20 - San Juan de Padornelo, 1,275m; a few farms and a church. Carry on straight ahead, north-west, aiming for the buildings at the col.

2.30 - Col del Poyo (also spelt Pollo, or Poio), 1,337m. Rejoin the road shortly before kilometre 26 and follow it.

3.00 - 150 metres before kilometre 24 take a track running along on the right of the road and only a few metres from it.

3.15 - Fonfría del Camino, 1,290m. Cross the village on the track parallel with the road, which is a few dozen metres to your left.

3.35 - Rejoin the asphalt 400 metres beyond kilometre 22, level with a col. The track follows the road to the right for about 300 metres in a wide bend.

3.40 - Cross the road and take another track also parallel with the road and a few dozen metres from it.

3.50 - Viduedo (or Biduedo): a chapel on your right as you enter the hamlet. Go through, heading north, with the road about a hundred metres to your right.

4.00 - On leaving the village the

BIDUEDO: BACK ON THE ROAD

The church at Biduedo is the smallest on the Camino. The village is an important reference point of the Pilgrim Way, for we leave the majestic mountain scenery at this point and return to the true Road to Santiago, which is clearly separate from the motor road and goes straight on from one ancient village to another.

A POSSIBLE ALTERNATIVE ROUTE

An alternative pilgrim itinerary led from Pedrafita, slightly to the north of Cebreiro and also on the León/Galicia boundary, to Triacastella via Doncos, Nogais and Laguna.

Doncos has a crenellated medieval tower, and the two palaces of the Dukes of Alba and of Saavedra.

Nogais, on a spur of the Sierra de Ancares, has a Roman bridge, a Romanesque church, and the palace of the Counts of Villapún.

ACCOMMODATION

Alto del Poyo:
- Posada del Peregrino, restaurant and grocery, 7 beds and an unequipped shelter.
- Cafe

Triacastela:
- Hostal-bar O'Novo, tel. 54.70.05
- Bar-Fonda Fernandez, 6 beds, tel. 54.70.48
- Fonda Villasente, tel. 54.70.16

FREE ACCOMMODATION

Triacastela:
- Enquire at the Town Hall about the hostel, tel. 54.70.47.

track bears westwards along the hillside.

4.07 - Ignore a turning to the right, down to Vilar.

4.13 - Go under the high-tension cables. The track continues to the south-south-west.

4.22 - Fork: bear right, south-west and down.

4.25 - Under the high-tension lines again.

4.30 - Continue down to the west-south-west.

4.40 - Filloval. Entering the hamlet bear left, south-west, to meet the road at kilometre 15.1; cross it and continue downhill.

5.00 - Meet the tarmac again at kilometre 13.3. Cross the road and take the track down to the near-by hamlet of As Pasantes.

5.05 - At the chapel bear down to the left.

5.12 - Turn left at the fork.

5.20 - Ramil, 700m. The track, which is suitable for vehicles, goes through the hamlet and on towards Triacastela.

5.35 - Triacastela church.

5.40 - Triacastela, 665m. Rejoin the LN634 road. Food supplies, fonda and a good hotel-restaurant.

TRIACASTELA
BaLsa

SandiL

Montan

fureLa
Pintin

SaMos

Nord

SARRIA

Stage 26 - 20 kilometres - 5 hours

TRIACASTELA TO SARRÍA

B*efore the building of the impressive abbey of Samos, pilgrims went to Sarría by a more direct route, which still has various Romanesque remains.*
We have kept to this interesting route, lined with picturesque hamlets, and well away from even minor roads.

The way into Sarría is marked by some more substantial remains: a Romanesque bridge and church, castle ruins. The most important monument on this stage, however, is Samos, lying beside the Triacastela-Sarría route which is waymarked in yellow. The most sensible way of getting there would be by bus from either of the two towns.

ON THE ROAD TO SAN-XIL

- At *San-Xil* (or Gil), the church contains a 15th-century chalice.
- *Montan*, to the left of the track, has a modest Romanesque nave.
- *Zoo*, to the right of the path, has a church of St James.
- Shortly before reaching *Furela*, away to the left of the road, the fine Romanesque church at *San Roman* is worth a visit. There is a chapel dedicated to San Roque in the village, next to a peasant house bearing a coat of arms.
- At *Calvor* the church, which retains Romanesque traces and a Visigothic capital used as a holy water stoup, lies on an ancient fortified camp.
- The last house in *Aguiada* is still called the 'Hospital'.

0.00 - Triacastela, 665m. Shortly beyond the hotel and 10 metres beyond kilometre marker 10, turn right, north-west, along a track suitable for cars. Ignore two turnings to the left, and cross over to the left bank of the River Valdoscuro.

0.30 - Turn left, west, down a track to Balsa which reaches the outlying houses almost immediately. The track goes through the hamlet and continues along the left bank of the River Valdoscuro.

0.35 - Bridge across the river. The track bears to the right, north-west;

165

SARRIA: BUT WHICH WAY DID AYMERY GO?

Aymery Picaud makes no mention of Sarría. He seems to have gone farther to the south through a 'San Michaél' which is not easy to identify. Most pilgrims, however, came to Sarría.

Along the road through the upper town, to which two flights of steps lead up, you will reach in turn:
- The modern church of *Santa-Marina*, on the site of a former medieval sanctuary.
- The *San Antonio Hospital*, now the Law Courts, where pilgrims could obtain a bed, a light, and medical care.
- The Romanesque *church of El Salvador* - Christ Our Saviour - with pre-Renaissance paintings, and a Gothic door, mentioned in 1094.
- The tower and octagonal walls which remain from the 14th-century fortress, destroyed in 1467.
- The *Monastery of the Magdalene*, which first belonged to the Augustinians and then until the 19th century to the Fathers of Mercy; it has a flamboyant cloister and the inscription *'Charitas Aedificat'* (with the h) on a door.
- The chapel of San Lazaro perpetuates the memory of a former lazaretto, where the sick and the lepers were cared for.
- The *Romanesque Aspera* bridge over the River Celeiro has a single arch and four openings.

OFF THE ROUTE: THE MONASTERY OF SAN JULIAN AT SAMOS

The existence of pilgrim tombs in the cemetery of the San Julián monastery proves that many of them made the detour here.

Founded in the 7th century, San Juliín was re-established in the 12th century by monks fleeing from Seville. Nothing remains of the original buildings except a Mozarabic arch, which may date from the 10th century, in the little chapel of the Saviour, some 150 metres from a thousand-year-old cypress tree. A Romanesque door dating from the 12th century can be seen in the corner of the Gothic cloisters, with the huge fountain of the Nereids. The 'great' cloister and the church are classical in style. In 1491 King Ferdinand and Queen Isabella linked the abbey with the community of Valladolid.

It is known that in the 18th century pilgrims could remain for three days, sharing the monks' meals in the

it tends to be muddy, and goes through a farmyard before a spectacular climb up a gully through the woods.

0.50 - Join a stony footpath and follow it for about 600 metres to the right.

1.00 - Col and hamlet of San Gil (or San Xil). An excellent path now follows the undulating hillside, heading generally west and up to a col.

1.30 - Col, 896m. Ten metres beyond it, leave the track to take a small footpath down to the right. This drops down north-westwards, and then north, crosses a stream and continues to Montán.

2.00 - Montán. You can go through the village or pass straight on, above it.

2.15 - Junction of tracks and a few houses (Fontearcuda). Leave a white house on your left and take a track to the north-north-west.

2.20 - Join a very small tarmac road from Montán and turn right along it. It bends round the valley bottom, climbs and heads for Furela (no tarmac surface at the time of writing).

2.50 - Furela. Leave the track as you enter the hamlet, and take a road to the left to go through it. Beyond the chapel are three successive forks: bear right each time, and rejoin the track to the north after 100 metres of grass path. Turn left, west, along the track.

3.10 - Pintín (bar, grocery). The village is linked with Sarría by a very quiet minor tarmac road which can be followed all the way. A side track 500 metres before a chapel makes it possible to cut off a loop of the tarmac and pick it up again 200 metres beyond the chapel, but this bypasses the chapel itself. A path through the brushwood cuts off the

refectory.

In 1824, sadly, with the law of 'disestablishment', the precious library was sold off in sack-loads to the peasants and in 1951 a fire destroyed what little remained. The buildings, however, have since been restored.

In the villages on the way from Triacastela to San Julián:
- *Lusio,* near its fortified house, has a *caballeriza de peregrinos,* a pilgrims' stable, in ruins but with a cross of St James.
- *Renche* has a figure of St James the Pilgrim on the altarpiece in its church.

NOTE

As this stage was checked by bicycle, walking times are approximate.

DETOUR VIA SAMOS

The footpath via Samos, which is also waymarked in yellow, follows almost exactly the same route as the ordinary Triacastela to Sarría road. There is a coach service between the two towns, so it is easy (and highly recommended) to visit this impressive abbey.

ACCOMMODATION

Sarría:
   - H** Londres, tel. 53.06.89
   - H* Roma, tel. 53.05.70
   - P Burgalesa

FREE ACCOMMODATION

Samos: Enquire at the Benedictine abbey, tel. 54.60.46.

Sarría: The Convent of Mercy of the Sisters of the Assumption, tel. 53.10.20.

next bend.

4.30 - Sarría. Cross the road from Triacastela and Samos and take the one-way street opposite, west; after 100 metres bear south-west. Before passing the school, on your left, a path heading north-west cuts off a loop of the road; rejoin the road to the north-west for 200 metres.

4.55 - Bridge over the River Sarría. Take the street opposite, north-west, then an avenue bearing right, north-west; after 50 metres go up steps on the left.

5.00 - Sarría church, 470m.

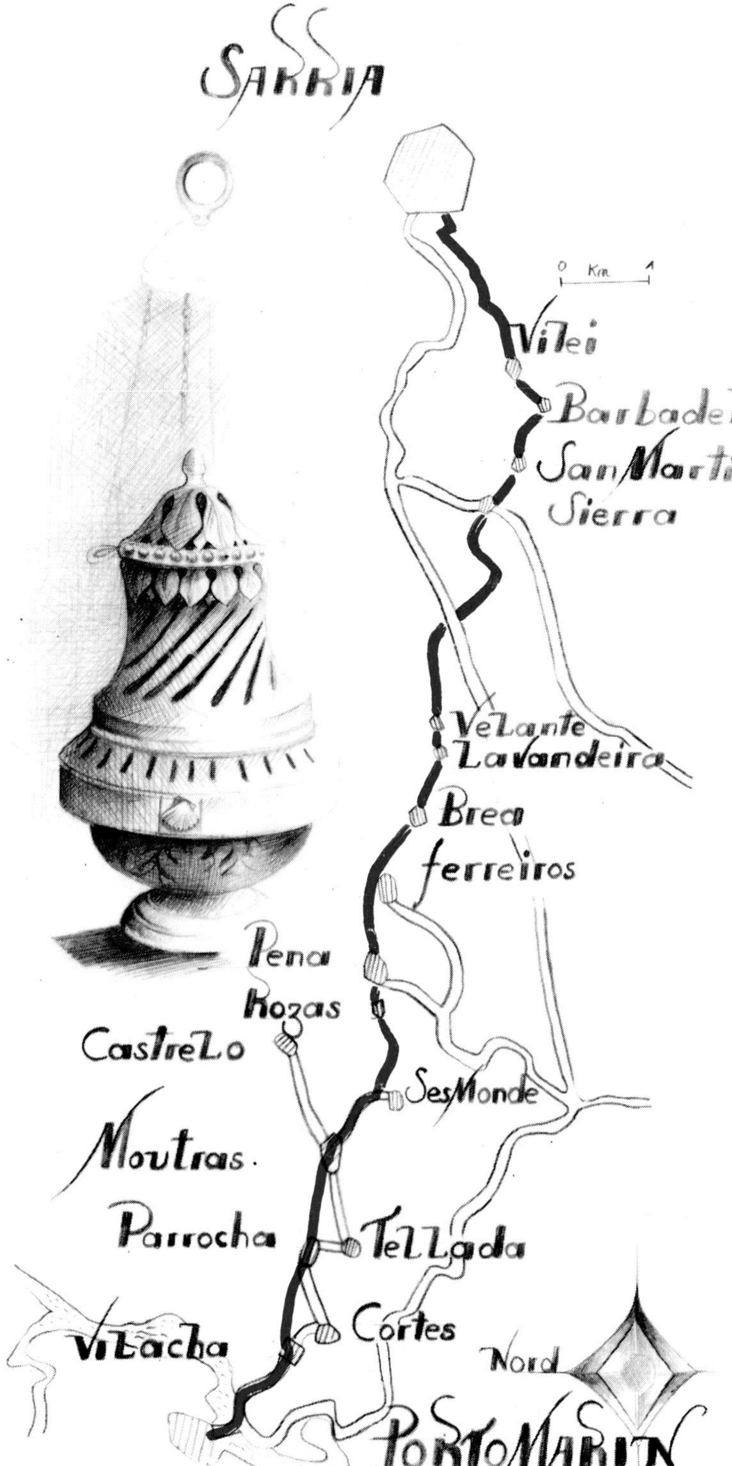

SARRIA

ViTei

BarbadeLo

SanMartin
Sierra

VeLante
Lavandeira

Brea
ferreiros

Pena
Rozas

CastreLo

SesMonde

Moutras.

Parrocha

TeLLada

ViLacha

Cortes

Nord

PORTOMARIN

0   Km.

Stage 27 - 28 kilometres - 7 hours

SARRIA TO PORTOMARÍN

A very pleasant stage, avoiding tarmac surfaces entirely and using a maze of tracks and footpaths through picturesque hamlets. The granite hillsides covered with heather, gorse and broom are somewhat similar to Brittany or Cornwall.
There are a few modest Romanesque remains along the way, but the most important can be seen at the end of the stage: 11th- and 12th-century churches, 16th- and 17th-century palaces, all rebuilt stone by stone on the heights, at the heart of the new village of Portomarín - for the old site and its bridge were drowned in 1962 by the newly-created artificial lake.

THE PAPAL BULL OF JOHN XXII

In Sarría, where we start out on this stage, the church of San Salvador preserved a Bull delivered in 1332 by the Avignon pope, John XXII. It is now kept in the national archives in Madrid. By this parchment the French pope granted indulgences to all who help pilgrims through hospitality or alms.

There are other historic connections - two notable individuals, one who died here and one who was born in the town.
- Alfonso IX of Castile met his death here while travelling to Compostela as a pilgrim.
- Luis de Sarría, who was born here, is better known to literature as Fray Luis de Granada (1504-1588); as the author of a Guide for Sinners he was one of the creators of the Castilian tongue, the origin of Spanish. He, of course, was Galician, and
it was only because they fought with King Ferdinand and Queen Isabella to recapture Granada that his parents took the Andalusian title.

THE BESTIARY OF THE CHURCH OF BARBADELO

The site of the church at Barbadelo and the house next to it retain the name of 'Mosteiro'; there was indeed a monastery there, as early as AD 874, a dependency of Samos; later it became a Benedictine house, which it

0.00 - Sarría, From the church, at 470m, go westwards up the Calle Mayor; at the top of the street leave the church of San Salvador on your left, and turn right into the Avenida a la Feria, with a panoramic view.
0.15 - 50 metres before reaching the convent (Covento de Mercadarios), turn left, south-west, down a track running beside the cemetery wall on your right.
0.20 - Fork: take the track to the right, north.
0.23 - Cross the bridge (Ponte Aspera) to the left, west, over the River Celeiro. Continue along a shaded track.
0.26 - Railway, Madrid to La Coruña; do not cross it, but continue along the track (which may be muddy in places) to the left.
0.35 - Cross the railway beside a small ruined house and turn left, south-west, along a track running beside the railway.
0.40 - Ford the River Regato, ignore a small tunnel on your left going under the railway, and turn right, west, onto a track up through the woods.
0.50 - Turn off onto a footpath up

remained until the 19th century. Only the 12th-century church still exists, with its fortified bell-tower; the church is particularly notable for its two tympanums and the decorated capitals of the north and west doors, rich in mythical animals.

FROM PEÑA LEIMAN TO BREA

- *Velante*, a hamlet 1,500 metres south of Peña, has a modest rural Romanesque church.
- *Cortinas*, mentioned in 1118, also has Romanesque relics in a small church 2 kilometres to the south, San Miguel de Viville.
- The etymology of Brea is *Vereda*, which means footpath.

to the left, south.

0.51 - Take a good track heading south.

0.55 - Continue on another track heading west across the plateau.

1.00 - Pass on your left a property surrounded by a wall. The track continues to the right, north, across the fields.

1.12 - Join a gravel path heading south to Vilei.

1.15 - Vilei. Carry on to the west.

1.20 - Fork: take the track to the right, west.

1.25 - Barbadelo church, 100 metres to the left of the route, but not to be missed. With your back to the church, head for the abandoned school and leave it on your right to take a track heading north-west.

1.35 - At a junction of tracks turn left, west.

1.40 - Fork: bear left, south-west, towards houses.

1.45 - Rente: go through the hamlet heading north-west.

1.50 - Continue in the same direction, north-west, along a track.

2.00 - Mercado da Serra. Cross a tarmac road and take a path north-west, then a track to the right, still north-west.

2.07 - Cross a gravel track and continue north-west.

2.15 - Take a track bearing left, south-west, and then at the junction another, just before reaching the wall and the transformer.

2.30 - Fork: bear right, north-west.

2.35 - Cross the Sarría-Portomarín road, with kilometre marker 38 slightly to your right, east, to continue along a wide track going north.

2.40 - Peña Leiman: continue along the track.

2.50 - Velante - the track continues to the west.

2.55 - Fork: bear left, south-west,

OFF THE ROUTE: PARADELA'S BELL, A SUPPORT IN CHILDBIRTH

From Cruceiro a motor road goes off to the left to Paradela, 7 kilometres along the C535 road.

Paradela's 12th-century church has a square apse and Romanesque vaulting. The sound of its bell, with a reputation known as far away as Orense, is said to be helpful during difficult births.

At a crossroads near this sanctuary a very fine Calvary bears carvings of the instruments of the Passion. Also on the C535, 3 kilometres farther on at Suar, is another Romanesque church.

FROM MIRALLOS TO VILACHA

- In *Mirallos* the little Romanesque church has a triple-arched doorway with lions' heads on the tympanum.
- Between Parrocha and Vilacha the route passes the ruins of Loyo monastery, away to the south; nothing of interest remains today, but in the 12th century the Order of Santiago came into being here, whose earliest knights were also called the *Freires de Loio*.

PORTOMARÍN: A VILLAGE DROWNED AND RECONSTRUCTED

The old village of Portomarín, lying on both sides of the River Miño, was deliberately submerged in 1962 by a dam which created a vast reservoir. The ruins can be seen when the water level is low, near the arch which still survives of the old Romanesque bridge, the Puente Miña dating from 1120, which was 150 metres long and 3.30 metres wide. Also surviving, because it stood fairly high, the chapel of Santa María of the Snows, much revered locally, lies close to the new bridge.

The important monuments, however, were preserved from the water and rebuilt stone by stone on the hillside among the new white houses:

- The church of *San Juan* (Romanesque, 13th century) was the fortified church of the Brothers of St John of Jerusalem. Ancient figures from the Apocalypse, plants, animals and symbolic characters share the doorway, and the vast single-span nave is decorated with restored Romanesque frescos.
- The major survival of the other Romanesque church,

then west.

3.05 - Lavandeira. Cross this new hamlet, taking tracks heading generally west.

3.10 - Follow a path to the right, north, for 30 metres, then a track to the left, west, between low walls.

3.15 - It drops down north-west and then north, merges with a small stream, then climbs south-west.

3.25 - Fork: bear right, west.

3.30 - Junction of tracks: go straight ahead, north-west.

3.35 - Take a path to the right, north-west, which goes through Brea and continues to the west.

3.45 - Morgade. Carry on along the footpath to the north, past a fountain on your right. The path runs between low walls.

3.50 - Fork: take the track facing you, north, which is sunken and sometimes muddy.

4.00 - The track bears west along the gravelly hillside (quartz sand) with broad views.

4.05 - Fork: both paths are waymarked, but the branch to the right is more direct, passing above Ferreiros.

4.10 - Broad track to the west.

4.15 - Houses on your left, junction of paths; go straight ahead, west.

4.20 - Chapel of Mirallos on your left. The track goes up to the north-west.

4.30 - Peña. Crossing of tracks: go up to the north-west, then take a gravel path north-west.

4.40 - Go through the hamlet of Rozas and carry on along the gravel path.

4.45 - Turn onto a track to the right, north-west.

4.50 - Fork: bear left, west-south-west, along the track across an undulating hilltop with panoramic views.

San Pedro, 1182, is the doorway with its triple arches.
- the Palacio de Berbetoros, a 17th-century arcaded 'palace', stands on the central square.
- the Casa de Condes, the seat of the Counts, dates from the 16th century.

THE GASTRONOMIC PILGRIM IN GALICIA

From the culinary point of view, Galicia is a land of sauces and crisp wines.

It is also, nearer the coast, notable for its fish and shellfish, and in the mountains, for its trout.

Worth looking out for:
- the 'pote gallego', a stew, a local variation of 'cocido';
- 'empañada', pâté in a pastry crust;
- 'truchas (trout) al Escabeche';
- sea-fish 'à la Gallega';
- 'lamprea estofada' - braised lamprey;
- 'lacon con grelos' - knuckle of ham with tender slivers of turnip;
- not forgetting the 'Vieira', 'the Coquille Saint-Jacques' - scallops; they can be cooked, but are also eaten raw with lemon, like oysters.

ACCOMMODATION

Portomarín:
- HR Mesón Rodriguez, tel. 54.50.45
- Posada del Camino, tel. 54.50.07
- Taberna Perez, tel. 54.50.40
- Restaurant Avenida, tel. 54.50.69
- Mirador Turistica
- Several bars near the church
- Hostel with beds for 37, hot water, kitchen, contribution to costs: apply to the Town Hall, tel. 54.50.70
- Near the bridge, the Youth Institute: contribution to costs, tel. 54.50.22

5.03 - Tracks cross: continue straight ahead, north-west.

5.05 - Cross a tarmac road and take the path facing you, north. A track then leads you through Moimentos heading north-west.

5.12 - Take the track to the left, west.

5.15 - Mercadoiro.

5.20 - Montrás. Take the tarmac track to the north-west, then a gravel one to the west.

5.35 - Turn left, south-west, along a track, then a turn to the right, north-west.

5.45 - Parrocha. Continue along the path.

5.50 - Turn right, north-west.

6.00 - Crossways: head north-west.

6.10 - Vilachá. Continue along the path north-west then north-east.

6.20 - Fork: bear left, north-west.

6.30 - Turn left, north-west, along a tarmac road.

6.35 - Reach the south-eastern end of the bridge over the stretch of water outside Portomarín.

6.40 - Continue to the north-eastern end of the bridge and up to the town.

7.00 - Portomarín. Fortified church of San Juan, with a Posada near it. To the east of the church, a bar-cafeteria which is modern, clean, and provides meals at reasonable prices. Enquire here for accommodation.

FREE ACCOMMODATION

Ferreiros:
- Proposed rest area in converted small school.

Portomarín:
- Campsite with full plumbing
- The changing room of the sports pavilion (hot showers, no beds)

PORTOMARIN

Nord

gonzar
Castromayor

hospital

Margan

Ventas
CoMeas

Ligonde

Monterroso

Reboredo
Zestedo
VaLos

MaMurria

Tarrio

Villajuan

0 Km

PALAS DE REY

Stage 28 - 25 kilometres - 6 hours

PORTOMARÍN TO PALAS DE REI

A n interesting stage, through typical Galician landscapes and villages. The route mostly avoids the roads between Portomarín and Palas de Rei (which owes its name to the residence of King Witiza). Reminders of the Romanesque and of the Pilgrim Way are frequent, if modest, all along the way.

FROM CASTROMAYOR TO PORTOS

- Castromayor derives its name from a prehistoric camp *(castrum)* on the edge of the village. The Romanesque church is very simple.
- The name of *Hospital* relates to the former 'hospital' of Saint Stephen, which disappeared after 1789.
- At *Ventas de Narón*, where in the year 820 the Christians defeated the Moors, there is a modest Galician chapel on the edge of the village, dedicated to St Mary Magdalene.
- At *Lameiros*, near Ligonde, the chapel of St Mark and the house next to it are decorated with heraldic stones.
- *Ligonde* played an important part in the pilgrimage from the 10th century onwards, although little remains today. Charles V came here on 24 March 1520, and Philip II also stopped here. The former introduced the right of asylum. There are houses bearing coats of arms. Facing No 7 is a house showing the name 'Nabal del Hospital.'

0.00 - Portomarín: from the church of San Juan, at 380m, go south-westwards down the Rúa de Chantada.
0.10 - On joining the C535 road, turn left along it for 50 metres.
0.11 - Go down to the right and cross a metal footbridge across the arroyo de Torres, an arm of the lake.
0.15 - Small tarmac road: turn right, south-west, along it for two minutes.
0.17 - Climb left, west, up a stony track.
0.45 - Rejoin the C535 at the turning to San Mamed; follow the C535 for about 4 kilometres, heading generally north-west.
1.40 - 200 metres beyond the kilometre marker, turn left onto a footpath and go north-west through

- *Ereixe* still has a fully semicircular Romanesque arch and a carving which may represent Daniel in the lions' den.

OFF THE ROUTE: VILAR DE DOÑAS

Sanctuary of the Order.
A track crossing the road between Portos and Lestedo leads to the Romanesque church of Vilar de Doñas, 2.5 kilometres to the right. The interest of this national monument justifies the 5-kilometre detour. In 1184 it was the professed house of the Order of Santiago, dedicated to combating the bandits who preyed on pilgrims. In addition it was often the final home for Knights of the Order, as indicated by several tombs. It has 14th-century murals of the Annunciation, and a Nuns' Doorway ('las Doñas'). There is a touching small granite retable on the High Altar.

FROM LESTEDO TO L'ALTO DO ROSARIO

- The church at *Lestedo,* which had a 'hospital', is dedicated to St James.
- A hamlet beyond *Valos* retains the name of 'Ave Nostre', an abbreviation of the pilgrim hymn, *'Ave Nostre Jacobus'*.
- *Alto do Rosario* is the point from which the pilgrims could, at long last, see the perfect cone of 'Pico Sacro', the 'sacred mountain' close to Compostela, and respond to the moment by saying a Rosary.

THE LEGEND OF THE PICO SACRO

The Pico Sacro, visible from Alto do Rosario, has its own legend about St James. When his disciples, who were bringing his body back from the Holy Land, disembarked at Padrón, they asked the cruel pagan Queen Lupa (a common name in medieval times, meaning 'Wolf') for a burial place. She replied, 'Go up that mountain and you will find a herd of oxen. Take two and harness them, and go wherever you wish'.

She knew she was really sending them into the midst of wild bulls, but, what a miracle!, the savage beasts allowed the disciples to approach and harness them. The furious Lupa tried to send her soldiers in pursuit of the disciples,

Gonzar.
1.50 - Turn left 100 metres beyond Gonzar along a gravel track. After another 100 metres bear right across heathland, along tracks heading north-west, parallel with the road.
2.05 - After passing a brick building and a house on your right, take a path to Castromayor.
2.10 - Castromayor (a hamlet several hundred metres to the left, west, of the C535). Go through the hamlet and take a gravel track in a generally north-west direction over a hilltop.
2.25 - Rejoin the C535, 300 metres before kilometre marker 65, and follow the road for 1,300 metres.
2.45 - 10 metres before marker 66, turn onto a track to the left, north-west.
2.50 - Go through Hospital heading north-west.
2.55 - Cross the N540 Orense-Lugo road - with a bar and the junction of the C535 with the N540 about 100 metres to your right. Continue straight ahead along a small tarmac road.
3.15 - Ventas de Narón. Go through the hamlet and carry on along the minor road.
4.00 - Go through Ligonde heading north-west.
4.15 - Pass a wayside Calvary 10 metres to your left, with a church 100 metres on your left. Continue north-west along the waymarked route.
4.25 - Cross a minor road running from Marco to Monterroso, and continue along the track opposite, which turns into a tarmac road, down to Portos.
4.35 - Portos. The new track runs through the hamlet going north-west.
4.40 - It continues through Lestedo and onward, north-west and then

but a river suddenly in spate protected them - and the fearsome queen was converted to Christianity.

THE 'KING'S PALACE'.

The name appears very grandiose now, but Palas de Rei is derived from *Palatium Regis,* 'King's Palace' in Latin, and refers to Witiza, who reigned 701-709 and is said to have lived here. He was the last Visigoth king, an enthusiastic adherent of Arianism - a 'pre-Muslim' according to the historian Ignacio Ollagüe.

The church of San Tirso has a Romanesque door; there are several medieval houses, one of which bears a carved St James's scallop-shell.

ACCOMMODATION

Palas de Rei:
- H Guest-house near the bridge, tel. 38.01.32
- Fonda Treni
- Fonda Casa Curro, tel. 38.00.86
- Bar Guntina (with rooms), tel. 38.00.80
- Cafe-bar-restaurant Los Madrileños (with rooms)
- Cafe-bar-restaurant Ultrella (with rooms), tel. 38.00.92
- A good hotel-restaurant beyond Palas de Rei, beside the C547, before reaching the bridge over the River Roxan.

FREE ACCOMMODATION

Ligonde:
- The disused school can be used as a shelter.

Palas de Rei:
- A hostel was being planned for summer 1989, near the sports establishment (with hot showers and bar); enquire at the Town Hall, tel. 38.00.01.
- Campsite planned with hostel (bedding, cold showers, no kitchen).

west.
4.50 - Go through Valos and continue along the road.
4.55 - Mamurria. Turn right along a gravel track, north-west then west, for 300 metres, to the next hamlet, and turn left, west-north-west, along a track which brings you near to the C547 and almost parallel to it.
5.05 - Outlying houses of Lamelas and shortly afterwards a junction of tracks; take the track opposite, west, running along close beside the road. On reaching a gravel path, turn right along it for 100 metres to rejoin the road.
5.15 - Join the C547 road, 300 metres from kilometre marker 544, and follow it for 300 metres.
5.20 - At a house on your right, turn left along a tarmac track which runs through the hamlet of Rosario.
5.25 - The track becomes a dirt track, and heads west.
5.30 - The track, now gravelled, leads past a football ground on your left. Continue along a gravel track, on the level, to the west and then downhill.
5.40 - Join a small tarmac road, Calle de Cruceiro, and turn right along it.
5.45 - The church is now visible on the left; go down the steps to the Avenida de Orense.
5.50 - Palas de Rei, 574m.

PALLAS DE REY

CarballaL

San julian

Orosa

Leboreiro

fureLos

MeLLid

MoLdes

San Martin

Baente

CasaL

Arzua

Stage 29 - 30 kilometres - 7 hours 30 minutes

PALAS DE REI TO ARZÚA

T he C547 road twists for 31 kilometres from Palas de Rei to Arzúa, and our route, never far
from it, plays hide-and-seek with the road along a maze of pleasant paths and tracks. The
gravelled road between Leboreiro and Disicabo is being restored.

Along the way there are some old bridges, wayside Calvaries, and a few modest churches. The most
extensive surviving group of buildings, however, is at Melide, about half-way through the stage.

FROM SAN XULIAN DO CAMINO
TO FURELOS

- The church at *San Xulián do Camino* (St Julian of the
Road) has a Romanesque apse, with a cross near-by.
- The name of *Leboreiro* or *Libureiro* comes from the Latin
Campus levurarius, the field of hares. It is an old village
with its modest transitional church of Santa María, and
facing it a former 'hospital' bearing the arms of the
noble Galician family of Ulloa. The old single-span bridge
over the River Seco is noted in the walking instructions.
- *Furelos*, on the river of the same name, also has a medieval
bridge, with four pointed arches and remains of the
ancient highway.

OFF THE ROUTE:
THE CASTLE OF PAMBRE

Lying on the River Pambre which flows through Outeiro
da Ponte but much further to the south, the 14th-century
Castillo de Pambre is a substantially complete medieval
fortress. It can be reached from Porto do Bois.

*0.00 - Palas de Rei, 574m. Beside
No 4, Avenida de Orense, turn
north-west down the steps of the
Traversia de la Iglesia. Cross the
C547, which runs through the town,
and take the facing Traversia del
Peregrino.*

*0.05 - Rejoin the C547 and turn
right, west, along it.*

*0.15 - Pass a hotel-restaurant on
your left, and cross the bridge over
the River Roxán.*

*0.20 - 200 metres beyond the bridge,
beside the Carballal sign, take a track
to the right, west.*

*0.24 - Pass Carballal de Arriba on
your left.*

*0.27 - At a junction of tracks go
straight ahead, west.*

*0.28 - Farm on your left, Gaiolo de
Riba, the last house in the hamlet.*

*0.29 - Fork: bear left, south-west,
with a barbed-wire fence on your*

MELIDE, CROSSROADS FOR SANTIAGO PILGRIMS

Melide once had several 'hospitals', and is a junction on the Pilgrim Way where travellers from Oviedo joined the *Camino Francés*. The region is rich in prehistoric remains such as camps and dolmens.

- On the way into the *Campo San Roque* the Romanesque doorway of the old church of San Pedro, with a richly ornamented triple arch, has been rebuilt. Beside it is a 14th-century Calvary carved on both sides, the oldest in Galicia.

- In the middle of the town, the *Casa Consistorial* is a former palace now used as the Town Hall, with a small local museum opposite.

- Facing the Casa Consistorial is the parish church with its 17th-century doorway and Gothic nave; this is the last remaining trace of the old 'hospital' of *Sanctus Spirite*, founded in 1375, with 12 beds for 24 pilgrims.

- On leaving the town and before reaching the River Lazaro - the name refers to a chapel, now gone - is the fine church of *Santa María de Melide;* this is Romanesque, 12th-century, with a single nave, circular apse, carved doorway and capitals, and 15th-century paintings.

FROM BOENTE TO ARZÚA

- *Boente* has its church of St James and pilgrims' fountain, some noble houses belonging to the Altamira family, with the arms bearing wolf-heads, and an old bridge.

- The first house on coming into *Ribadizo de Baixo* (the name means Bank of the River Iso: medieval bridge) was a 'hospital' in 1523. Before that, as the name of the village indicates, an old bridge with a single arch linked the 'banks of the River Iso'.

- *Castañeda*, (The Chestnuts), is where Aymery Picaud noted the lime-kilns working for the Compostela building site, to which each pilgrim brought a stone from Cebreiro.

- Off the route but, not far away, on the right towards the north, is the castle of Paso de Sedor, home of Pita da Veiga who in 1515 held François I of France prisoner in Pavia.

- At *Arzúa* the Romanesque church of St James served as a shelter for pilgrims. Shortly before it, on the left of the Magdalene chapel which has tombs inside, are the remains of the former 'hospital' founded in the 14th century by the Augustinians from Sarría.

left.

0.32 - Rejoin the C547 road beside another Carballal sign, and follow it for 200 metres to the right.

0.35 - Turn off the road on a bend, to take a track to the left, north-west.

0.42 - Take a gravel path to the right, north.

0.43 - After 50 metres turn left onto a muddy track heading north-west.

0.46 - Fork: go straight ahead, north-west, down a pleasant sunken track.

0.48 - San Xulián do Camino. Turn left, west, along a gravel path.

0.50 - Wayside Calvary; turn left, south-west.

0.51 - Church on your left; the path goes down to the north-west, with a public wash-house on your right, a little lower down.

0.56 - Crossing of tracks: go straight ahead, north-west, leaving a farm, La Pallota, on your left; 20 metres farther on, turn north-north-west down a slightly overgrown sunken track.

1.04 - Bend in the path; go down it to the west.

1.05 - Bridge over the River Pambre.

1.06 - Turn off the path onto the track facing you, northward.

1.07 - Bear left, north-west.

1.10 - Tracks cross; go north-west along a good track through brushwood.

1.14 - Continue straight ahead, west, beneath oak-trees.

1.23 - Continue in the same direction along a more heavily used track.

1.25 - Take a path heading west through Casanova.

1.30 - At the top of the slope bear left at the fork, north-west.

1.32 - Fork: head westward.

1.45 - Crossing of broad tracks; continue straight ahead, north-west.

1.47 - Stream and marshy area, then

- On the way out of Arzúa the Fuente de las Franceses, the fountain of the French, is now derelict.

THE 'ROMANCE' OF THE OLD PILGRIM

This is the proper time and place for the weary pilgrim to recite the very fine 'Romance of Don Gaiferos of Monmaltán' in Galician dialect, quoted by Eusebius Goicoechea Arrondo in his *Rutas Jacobeas*.

'A onde ira meu romeiro,
Meu romeiro a onde ira?
Camino de Compostela,
Non sei si chegará/
O seus pés cheos de sangre
Xa non poden meis andar;
Vai tocado o pobre vello
Non sei si ali chegará ...
I si ago non teno forzas
Meu Santiago m'as dará!
Chegarón a Compostela
E forón a Catedral.
D'esta manera falou
Gaiferos de Mormaltán:
Gracias, meu Señor Santiago,
A vosos pés me tés xa.
Si queres tiram'a vida
Podesm'a, Señor, tirar
Porque morrerei contento
N'esta Santa Catedral'.

Translation: Where he is going, my pilgrim/My pilgrim, where is he going?/On the road to Compostela/I don't know if he will get there.
- His feet covered in blood/Cannot take him any further/He is done for, the poor old man/I don't know if he will get there...
- Now, if I have no strength left/My Saint James will send me strength!/So they did reach Compostela/And were there in the Cathedral.
- These were the words spoken by/Gaiferos de Mormaltán:/Thank you my lord St James/See, I am here at your feet.
- If you wish to take my life from me/You may take it, Lord/For I shall die happy/In this holy Cathedral.

In its touching simplicity, this outstanding poem is surely an impressive act of faith.

a footpath beside grassland. Continue along a track going uphill.
1.50 - Take another broad track to the west which goes under high-tension wires.
1.55 - House 50 metres to your right. Continue west along the track.
1.57 - Minor tarmac road linking the C547 with Sambreixo; turn north-west along it to the C547.
2.05 - On to to the C547 again, with a bar (Coto) slightly to the south-east of kilometre marker 555. Here we leave the province of Lugo and enter the province of Coruña. Turn left along the road, north-west.
2.07 - Take a track to the left, and after 100 metres another to the right, north-west.
2.10 - Continue along a footpath, and then the remains of an old stony track.
2.14 - Continue north-west along a footpath.
2.15 - Wayside Calvary. The paved path goes through Leboreiro and continues beyond it.
2.20 - Hump-backed bridge across the River Seco.
2.23 - Farm on your right. Muddy track, and junction of tracks: turn right, north-west, along a broad track or path.
2.25 - As this track bears right, turn left on a path across the heathland, towards a very large shed (for coaches).
2.30 - Rejoin the C547 once more and turn left, north-west, along it.
2.37 - Restaurant on your left.
2.40 - Kilometre marker 557 - continue along the road, or walk beside it through the heathland on the left.
2.55 - Leave the highway no later than kilometre marker 558, where the road bears right, and follow the waymarking across the heathland

stamp here

to the west-north-west.

3.00 - *Junction of tracks: continue straight ahead, north-west, and follow other tracks leading in the same direction.*

3.07 - *Junction of tracks: continue opposite, down a distinct sunken track, first between scrubby hedges and then between trees.*

3.14 - *Tarmac track: turn left, west, along it.*

3.15 - *Cross the pretty medieval bridge, restored, over the River Furelos, on your right.*

3.16 - *Furelos church. Go through the hamlet, heading roughly west, along tarmac lanes.*

3.20 - *Gravel track leading north-west, across waste ground on the edge of Melide.*

3.26 - *Continue to the west along a wide road through the middle of a saw-mill.*

3.28 - *Next take the track facing you, heading west.*

3.32 - *Join the C547 to go into Melide, on your left.*

3.33 - *Pass in front of the church of San Pedro, on your right.*

3.35 - *Centre of Melide. Go on to the north-west, taking the Calle Principal, running roughly westward through the old town, and parallel with the C547.*

3.45 - *Cemetery on the left. Take a grassy path down to the C547.*

3.50 - *Cross the C547 and continue south-west at first along the minor tarmac road towards Santa María; after 300 metres turn right, west.*

3.55 - *Wayside Calvary on your left, then a church on the right. Continue westward along a narrower road which becomes a broad track suitable for cars, running parallel with the C547 a few dozen metres to your right.*

4.05 - *The track becomes tarmac*

TESTIMONY OF A PRESENT-DAY PILGRIM

If this book succeeds in encouraging readers to rediscover the Pilgrim Road it will have achieved its aim.

But once on your way to Santiago de Compostela, do remember that guides exist to provide useful information and are not simply to be followed blindly. The difference between these two definitions of the same word will be recognised in the thrill of active discovery and the thirst for adventure that we all share, whether in spiritual matters or in more mundane sorts of activity.

Armed beforehand with good intentions, full of noble aspirations or more moderate aims, working out a mass of plans to make the most of the expedition, intending travellers will from the outset have to abandon many preconceived notions, as the vicissitudes of the journey modify the importance and priority of each one - and will perhaps drop others along the way. Many possessions, from cameras to bedside books, have finished the journey via the services of the post office!

With the benefit of hindsight, I offer my own discoveries -which no-one is obliged to follow - in no particular order:
- Properly speaking, the Santiago pilgrimage means, first of all, travelling the whole route without interruption, and only sleeping in hotels when unavoidable.
- At the end of each stage the pilgrim seeks only enough ground to sleep on: a tap nearby is a luxury.
- The starry skies and church porches make the finest bedroom ceilings.
- Eat little and often; occasionally copiously - and well - and well washed down;
- In summer, water, and more water - and more for drinking than for washing;
- Weight is the great enemy - but may mean freedom: in the form of a tent, for example.
- Blisters on your feet are like changes in the weather; they come and go for no apparent reason.
- Let cock-crow find you already awake; by dawn, be well on your way.
- If you are showing signs of wear at the end of a long stage, you will never be treated like a tramp in the small villages. Go into big towns to see the sights and buy what you need, but move on again to finish the stage.
- You will find some cathedrals locked and cottages open; this may not always be a loss.

again. Continue along a good track heading north-west through the woods.
4.10 - The track veers left, north-west, and becomes narrower.
4.15 - Cross the River Raído and continue up to the right, north.
4.17 - Fork: bear left, west.
4.22 - Keep left, west-north-west; you could use the C547 a few metres to your right. 4.24 - Turn right along a path.
4.25 - Rejoin the road at Raído and turn left, west, along it for 150 metres.
4.27 - Turn left, south, along a muddy track which bends to the right, south-west then west.
4.33 - Continue straight ahead along a path, west.
4.36 - Follow a track continuing in the same direction.
4.39 - Junction: take a track straight ahead, west, going downhill.
4.43 - Cross a stream, the Regato Valverde, and climb up the track which is much wider and suitable for cars, heading west.
4.48 - Boente de Riba. Go through the hamlet, to the west.
4.53 - Fork: take the path to the left.
4.55 - The path veers right in the hamlet.
5.00 - C547, with Fuente de la Saleta on your right. Go left along the road for 100 metres.
5.02 - Pass the church on your right and the road on your left, and go down a track suitable for cars to cut off a loop of the C547.
5.12 - Cross the C547 and go down a broad track suitable for cars, facing you.
5.20 - Bridge over the River Boente. Continue along a track not suitable for cars, going uphill.
5.25 - A further track going up, to the north-east.
5.27 - Junction: turn left, west, along

- You will discover places that match your dreams, and others to be shunned like the plague;
- Consult and converse with your conscience often, or pray according to your beliefs; this will delay the onset of fatigue.
- Make friends with the people you meet along the way: you will be all the richer for it.
- Salute the important places for me, and treasure the precious moments and sacred things.
- Even in a group or with a guide, the pilgrimage is something special ...

Michel Casamitjana

a splendid sunken track.

5.35 - Rejoin the C547 at Cobelo and walk along it.

5.50- Castañeda. 200 metres beyond kilometre marker 570, turn left, west, onto a small tarmac road to Río, Pomar, and Dorona, then after 100 metres take a smaller road facing you.

6.02 - Fork: turn left and cross a bridge over the Regato Rebeiral.

6.10- Take a track facing you, north-west.

6.16 - Fork: turn right, north.

6.17 - Keep straight on, north-west.

ACCOMMODATION

Melide:
- H* Estilo, tel. 50.51.03.
- H Sony, tel. 50.54.73.
- Fonda Avenida.
- Fonda Osel, tel. 50.53.54.
- Fonda Continente, tel. 50.61.82.
- Fonda Xaneiro, tel. 50.50.15.

Arzúa:
- H* El Retiro, on the way into the town, tel. 50.03.37.
- Restaurant-bar Paco, near the sports ground, tel. 50.04.52.
- Fonda-casa Teodora, tel. 50.00.80.
- Fonda-casa Frade, tel. 50.00.19.
- CH Esmeralda, tel., see Frade.
- Bar Caballeira (with rooms), tel.50.00.94.

FREE ACCOMMODATION

Melide:
- Enquire at the Parish House, tel. 50.51.20.
- Monastery of the Passionist Fathers, tel. 50.50.54.

Arzúa:
- Parish hostel.
- Pilgrims' Hostel, due to open in 1989, free. 10 places (bedding, washing facilities), apply to the Town Hall, tel. 50.00.00.

6.18 - Turn right, north. The track crosses a hilltop and goes down across heathland planted with pines.
6.20 - Fork: turn left, west.
6.30 - Cross the road beside kilometre marker 573 and take a broad track down to the west.
6.40 - Bridge over the River Iso. Go up a small tarmac road, heading north-west.
6.45 - Take another small road to the left, south-west.
6.50 - Join the C547 at the top of the hill, to reach Arzúa, or nearly...
7.20 - 300 metres before reaching the middle of the town, follow the waymarking along a lane to the left, Calle Cima del Lugar, leading to the church.
7.30 - Arzúa.

ARZUA

Cortobe et
fonteviza
quintas

Calzada

ferreiros

Nord

Boavista
Salceda

Brea

Ras

Astrar
Rua

El Pino

San Anton

Vilacha
Amenal

Beis Sada

aerodrome

Lavacolla

1 Km.

Stage 30 - 28 kilometres - 7 hours

ARZÚA TO LABACOLLA

Stage number 30, almost the end of the Road: in fact we could reach Santiago this evening, but why hurry?

It seems more sensible to stay in one of the two hotel-restaurants in Labacolla, to wash - as the name indicates - and to follow the example of Aymery Picaud and his companions of the GENS GALLICA.

And then next morning we go quietly on to Compostela, to explore the great treasures of the town at the leisurely pace they deserve.

In the meantime, on the way from Arzúa to Labacolla we shall continue the game of hide-and-seek with the C547, although on the way out of Arzúa the previously unusable part of the Road has been restored.

FROM BREA TO RUA, WHERE THE PLACE-NAMES REFLECT THE ROAD

- *Brea* (derived from Vereda, footpath) is one of the synonyms of Path or Road that we have already encountered.
- The setting of the modest chapel of *Santa Irena*, surrounded by trees, is ideally peaceful.
- Rúa - like Calzada and Brea - is one of the place-names frequently occurring along the Road to Santiago.

THE MOMENT FOR WASHING

Labacolla, or Lavacolla, which one might nowadays be tempted to translate as 'wash-your-collar', was entered in the *Codex* as 'Lavamentula', the smaller toilette...

Faithful to this etymology, Aymery Picaud and his companions of the *Gens Gallica* stripped off their clothes there, to wash themselves and prepare for a clean and fitting entry to the sacred city.

There is a baroque church, and a very simple wayside Calvary.

0.00 - Arzúa, 388m. From the church go west down the Calle del Carmen, then continue in the same direction along a gravel track suitable for cars. The track broadens out, then becomes a path down to a stream, Regato das Barrosas.

0.15 - Use the stepping stones to cross the stream, then take a muddy track north-west up the slope. Chapel of San Lazaro on your left.

0.18 - Go across a path.

0.20 - Join a track suitable for cars, and turn right, north, along it.

0.23 - Rejoin the C547 at the top of the slope, at Laberco, and turn left, west, along it.

0.27 - Where the road veers to the right, turn onto a sunken track below and to your left, which takes you down generally heading west.

0.31 - After stepping stones across the River Raído the track climbs,

SOME 1985 PILGRIMS

Like all who undertake this long march, you will have been surprised at first to find you are not alone, as you might have expected. For many reasons, the pilgrimage to Santiago has gained its vigour again.

To take another example: on 24 July 1985 Jacques Pédehontaà, 27, the young mayor of Laàs in the Pyrénées Atlantiques, with four friends aged between 21 and 24 (Marie-Hélène Escudé, Brigitte Casanova, Jean-Philippe Ros and François Saspiturry) entered Compostela in striking style on their farm tractor, towing a caravan and decorated with streamers. Maintaining a steady 25 kilometres per hour, they had left Béarn on 12 July and followed the *Camino Francés* as far as Ponferrada. With time in hand, they took an alternative route for the final stage, by way of Vigo and Orense along the *Camino Portugués*.

Back home again, Jacques Pédehontaà described his encounters in the *Clocher de la Vallée*, his local newspaper:

stamp here

'At Sauveterre-de-Béarn, 8 kilometres after setting out, we met four pilgrims on bicycles: a man with his 14-year-old son, from Nantes, and a retired couple from Marseille. They had met each other at Notre-Dame des Cyclistes, at Créon d'Armagnac.
- Further on, there were two young girls on horseback, then a Dutch couple, then two worker-priests from Nay in the Pyrenees, then someone from Oloron ...
- And again: in Santiago itself there was Pierre Jean, from Navarrenx, also in the Pyrenees, who had cycled with Belgian friends and some from Pau; along the way they met James and made friends with him; James was an Englishman who had set out from London, never having ridden a bicycle before, and who reached Santiago without any difficulties except a puncture within 20 kilometres of setting out.'

crosses a small stream, passes a farm on your right, and rejoins the C547 again.

0.35 - Rejoin the C547 at the top of the hill, with a wayside Calvary on your right, and follow the road for about 400 metres.

0.41 - Turn right, north-west, along a road for about 300 metres.

0.45 - Next take a path to the left, west.

0.47 - Follow the path through Fondevilla.

0.50 - Go through Cortobe then continue along a broad track suitable for vehicles.

0.55 - Pereirina. Fork: bear left, west, down a track not suitable for vehicles.

1.03 - Through the valley bottom, with a stream, the Regato Ladron, and junction of tracks: go up to the north-west.

1.12 - Cross a small tarmac road linking the C547 with Fontelas, and take a track to the north-west.

1.20 - Next take a wide track to the south-west.

1.21 - The houses of Quintas; take a wide track suitable for vehicles, heading west.

1.35 - Calzada, a hamlet about 400 metres north of the C547, on your left. Cross a small tarmac road and take a track to the south-west. After passing two right turns it becomes grassy and bears to the right, west.

1.44 - Fork: bear right, west, on a good track through eucalyptus trees.

1.47 - Junction of tracks: continue straight ahead, west.

1.50 - Fork: bear right, west.

1.53 - Calle, part of Fereiro: at the fountain go down the track to the right, north-west, which is often muddy.

1.55 - Turn right, north-west, along a minor road for 50 metres.

1.56 - Turn left, west, onto a track

WHAT ABOUT RETURNING ALONG THE OLD COAST ROAD?

Although the *Camino Francés* has seen the greatest tide of pilgrims to Santiago down the centuries, it is not the only route. Nor is it the oldest, for the simplest of reasons: in the earliest days a substantial part of the territory we have crossed was under Moorish domination. Only a few Pyrenean valleys and the Cantabrian coast of northern Spain were Christian-ruled; and the earliest pilgrim route therefore followed the sea.

This original route can thus be used for the return, and some possible stages are suggested below, though today it is more suitable for road transport than for walking.

- Arzúa, Sobrado de los Monjes (monks): a large 17th-century abbey with some Romanesque remains.
- Lugo, 2 kilometres of walls, partly Roman, flanked by 50 towers.
- Mountain road via Tinéo: Asturian houses and 'horréos', granaries built up on piles.
- Oviedo, the first capital city of Asturias. Inside the cathedral the 8th-century Cámara Santa contains rich treasures. On a hill overlooking the town are the two pre-Romanesque 9th-century sanctuaries of striking style, Santa María de Naranco and San Miguel de Lillo.
- San Salvador de Valdedios: parts of the Benedictine monastery date back to 893, with horseshoe arches.
- Villaviciosa is rich in old houses.
- Covadonga, together with Pelayo, was in 711 the prime refuge of the Christian monarchs. The mountain setting is impressive, away from the road; but development there is quite recent.

which winds up and down through Ferreiro.

2.05 - Fork: bear right, north-west, and then shortly afterwards right again at another fork.

2.12 - Cross a small tarmac road and take the facing track, north-west.

2.14 - After 100 metres turn left, west, onto a wide track.

2.19 - Boavista: cross a path in the hamlet and take the track opposite, west. Pass a clump of pine-trees on your right. The path undulates, passing a public wash-house on your left, and descends to the north-west.

2.26 - Farmland on your right, and junction of paths: continue west for about 100 metres then take a track in the same direction.

2.30 - Fork: bear left, north-west.

2.38 - Junction of paths: go straight ahead, north-west, and through Salceda.

2.39 - Fork: go straight ahead, west-north-west, along a gravel track.

2.40 - Turn off onto a footpath heading west-north-west.

2.43 - Back to the C547 again! Turn right along it for 400 metres.

2.49 - Bus shelter; turn right, west, onto a track.

2.52 - Farm on your left.

2.55 - Cross another track and continue straight on, west-north-west.

2.58 - Turn right along the C547 for 100 metres.

3.00 - Plunge on to an overgrown footpath to your left, then onto a track.

3.05 - Cross a small road running from the C547 on your right to Xen. Go straight ahead, west-south-west, along a track which is level at first, then goes downhill.

3.17 - Cross a stream, and up the other side.

3.20 - Cross the C547 and take a track down, west-south-west, for 400 metres.

- Cangas de Onis has a Roman hump-backed bridge.
- Santillana del Mar is an ancient and well-preserved town.
The prehistoric (Magdalenian) caves of Altamira are not far away, but unfortunately visitors can see only photographs of the wall-paintings.
- Beyond Santander with its fashionable beach, and the modern metropolis of Bilbao, lies a string of old Basque fishing villages, each on its own inlet, such as Ondarroa. Guernica (or Gernika), immortalised by Picasso, has its oak-tree, symbol of Basque independence.
- A visit to the sanctuary of Ignatius of Lóyola, founder of the Jesuits, in the town of his birth, means leaving the coast-line.
- From this point the crowds along the coast can be avoided by continuing through Tolosa - the 'Armeria' of the 12th century with its baroque churches, Leiza, Santestebán, Elizondo where there are houses with armorial bearings, and so back to the French Basque coast.

FREE ACCOMMODATION

Arca (Pino district):
- Hostel for 40-50 people (showers), enquire at the Town Hall, tel. 51.10.02.

3.26 - Brea. Turn left along a gravel path for 30 metres; the C547 is 100 metres away, with kilometre marker 592, and a bar-grocery offering snacks or an omelette. Turn right, north-west, along a track suitable for vehicles.

3.32 - Pass a farm on your right, and a large concrete shed. Continue west along the track.

3.34 - Turn left for about 100 metres to rejoin the C547, and follow the road for 1 kilometre.

3.50 - Restaurant de Pau on the left of the road.

3.51 - At the top of the hill (Alto de Santa Irena) turn right, north-east, along a track for 100 metres.

3.53 - Turn left, west, onto another track through eucalyptus trees, running almost parallel with the road.

3.58 - Rejoin the road and turn down to the west, with the church of Santa Irena below, to your right. Continue along the road for 600 metres beyond the church.

4.10 - 50 metres beyond kilometre marker 595 turn right onto a track heading west-south-west.

4.15 - The track fades out shortly before you reach a saw-mill beside the C547.

4.18 - Cross the road and go west down a path suitable for cars - 5.5 tons limit - for 200 metres.

4.21 - Take a track to the right, and almost immediately, at a fork, bear left, west, along a broad well-shaded track.

4.24 - The track veers to the right, north-west, and down to the hamlet of Rúa.

4.25 - On a bend take a tarmac track coming from the C547, to go straight ahead, west, through Rúa.

4.30 - Fork: continue on the track facing you, south-west, along to a

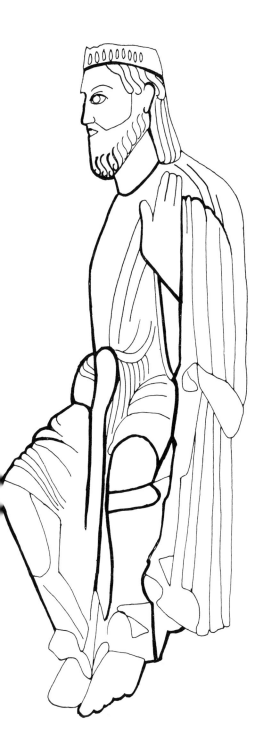

fork 100 metres ahead. Bear right, west, down the track, cross a stream, *Regato del Burgo*, and back up to the C547.

4.36 - 30 metres before the kilometre marker 597 take a track to the south-west, and at each intersection or fork, continue heading south-west.

4.46 - Follow a path beside the football ground on your right.

4.48 - Take a small road to the right for 200 metres.

4.51 - Take a pleasant well-shaded track left, south-west.

4.52 - Fork: bear right, south-west.

4.58 - Hamlet of San Antón; at a junction of three tarmac tracks turn left, south, for about 100 metres.

5.00 - Fork: bear right, south-west.

5.15 - Cross a rough track, suitable for cross-country vehicles, and then another running at right-angles; take a track to the west which soon after becomes sunken and brambly.

5.20 - Farm on your left, and junction of paths; take the one heading north-west.

5.26 - Fork: bear left, south.

5.27 - Fork: take the right branch, straight ahead!

5.30 - Cross the C547 at Amenal, continue opposite between two houses along a sunken track heading west.

5.34 - Farm on your right, Cima de Vila.

5.36 - Cross a gravelled road and take the track opposite leading to a eucalyptus wood.

5.41 - Cross a forest track, and continue to the west.

5.53 - Junction of paths, turn right.

5.58 - On reaching a broad forest track, turn right, north. Airport runway visible on the left.

6.05 - Timber yard alongside the N634 road close to a major crossroads. Take the C547 road to Labacolla.

No.	Start and End of each stage	distance (km) (1)	(2)	approx. walking time (hours)
1.	SAINT JEAN PIED DE PORT - BURGUETE	21	28	7.30
2.	BURGUETE - ZUBIRI	15	20	5
3.	ZUBIRI - PAMPLONA	17	23	5.30
4.	PAMPLONA - PUENTE LA REINA	21	28	7
5.	PUENTE LA REINA - ESTELLA	16	20	6
6.	ESTELLA - LOS ARCOS	18	22	5.30
7.	LOS ARCOS - LOGROÑO	24	28	7
8.	LOGROÑO - NAJERA	24	32	8
9.	NAJERA - SANTO DOMINGO DE LA CALZADA	19	24	6
10.	SANTO DOMINGO DE LA CALZADA - BELORADO	19	28	7
11.	BELORADO - SAN JUAN DE ORTEGA	22	25	6.30
12.	SAN JUAN DE ORTEGA - BURGOS	21	28	7
13.	BURGOS - CASTROJERIZ	36	40	10
14.	CASTROJERIZ - FROMISTA	21	24	6
15.	FROMISTA - CARRION DE LOS CONDES	18	22	6
16.	CARRION DE LOS CONDES - SAHAGUN	35	40	10
17.	SAHAGUN - MANSILLA DE LAS MULAS	35	40	10
18.	MANSILLA DE LAS MULAS - LEON	17	22	5.30
19.	LEON - HOSPITAL DE ORBIGO	29	35	8.30
20.	HOSPITAL DE ORBIGO - ASTORGA	14	17	4
21.	ASTORGA - ACEBO	33	37	9
22.	ACEBO - PONFERRADA	13	18	4.20
23.	PONFERRADA - VILLAFRANCA DEL BIERZO	19	22	5.15
24.	VILLAFRANCA DEL BIERZO - CEBREIO	22	40	10
25.	CEBREIO - TRIACASTELA	17	28	5.30
26.	TRIACASTELA - SARRIA	14	20	5
27.	SARRIA - PORTOMARIN	17	23	7
28.	PORTOMARIN - PALAS DE REI	22	25	6
29.	PALAS DE REI - ARZUA	25	30	7.20
30.	ARZUA - LABACOLLA	23	28	7
31.	LABACOLLA - SANTIAGO	8	12	3
	(1) Distance as the crow flies (2) Approximate distance walked	655	829	207.25

Nord

LABACOLLA
ViLLaMayor

Casa Meiro

zarraMacedo

Bando de Abajo
San Marcos

1 Km

Stage 31 - 12 kilometres - 3 hours

LABACOLLA TO SANTIAGO DE COMPOSTELA

*S*antiago is less than 10 kilometres away by road: but let it wait awhile. We could perhaps climb to the modest peak of Monxoi, like the pilgrims of olden times; in any case, we will do our utmost to avoid the tarmac of the C547.

But try as we may, the Road wins through in the end, like a good detective, in the last thirty minutes of the story; the Road that will take us into Santiago de Compostela and right up to the cathedral door, following the Pilgrim Way.

MONXOI: THE GALICIAN 'HILL OF JOY'

Lying to the left of the hamlet of San Marcos, the hill of Monxoi, or Monte del Gozo in Castilian, at 368m is the highest of the surrounding hills.

Its name, from the Latin *Mons Gaudii*, is the exact equivalent of the French *Mont-joie*, the word used for a cairn marking a road or as a memorial.

From this viewpoint the pilgrims, giving thanks to God, first caught sight of the whole of Compostela. A chapel dedicated to St Mark and three simple wooden crosses at the top of the hill mark the solemnity of the site.

0.00 - Labacolla (or Lavacolla), 300m. Cross the C547 beside the sign marking the end of the town of Labacolla, 120 metres before kilometre marker 607, and take a track heading south.

0.05 - Turn right up the very small road to Villamayor.

0.25 - Villamayor (or Vilamaior). In the hamlet turn left up the tarmac to the junction of three tracks suitable for vehicles. Turn right, west, on a track along the edge of the hamlet on your right. Continue along it as

A FINAL LEGEND: THE 'HOME SANTO'

On the way into the town through the *Puerta del Camino* or *Puerta Francigena* pilgrims will see a magnificent 14th-century Calvary with thirteen scenes illustrating the legend carved in the stone. In Galician, this is *O cruceiro do Home Santo.*

This 'holy man', the legend tells, was one Jean Touron, unjustly condemned for a crime. Passing a figure of the Virgin, on his way to the place of execution, he prayed to her: 'Ven e valme!' - 'Come and save me! - a prayer which led to the name of the street, Calle Bonaval.

The compassionate Virgin granted him the blessing of instantaneous death, which was immediately accepted as a miracle.

SANTIAGO OF COMPOSTELA, CROWNING POINT OF THE PILGRIMAGE.

In a guide designed to lead travellers to Compostela - a task now accomplished - it is impossible to describe all the treasures of a town which has 46 churches, 114 bell-towers, 288 altars, 36 brotherhoods, a university, city gates, palaces .. We have to restrict ourselves to a few general points.

We know (see the general history section in the Introduction) that St James the Apostle, brother of John and son of Zebedee, was buried here in about AD 44; that following persecution in the 3rd century the sanctuary was rebuilt in 899; and that the Moorish king Almanzor destroyed it in 997.

The first cathedral to survive into the modern era was built between 1075 and 1112 by Gelmirez, the first archbishop; in the 12th century the Palace of Gelmirez was added; between the 15th and 17th centuries, the Clock Tower; in the 16th century came the Gothic cloisters, and in the 18th century the baroque façade.

Thus starting from its single Romanesque nave in the Toulouse style, the centuries have turned it into a vast and complex treasure-house of stone ... In Compostela you will want to visit everything, but whatever else you fail to see, you must not miss:
- In the *Cathedral,* the two magnificent doorways of 'las Platerias' (11th century), and the 'Portico de la Gloria' (12th century), which alone constitute a veritable museum of Romanesque art; also the choir, the chapels,

it becomes a tarmac surface.

1.00 - Television transmitters and relay station on your right, Galicia Television Centre. Continue along the tarmac track for about 400 metres.

1.06 - Leave the tarmac as it rejoins the C547, and turn left, south, along an unsurfaced path.

1.10 - Turn right along a broad track up and over a hilltop, then down again.

1.28 - Take a small tarmac road to the right for 100 metres.

1.30 - Ignore the C547, 100 metres ahead, and turn left along a minor tarmac road through San Marcos.

1.35 - 300 metres beyond the hamlet pass the Chapel of San Marcos on your left, near the top of Monxoi, or Monte del Gozo, 368m, the point from which the pilgrims, deeply moved at reaching the end of their journey, first caught sight of Santiago.

2.00 - Crossing of minor roads: go straight ahead up a one-way street to reach the C547 after a few dozen metres, rejoining this old acquaintance 200 metres beyond kilometre marker 612 and 200 metres before a bridge. Follow the road, for the final time, for about 2 kilometres.

2.30 - SANTIAGO. The Pilgrim Way runs as follows: Calle de Los Concheiros - Rúa de San Pedro - the Cross of the HOME SANTO (passed on your right) - Puerta del Camino - Calle Casas Reales - Plaza de Salvador Parga - Plaza de Animas - Plaza de Cervantes - Calle Azabacheria, leading to the Cathedral by the north door (the Azabacheria door).

3.00 - Cathedral of Santiago. The immense Obradoiro square is an astonishing ensemble, its sides formed by the Cathedral, the Colegio

the crypt, the museums of archaeology and tapestry, and the archives.

- the 12th-century archbishop's palace, the *Palacio de Gelmirez* next to the Cathedral,

- the *'Hospital Real'*, dating from the 15th-18th centuries, now the luxurious and splendid 'Hostal de Los Reyes Católicos',

- the 18th-century *Monastery of San Martín Pinario*,

- the *Colegio de Fonseca* (16th century),

etc.

Access to the Cathedral is normally from the Plaza de la Immaculada, and in 'Jubilee years' - when St James's Day falls on a Sunday - through the door in the Via Sacra.

de San Jerónimo, the Palacio de Rajoy, and the Hostal de Los Reyes Católicos. But you should also wander through the little streets, often glistening with rain, sometimes crowded with peasants selling poultry and vegetables.

And beware of the cowboys who persist in trying to sell you records, cassette tapes, or other souvenirs!

Above all, do not fail to visit Santo Domingo and its museum and then climb one of the three spiral stairways - the highest - to contemplate the whole city, and take your final photographs.

ACCOMMODATION

Santiago:
- A great many hotels, restaurants, fondas: enquire at the Tourist Office.

FREE ACCOMMODATION

Enquire at the Cathedral office for a copy of 'La Compostela'.

ALTERNATIVE ROUTE

It is possible to avoid the C547 on the way into Santiago, as follows:

On rejoining the C547 (2.00), turn left along it for a few metres around the remains of a cement bridging construction, then turn left along a track suitable for cars, beside a stream. This leads to a small farm; next turn right along a footpath which crosses the stream and continues to the left beside it. Cross the bridge over the railway.

The track continues beside the railway, past the foot of a hill, to a tarmac street. Turn right up this to the Avenida de Lugo, close by, and cross over by way of a footbridge.

Go to the right up the Cuesta del Veedor, and at the top turn into the Rúa de San Pedro, to rejoin the Pilgrim Way.

EL CAMINO ARAGONÉS: THE ARAGON ROAD

The swelling tide of pilgrims from all over Europe travelled through France along four main routes leading them onward to the Pyrenees:

- The three routes from Paris, Vzelay and Le Puy converged at Ostabat; from this village in lower Navarre, the pilgrims continued to Saint-Jean-le-Vieux and then Roncesvalles. This Basque Road, the most famous and most heavily used, forms the basis of our main itinerary of the Road to Santiago across Spanish territory.

- The Arles route went through Montpellier and Toulouse, through the heart of Béarn, then across the Pyrenees by the Somport col or the Col des Moines. On the Spanish side, where these two routes came together, stood one of the most substantial establishments ever built to shelter Christian pilgrims: the imposing 'hospital' complex of Sainte Christine, or Santa Cristina. Today only its foundations remain.

From here the *Camino Aragonés* followed the high valley of the River Aragón, due south down to Jaca and its magnificent 11th-century cathedral.

The river and the pilgrims flowed on westward to Tiermas, Yesa and Sangüesa, where Santa María La Real is one of the great treasures of the pilgrimage and a high point of Romanesque art.

Leaving the River Aragón, the *Camino Aragonés* (in Navarre now for about the last dozen kilometres) plunges into a deep gorge on its way to Monreal, Tiebas and Campanas, then Obanos on the main Pilgrim Way. A few kilometres before the junction of the Basque and Aragonese Roads lies the magnificent Romanesque church of Eunate, well worth a slight detour on the way from Roncesvalles and which, together with Jaca and then Sangüesa, justifies the choice of the Somport route.

What was the *Camino Aragonés* like then, when this Guide was planned early in 1986? On its 150-odd kilometres from Le Somport to Puente la Reina there was no waymarking. And as far as we are aware none of the rare publications describing this route, mostly in Spanish, has indicated any itinerary offering greater calm or more picturesque surroundings than the busy trunk roads.

Since it is impossible, for practical reasons, to describe these 150 kilometres with the same detail as for the main route, we offer here a breakdown into stages linked with overnight accommodation.

A detailed description of the *Camino Aragonése* will form part of the guide devoted to the *Via Tolosana,* or Provence Road. That guide, planned for late 1990, will be a co-production of the Randonnées Pyrénéennes and the FFRP.

Stage 1	Somport to Jaca	30 km
2	Jaca to Puente la Reina	20
3	Puente la Reina to Mar del Pirineo (the Yesa reservoir), eastern end	23
4	Mar del Pirineo to Yesa	22
5	Yesa to Monrea	25
6	Monreal to Obanos and junction with the main Road to Santiago	30

With detours to the Leyre Monastery in stage 4 and

Sangüesa in stage 5.

SANTA CRISTINA OF SOMPORT, 'ONE OF THREE IN THE WORLD'

Immediately beyond the Somport col - in Latin *Summus Portus*, the highest passage - pilgrims arriving from Aspe through the valley or from Ossau via the Col des Moines, often through snow, found the 'Hospital' of Sainte-Christine or Santa-Cristina. There may have been a Benedictine monastery there since 1108, but it is known that on his return from the reconquest of Saragossa, Gaston IV the Crusader, Viscount of Béarn, built or rebuilt it and handed it over to the Canons of St Augustine. In 1216 Pope Innocent III called it *'Unum de tribus mundi'*, one of only three in the world (along with the Great St Bernard and Jerusalem) - referring not to its size, but to its strategic importance. A few ruins remain, at ground level only, but making it possible to perceive the lay-out, at the foot of the ski-resort of Candanchú and above the cliff overlooking the Santa Cristina Bridge. Slightly further on, before reaching the 'Russian Bridge' there must have been a fortified tower, of which nothing remains but the base.

THE INTERNATIONAL RAILWAY STATION AT CANFRANC

The size of the International Station at Canfranc comes as a surprise. It was built for the railway between Pau and Saragossa, which leaves the tunnel near here, but there are no longer any trains, since the Lestanguet bridge in the Aspe valley collapsed in 1970. The station is now the terminus for the Spanish railway service, with a coach connection across the Pyrenees to Oloron.

The town was originally called Los Arañones, and the real village of Canfanc, burnt and badly rebuilt, is lower down. The name is typical of the Road to Santiago: 'Camp Franc'. A 16th-century fort can be seen further on, beside the road.

FROM CANFRANC TO JACA

- *Villanua* (Villeneuve) has a medieval bridge, and the church contains a 13th-century Virgin and a 15th-century figure of St James.
- *Aruej* is a very modest 11th-century Romanesque church with a semi-circular apse, now deconsecrated.
- *Castiello* owes its name to the castle of which only a few traces remain. The Romanesque church was restored in the 16th century.

OFF THE ROUTE:
- *San Adrién de Sasabe,* on the right before reaching Castiello, and *Iguacel* on the left of the village, each have a fine 11th-century Romanesque church, oddly built high up in the mountains, each about ten kilometres off our route.
- the *Ermita San Cristóbal,* of which nothing remains except some ruins on the way into Jaca, was a medieval chapel.
- The capital of the *Arbol de la Salud* (the Tree of Salvation, and of Health) indicates the site of the Hospital which bore this name.

JACA, A CAPITAL SINCE 1025

Jaca was the cradle of the first Christian kingdom of Aragon. Ramiro I, natural son of Sancho the Great of Navarre, established his court here in 1035. In 1063 an imposing *Romanesque cathedral* was built here, with sculptured doorway, capitals carved with great realism, three aisles, twelve chapels; but with a Spanish characteristic: the central cupola on its crossed rib vaulting. A 16th-century statue of St James stands in the porch. Visitors should see the museum of Romanesque painting housed in the cloisters, with a collection of 11th-13th century frescos from abandoned mountain churches.

Also worth seeing is the Romanesque tomb of Doña Sancha, 11th century, in the *Benedictine monastery;* the Visigoth remains of the former *church of Santiago,* now the presbytery; and the *Casa Consistorial,* 16th-century baroque, containing a 13th-century copy of the *Fueros,* a code of laws.

OFF THE ROUTE: SANTA CRUZ DE LA SERÓS AND SAN JUAN DE LA PEÑA

On the left at the foot of the mountains, *Santa Cruz de la Serós*, derived from the old word Soror, sister, has a beautiful Romanesque Benedictine church with three apses, and its chapter-house in a cupola above the vaulting. Also the 11th-century Romanesque church of San Caprasio, on the way into the village.

Higher up the mountain, the monastery of *San Juan de la Peña* (of the rock), with access along a recently-constructed road, was one of the cradles of the Christian reconquest of Spain. It occupies an astonishing rocky setting; its crypt is an early Mozarabic church of the 10th century, with horseshoe arches, the chapter-house and upper church date from the 11th century, the tombs of the nobles from the 12th-14th centuries, and most impressive of all are the outstanding 12th-century capitals in the cloisters.

FROM SANTA CILIA TO TIERMAS

- *Santa Cilia de Jaca* had a Chapel of St James, now vanished.
- *Puente de la Reina,* the bridge over the River Aragón, was once neighbour to a royal establishment called Astorit which has now completely disappeared.
- *Berdün,* a name of Celtic origin, related to the French Verdun, and Esco, an abandoned village, are perched on the tops of truncated cone-shaped hills.
- *Tiermas* is also perched high, and still has medieval houses; but sadly it no longer has the hot springs from which it takes its name, which have recently been submerged by the waters of the Yesa reservoir.

LEYRE, CRADLE OF THE RECONQUEST.

As with San Juan de la Peña for Aragon, the San Salvador monastery at Leyre, refuge of Christian princes and bishops, was Navarre's birthplace of the Reconquest. Originally a Visigoth monastery, it was rebuilt in the 9th century and enlarged by King Sancho the Great in the 11th century. The present monastery, built above an extraordinarily strong and substantial crypt, has a large Romanesque church with 11th-century apses and a 12th-13th-century nave.

Expropriated during the 19th century, in 1954 it was handed back to the monks who now offer hospitality there.

SAN VIRIDA ENCHANTED BY A BIRD

The fountain of San Virida, near the Leyre monastery, preserves the name of a 10th-century monk who re-established the Galician monastery at Samos and was probably born in Tiermas.

The *Cantigas* of Alfonso X The Wise tell a less historically sound - but very attractive - tale: San Virida very foolishly feared that he would be bored during Eternity: God sent him a small bird whose singing plunged him into a deep trance which lasted for 300 years, so that when he awoke he no longer recognised the monks of Leyre.

SANGÜESA, MEDIEVAL TOWN

The 12th-century church of Santa Maróa la Real is a 'National Monument', a distinction justified by the amazing façade-porch alone, overflowing with statues and carvings. It has three apses, each with an aisle, from the Romanesque-Gothic transitional period, and a 14th-century statue of Our Lady of Rocamadour.
The medieval city still preserves:
- The *church of St James:* 12th and 13th centuries, with a Gothic statue of the saint;
- The *churches of San Salvador and San Francisco,* 13th century, with Gothic and Renaissance altar-pieces;
- The 15th-century Gothic *Palace of the Dukes of Granada;*
- The royal *Palace of the Princes of Viana* who were the 'Dauphins', the heirs of the Kingdom of Navarre in the 12th and 14th centuries.

On the opposite bank, Rocaforte was undoubtedly

the original site of Sangüesa, and St Francis of Assisi would have passed through here.

FROM SANGÜESA TO PUENTE LA REINA

- *Idocin* has a small Gothic church. It was the birthplace of Espoz y Mina, the Navarrese leader in the War of Independence against Napoleon.
- *Monreal* takes its name from an ancient ruined castle.
- *Tiebas* has a Gothic church with statues; there was also a castle here, built by Thibaut I in the 13th century and demolished in the 16th century.

OFF THE ROUTE: JAVIER, BIRTHPLACE OF SAINT FRANCIS XAVIER

The castle at Javier, 4 kilometres to the left of Yesa, was the birthplace of St Francis of Jassu, known as St Francis Xavier, Francisco Javier in Spanish. Born in 1506, companion and fellow-Jesuit of Ignatius de Loyola, he evangelised Goa in India, Malacca and Japan, and died on the frontiers of China.

EUNATE, FUNERARY CHAPEL OF SANTIAGO PILGRIMS

The Basque meaning of the name Eunate is probably 'the Hundred Doorways', an allusion to the band of arcading forming a cloister round the monument which has its own intrinsic interest; its
octagonal shape was inspired by the Holy Sepulchre in Jerusalem. The discovery of bones and scallop-shells appears to explain its origins, which for long remained mysterious: it was a funerary chapel for pilgrims who died along the Road. It has a Mozarabic cupola and a 12th-century 'lantern tower of the dead'.

MAPS

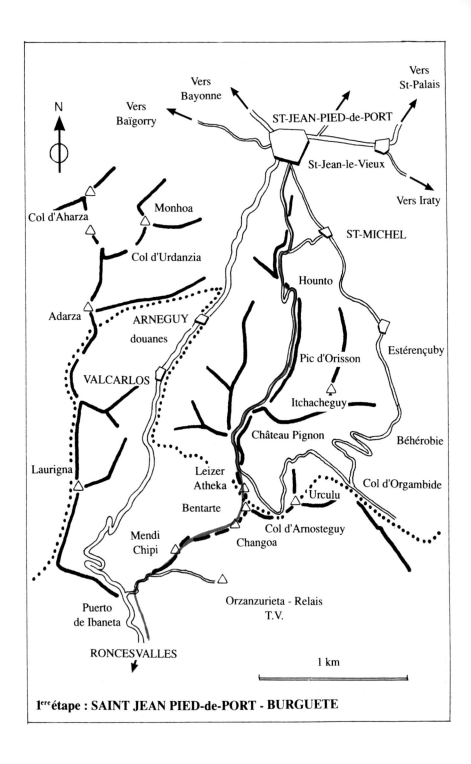

1ere étape : SAINT JEAN PIED-de-PORT - BURGUETE

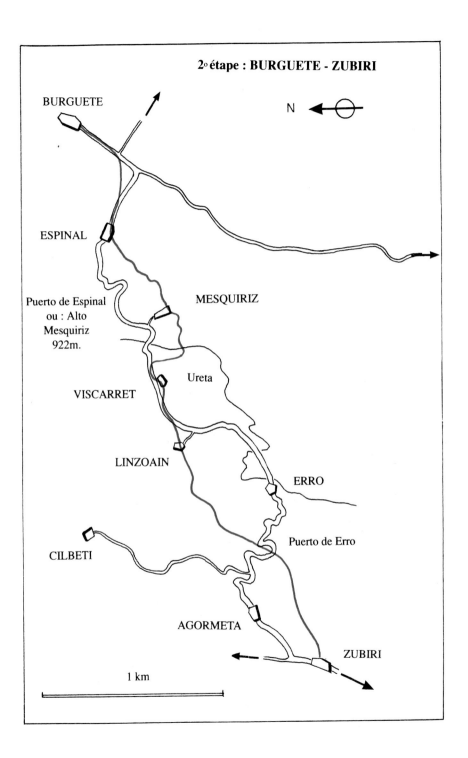

2º étape : BURGUETE - ZUBIRI

BURGUETE

N

ESPINAL

Puerto de Espinal
ou : Alto
Mesquiriz
922m.

MESQUIRIZ

Ureta

VISCARRET

LINZOAIN

ERRO

CILBETI

Puerto de Erro

AGORMETA

ZUBIRI

1 km

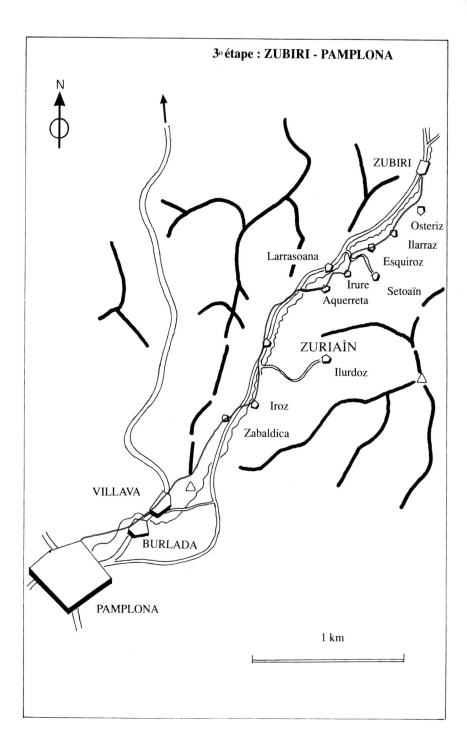

3º **étape : ZUBIRI - PAMPLONA**

N

ZUBIRI

Osteriz

Ilarraz

Larrasoana

Esquiroz

Irure

Setoaïn

Aquerreta

ZURIAÌN

Ilurdoz

Iroz

Zabaldica

VILLAVA

BURLADA

PAMPLONA

1 km

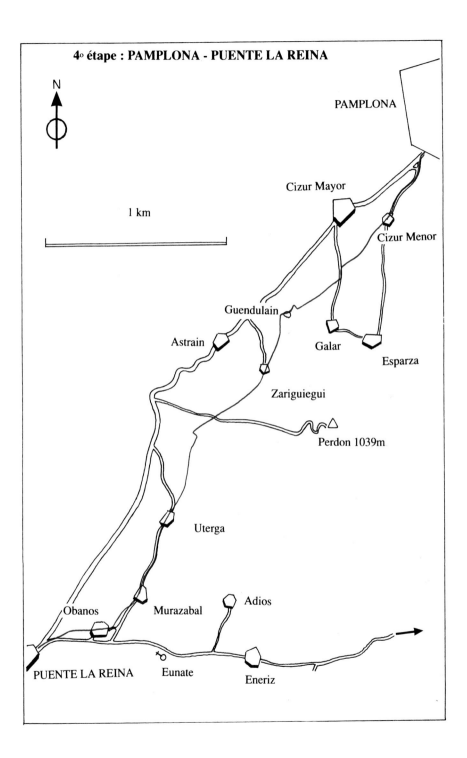

4o étape : PAMPLONA - PUENTE LA REINA

N

1 km

PAMPLONA

Cizur Mayor

Cizur Menor

Guendulain

Astrain

Galar

Esparza

Zariguiegui

Perdon 1039m

Uterga

Adios

Obanos

Murazabal

PUENTE LA REINA

Eunate

Eneriz

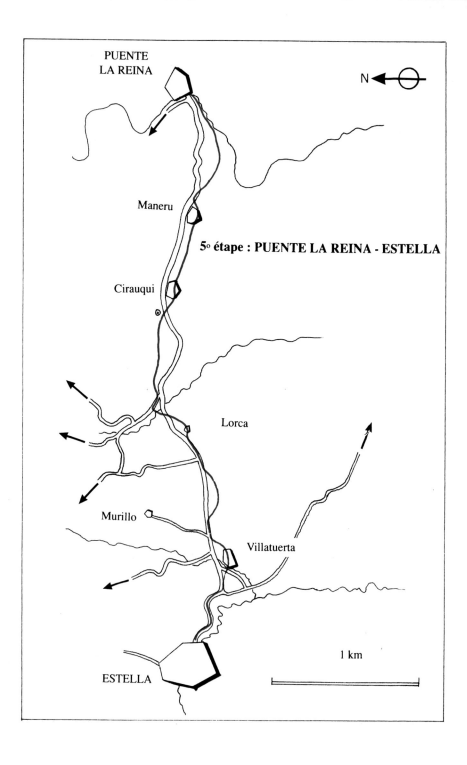

PUENTE
LA REINA

N

Maneru

5o étape : PUENTE LA REINA - ESTELLA

Cirauqui

Lorca

Murillo

Villatuerta

1 km

ESTELLA

6º étape : ESTELLA - LOS ARCOS

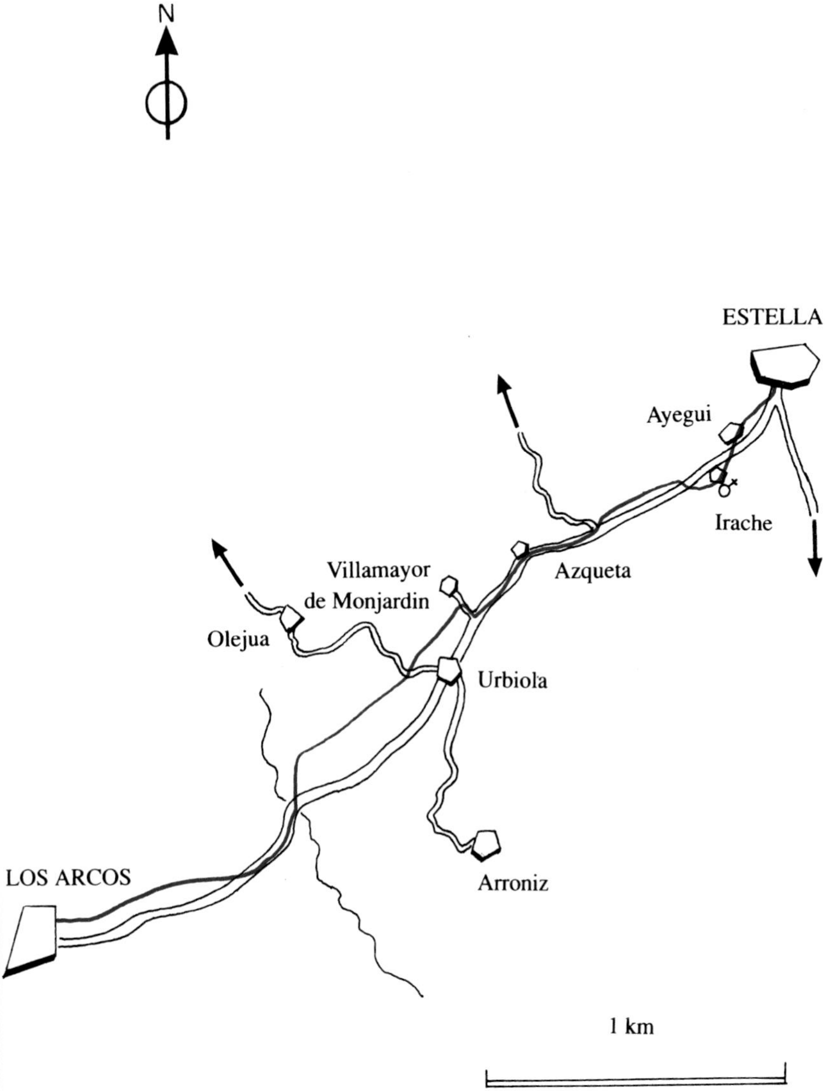

N

ESTELLA

Ayegui

Irache

Villamayor
de Monjardin

Azqueta

Olejua

Urbiola

LOS ARCOS

Arroniz

1 km

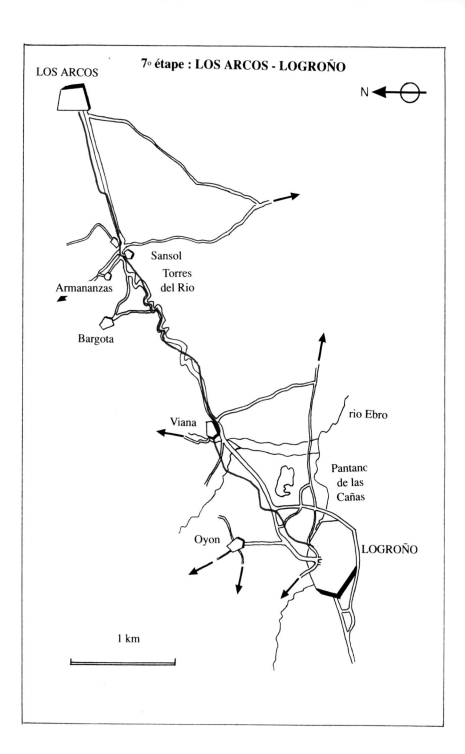

7º étape : LOS ARCOS - LOGROÑO

LOS ARCOS

N

Sansol

Torres
del Rio

Armananzas

Bargota

Viana

rio Ebro

Pantanc
de las
Cañas

Oyon

LOGROÑO

1 km

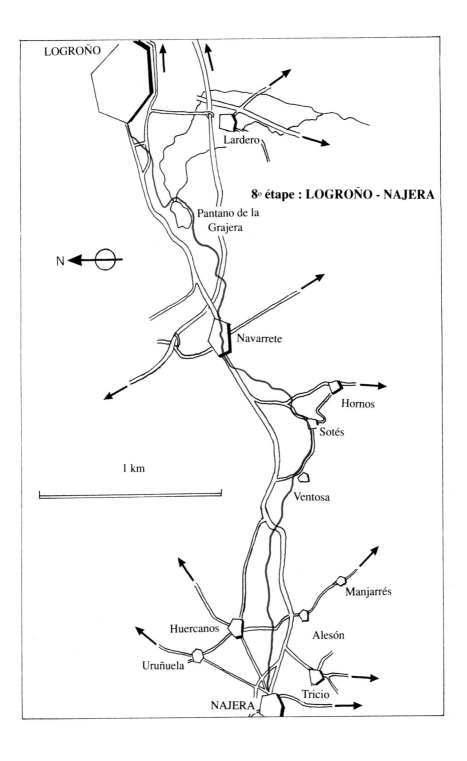

LOGROÑO

Lardero

8º étape : LOGROÑO - NAJERA

Pantano de la
Grajera

N

Navarrete

Hornos

Sotés

1 km

Ventosa

Manjarrés

Huercanos

Alesón

Uruñuela

Tricio

NAJERA

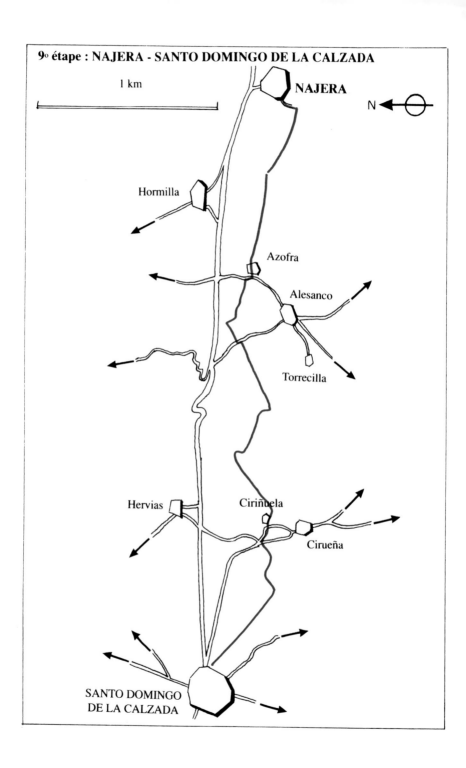

9º étape : NAJERA - SANTO DOMINGO DE LA CALZADA

1 km

N

NAJERA

Hormilla

Azofra

Alesanco

Torrecilla

Hervias

Ciriñuela

Cirueña

SANTO DOMINGO
DE LA CALZADA

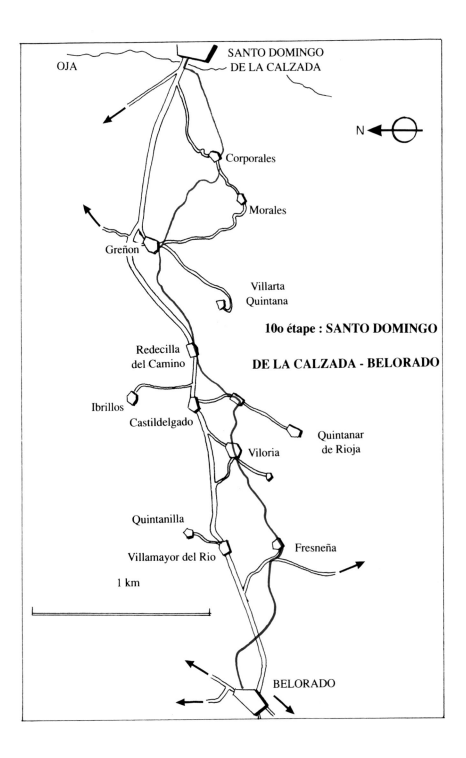

OJA

SANTO DOMINGO
DE LA CALZADA

N

Corporales

Morales

Greñon

Villarta
Quintana

10o étape : SANTO DOMINGO

Redecilla
del Camino

DE LA CALZADA - BELORADO

Ibrillos

Castildelgado

Viloria

Quintanar
de Rioja

Quintanilla

Villamayor del Rio

Fresneña

1 km

BELORADO

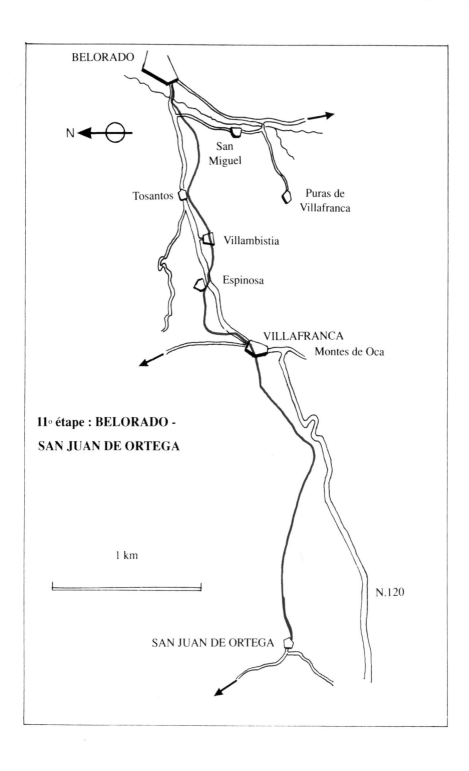

BELORADO

N

San
Miguel

Tosantos

Puras de
Villafranca

Villambistia

Espinosa

VILLAFRANCA
Montes de Oca

11º étape : BELORADO -
SAN JUAN DE ORTEGA

1 km

N.120

SAN JUAN DE ORTEGA

12º étape : SAN JUAN DE ORTEGA - BURGOS

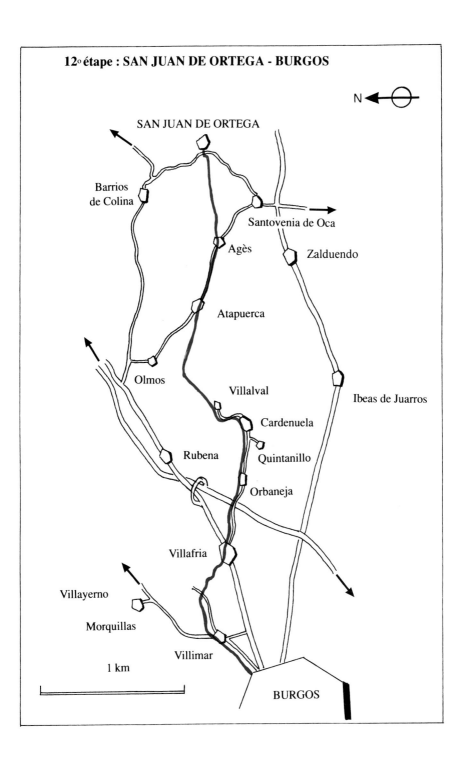

N

SAN JUAN DE ORTEGA

Barrios
de Colina

Santovenia de Oca

Agès

Zalduendo

Atapuerca

Olmos

Villalval

Ibeas de Juarros

Cardenuela

Rubena

Quintanillo

Orbaneja

Villafria

Villayerno

Morquillas

Villimar

1 km

BURGOS

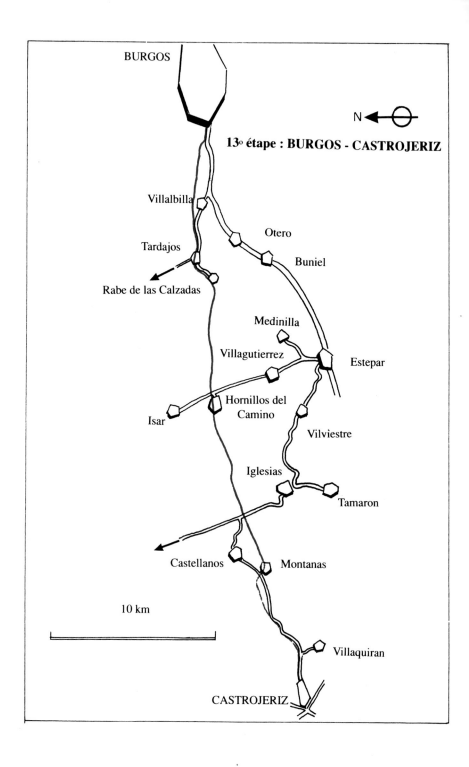

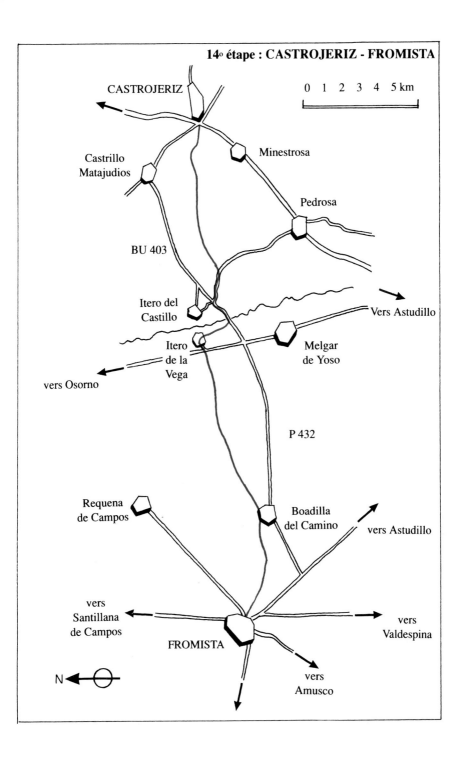

14° étape : CASTROJERIZ - FROMISTA

0 1 2 3 4 5 km

CASTROJERIZ

Minestrosa

Castrillo
Matajudios

Pedrosa

BU 403

Itero del
Castillo

Vers Astudillo

Itero
de la
Vega

Melgar
de Yoso

vers Osorno

P 432

Requena
de Campos

Boadilla
del Camino

vers Astudillo

vers
Santillana
de Campos

vers
Valdespina

FROMISTA

N

vers
Amusco

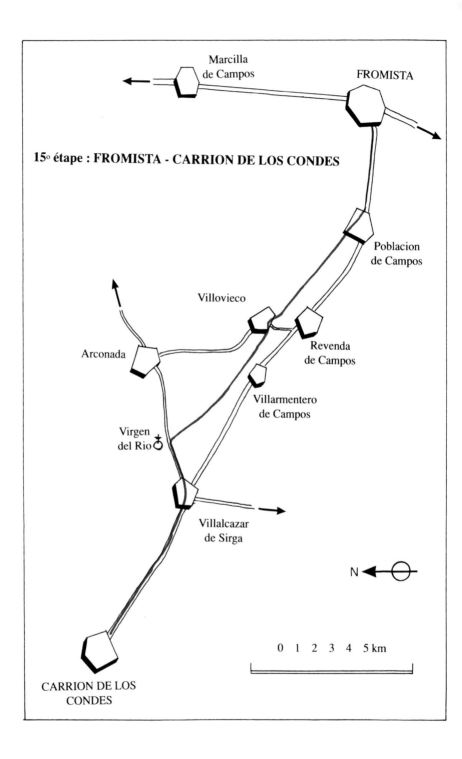

15º étape : FROMISTA - CARRION DE LOS CONDES

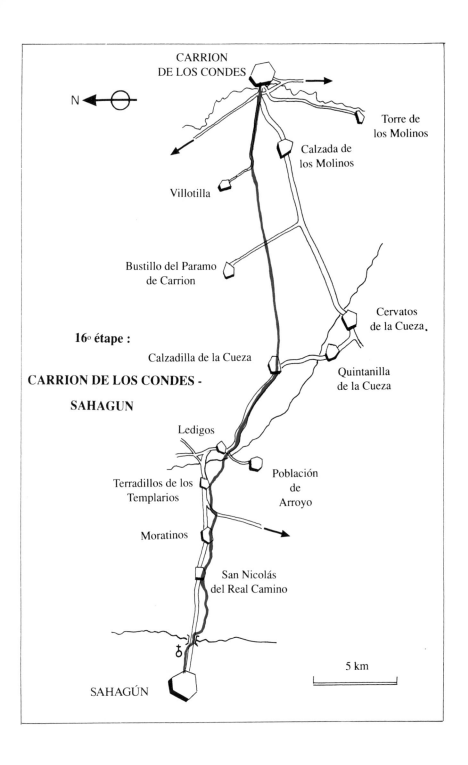

N

CARRION
DE LOS CONDES

Torre de
los Molinos

Calzada de
los Molinos

Villotilla

Bustillo del Paramo
de Carrion

Cervatos
de la Cueza.

16° étape :

Calzadilla de la Cueza

Quintanilla
de la Cueza

CARRION DE LOS CONDES -

SAHAGUN

Ledigos

Población
de
Arroyo

Terradillos de los
Templarios

Moratinos

San Nicolás
del Real Camino

5 km

SAHAGÚN

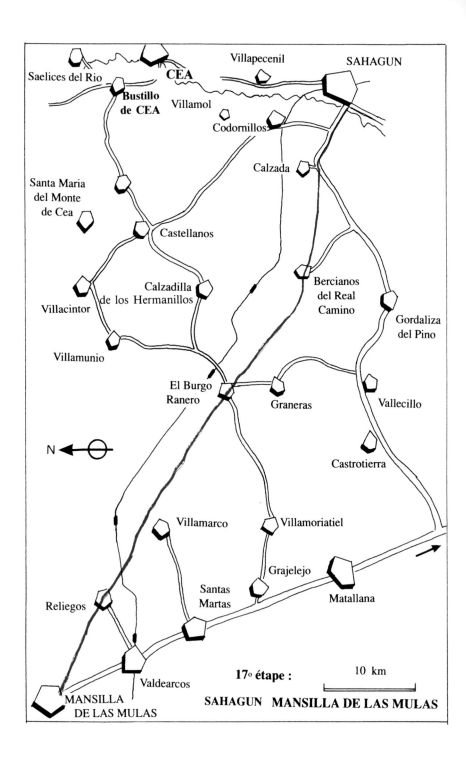

Saelices del Rio
CEA
Villapecenil
SAHAGUN
Bustillo de CEA
Villamol
Codornillos
Calzada
Santa Maria del Monte de Cea
Castellanos
Calzadilla de los Hermanillos
Bercianos del Real Camino
Gordaliza del Pino
Villacintor
Villamunio
El Burgo Ranero
Graneras
Vallecillo
N
Castrotierra
Villamarco
Villamoriatiel
Grajelejo
Reliegos
Santas Martas
Matallana
Valdearcos
MANSILLA DE LAS MULAS

17o étape :   10 km

SAHAGUN MANSILLA DE LAS MULAS

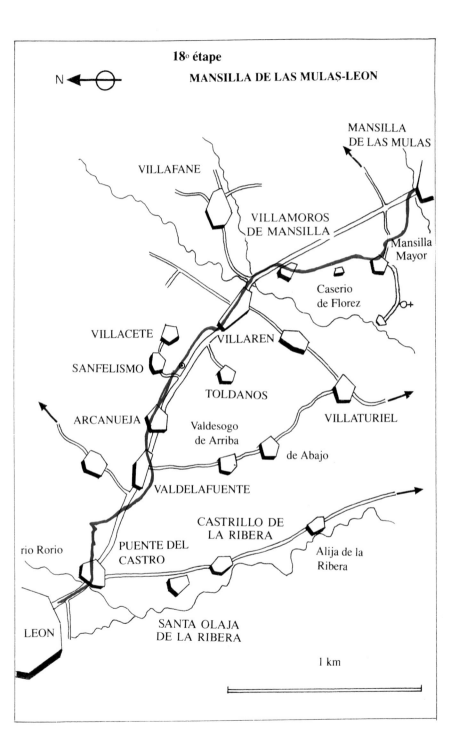

18° étape

MANSILLA DE LAS MULAS-LEON

N

MANSILLA
DE LAS MULAS

VILLAFANE

VILLAMOROS
DE MANSILLA

Mansilla
Mayor

Caserio
de Florez

VILLACETE

VILLAREN

SANFELISMO

TOLDANOS

VILLATURIEL

ARCANUEJA

Valdesogo
de Arriba

de Abajo

VALDELAFUENTE

CASTRILLO DE
LA RIBERA

rio Rorio

PUENTE DEL
CASTRO

Alija de la
Ribera

LEON

SANTA OLAJA
DE LA RIBERA

1 km

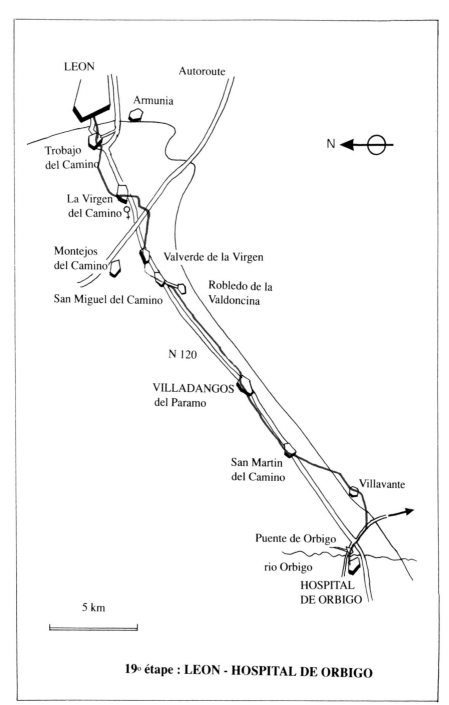

LEON

Autoroute

Armunia

N

Trobajo
del Camino

La Virgen
del Camino

Montejos
del Camino

Valverde de la Virgen

Robledo de la
Valdoncina

San Miguel del Camino

N 120

VILLADANGOS
del Paramo

San Martin
del Camino

Villavante

Puente de Orbigo

rio Orbigo

HOSPITAL
DE ORBIGO

5 km

19° étape : LEON - HOSPITAL DE ORBIGO

20° étape : HOSPITAL DE ORBIGO - ASTORGA

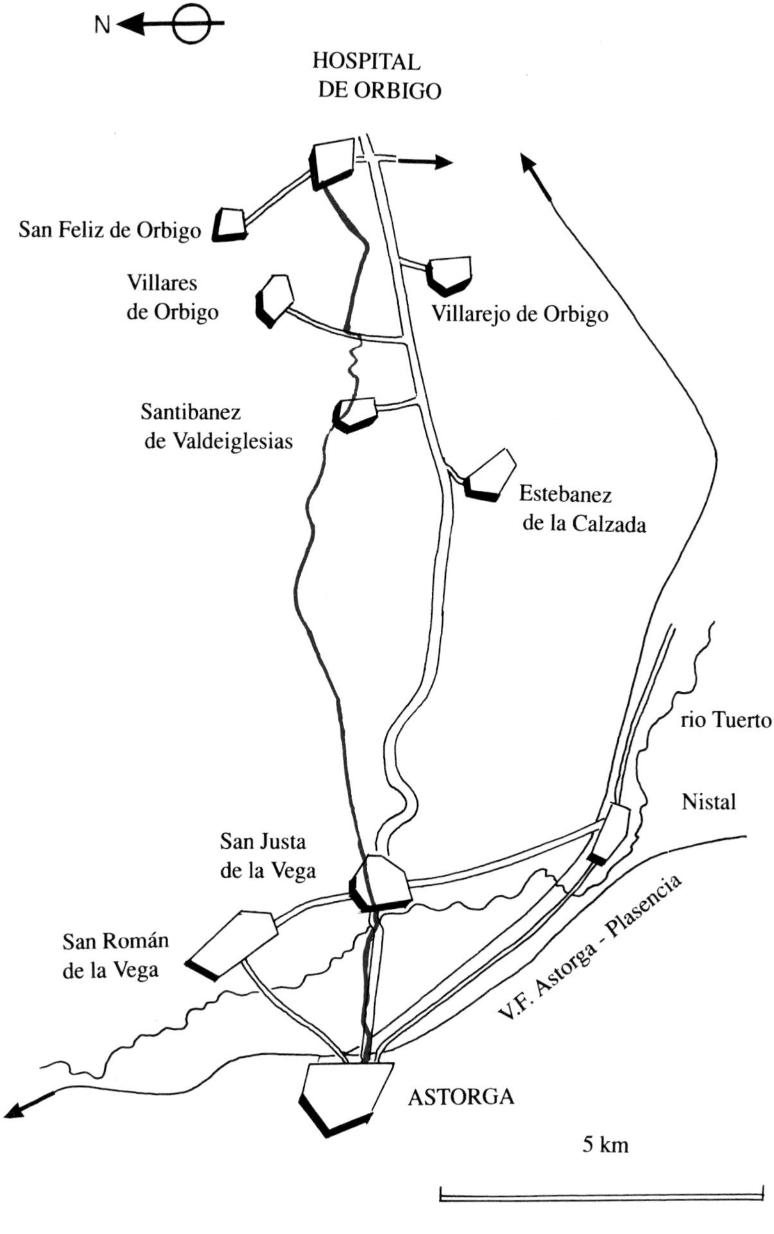

N

HOSPITAL
DE ORBIGO

San Feliz de Orbigo

Villares
de Orbigo

Villarejo de Orbigo

Santibanez
de Valdeiglesias

Estebanez
de la Calzada

rio Tuerto

Nistal

San Justa
de la Vega

San Román
de la Vega

V.F. Astorga - Plasencia

ASTORGA

5 km

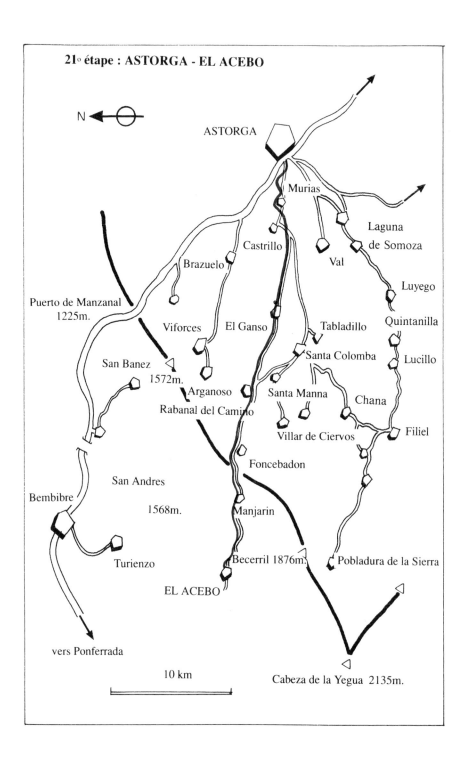

21º étape : ASTORGA - EL ACEBO

N

ASTORGA

Murias

Laguna
de Somoza

Castrillo

Brazuelo

Val

Luyego

Puerto de Manzanal
1225m.

Viforces   El Ganso

Tabladillo   Quintanilla

San Banez

Santa Colomba   Lucillo

1572m.

Arganoso   Santa Manna   Chana

Rabanal del Camino

Villar de Ciervos   Filiel

Foncebadon

San Andres

Bembibre

1568m.   Manjarin

Turienzo

Becerril 1876m.   Pobladura de la Sierra

EL ACEBO

vers Ponferrada

10 km

Cabeza de la Yegua 2135m.

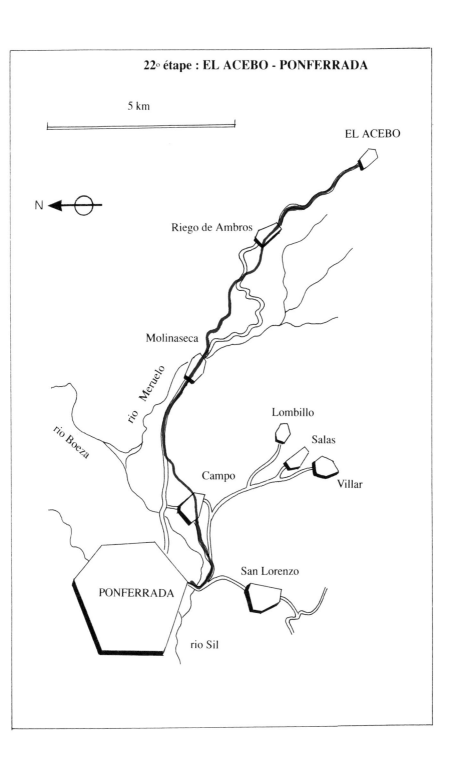

22° étape : EL ACEBO - PONFERRADA

5 km

EL ACEBO

N

Riego de Ambros

Molinaseca

rio Meruelo

rio Boeza

Lombillo

Salas

Campo

Villar

PONFERRADA

San Lorenzo

rio Sil

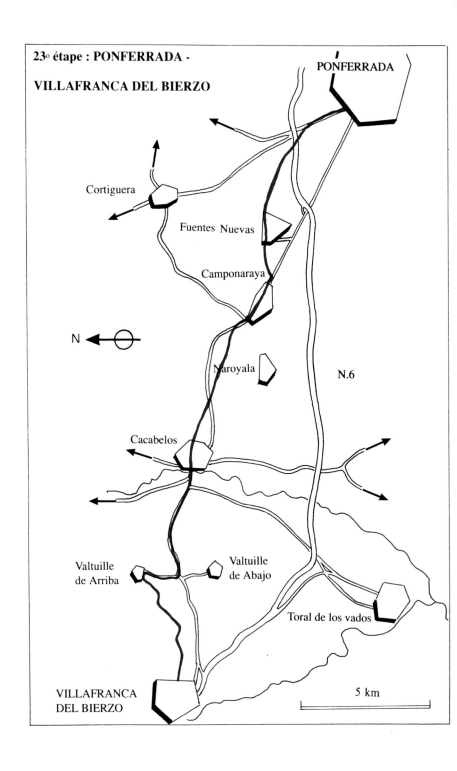

23o étape : PONFERRADA -

VILLAFRANCA DEL BIERZO

PONFERRADA

Cortiguera

Fuentes Nuevas

Camponaraya

N

Naroyala

N.6

Cacabelos

Valtuille
de Arriba

Valtuille
de Abajo

Toral de los vados

VILLAFRANCA
DEL BIERZO

5 km

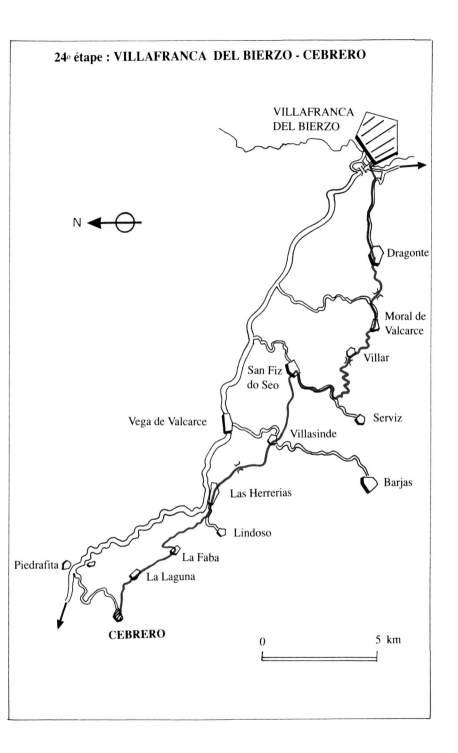

24° étape : VILLAFRANCA DEL BIERZO - CEBRERO

VILLAFRANCA
DEL BIERZO

N

Dragonte

Moral de
Valcarce

Villar

San Fiz
do Seo

Serviz

Vega de Valcarce

Villasinde

Barjas

Las Herrerias

Lindoso

Piedrafita

La Faba

La Laguna

CEBRERO

0   5 km

25º étape : CEBRERO - TRIACASTELA

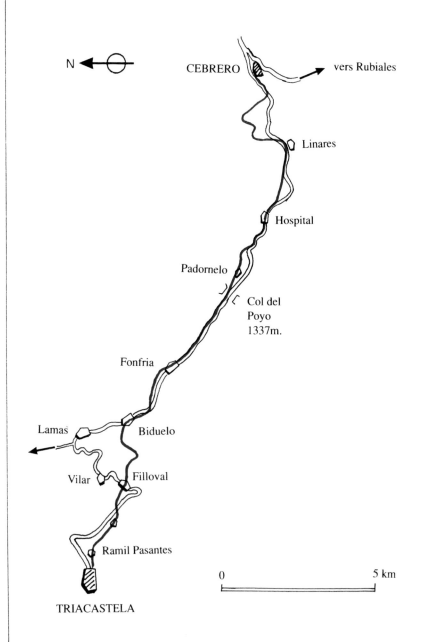

N

CEBRERO

vers Rubiales

Linares

Hospital

Padornelo

Col del
Poyo
1337m.

Fonfria

Lamas

Biduelo

Vilar

Filloval

Ramil Pasantes

0

5 km

TRIACASTELA

26º étape : TRIACASTELE - SARRIA

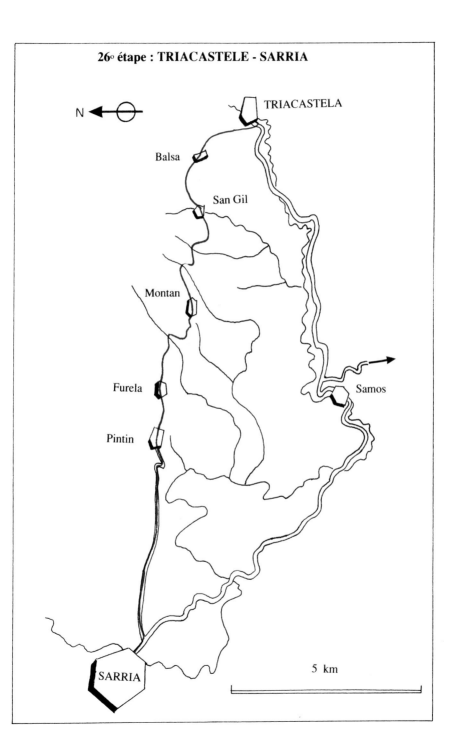

N

TRIACASTELA

Balsa

San Gil

Montan

Furela

Pintin

Samos

SARRIA

5 km

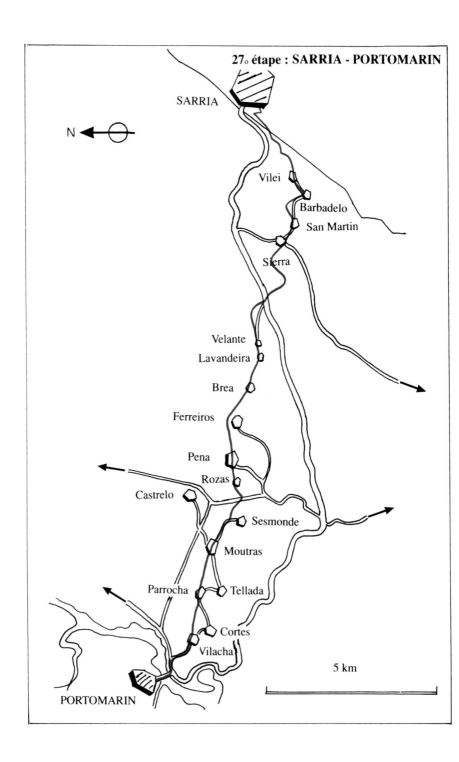

27o étape : SARRIA - PORTOMARIN

SARRIA

N

Vilei

Barbadelo
San Martin

Sierra

Velante
Lavandeira

Brea

Ferreiros

Pena
Rozas

Castrelo

Sesmonde

Moutras

Parrocha   Tellada

Cortes

Vilacha

5 km

PORTOMARIN

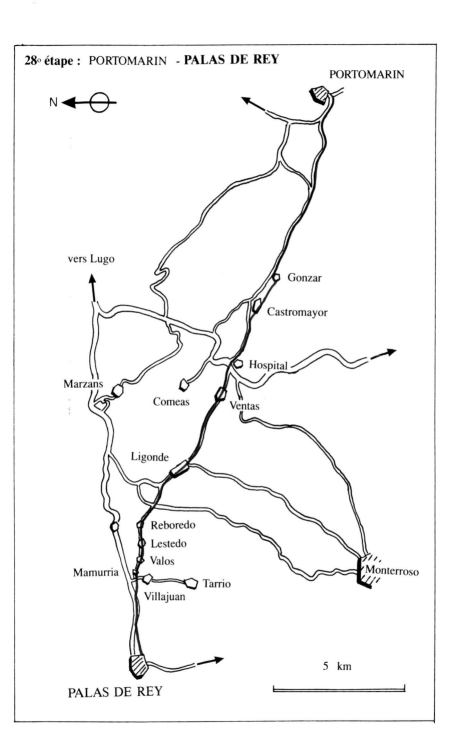

28° étape : PORTOMARIN - **PALAS DE REY**

PORTOMARIN

N

vers Lugo

Gonzar

Castromayor

Hospital

Marzans

Comeas

Ventas

Ligonde

Reboredo

Lestedo

Valos

Mamurria

Tarrio

Villajuan

Monterroso

PALAS DE REY

5 km

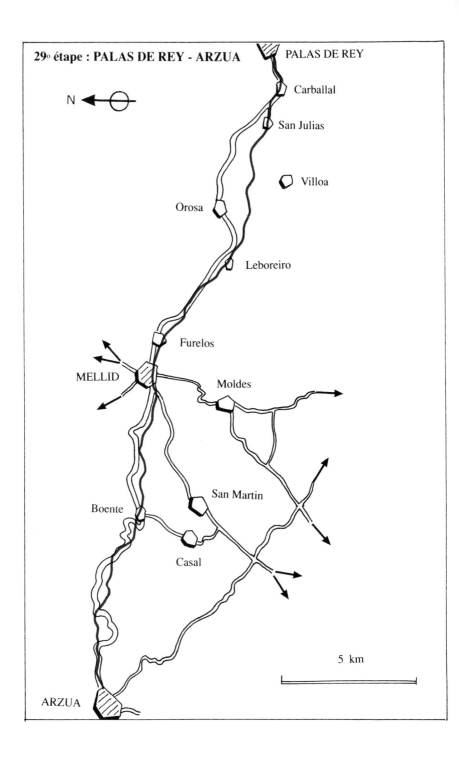

29º étape : PALAS DE REY - ARZUA

N

PALAS DE REY

Carballal

San Julias

Villoa

Orosa

Leboreiro

Furelos

MELLID

Moldes

San Martin

Boente

Casal

5 km

ARZUA

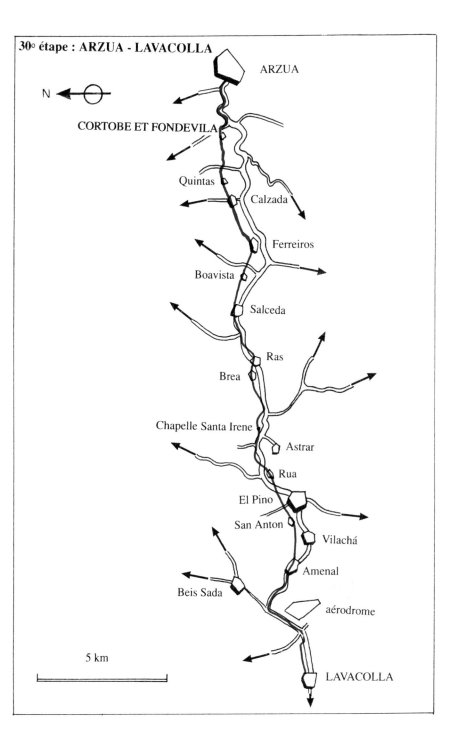

30° étape : ARZUA - LAVACOLLA

N

ARZUA

CORTOBE ET FONDEVILA

Quintas
Calzada

Ferreiros

Boavista

Salceda

Ras

Brea

Chapelle Santa Irene

Astrar

Rua

El Pino
San Anton

Vilachá

Amenal

Beis Sada

aérodrome

5 km

LAVACOLLA

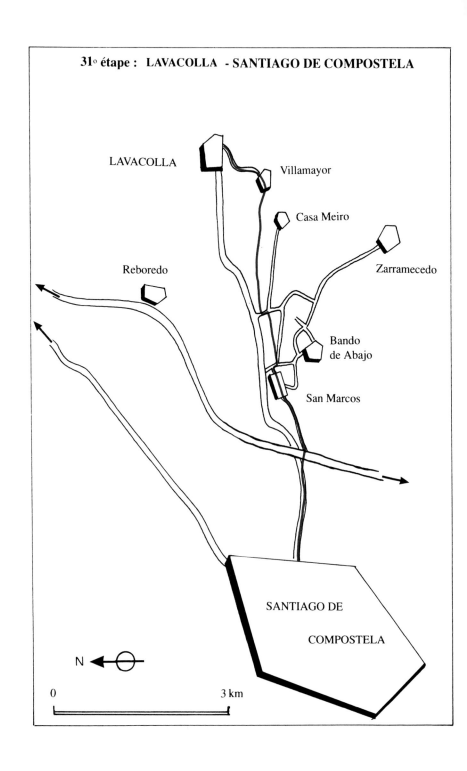

31° étape : LAVACOLLA - SANTIAGO DE COMPOSTELA

LAVACOLLA

Villamayor

Casa Meiro

Reboredo

Zarramecedo

Bando
de Abajo

San Marcos

SANTIAGO DE

COMPOSTELA

N

0   3 km

INDEX

ABELDA DE IRUEGA   73
AGÉS   100
AQUERRETA (hameau de)   50
ARCA   190
ARCAHUEJA   131
ARLETA   50
ARNÉGUY   38
ARNOSTÉGUY (COL DE)   38
ARZÚA   179/185
ASTORGA   139/141
ASTRAÍN   56
ATAPUERCA   100
AYEGUY   69
AZOFRA   84/86
AZQUETA   68

BASCUÑANA   91
BAZONGAIZ   56
BELORADO   89/91/92/94
BENEVIVERE   119
BENTARTE (CABANES DE)   40
BERCIANO DEL REAL   124
BIDUEDO   161/163
BOADILLA DEL CAMINO   111
BOAVISTA   189
BOENTE DE RIBA   184
BURGOS   99/100/102
BURGUETE   37/41
BURLADA   49/51/52

CACABELOS   152-153
CALZADA   188
CALZADILLA DE LA CUEZA   119/121
COMPLUDO   144
CAMPO   148
CAMPONARAYA   153
CANAS   84
CANFRANC   201
CARDENUELA   99/101
CARRION DE LOS CONDES   113/117
CASTROJERIZ   107
CASTROMAOR   176
CASTENADA   184
CEBREIRO   157
CHANGOA   40
CHARTREUSE DE MIRAFLORES   101
CIRAUQUI   61/62
CIRINUELA   85
CIZUR MENOR   55/56

CLAVIJO	73
CORPORALES	90
DICASTILLO	68
DRAGONTE	156
EL ACEBO	143/145
EL CEBRERO	155/159
EL ESPINAL	43/46
ELHURSARO (COL DE)	39
ELIZACHARRA	40
ESPINOZA DEL CAMINO	96
ESQUIROZ	50
ESTELLA	61/63/64/67
ESTERIZ	50
EUNATE	55/56/205
FILLOVAL	163
FONCEBADON	145
FONDEVILLA	188
FONFRÍA DEL CAMINO	162
FRESNENA	92
FRÓMISTA	109/110/111
FURELA	166
GAÑECOLETA	38
GAZOLAS	56
GRAÑON	90
GUENDULAÍN	57
HERRERIAS	156/158
HORNILLOS DEL CAMINO	105/107
HONTANAS	106/107
HOSPITAL DE LA CONDESA	162
HOSPITAL DE ORBIGO	133/137
HOSTATÉGUY (PIC DE)	39
HUARTE	50
IBAÑETA (CHAPELLE DE)	38
IGLESIA DEL CRUCIFIJO	59
IROZ	50/51
IRACHE	67/68
IRANZA (ABBAYE)	65
IRUÑA	51
IRURE	50
JACA	200/202
LA FABA	159
LAGUNA DE CASTILLA	159
LAGUARDIA	74
LARRASOAÑA	49

LABACOLLA	187/190
LAVANDEIRA	171
LEDIGOS	121
LEIZAR ATHÉKA	39
LÉMOVICENCIS (VIA)	23
LEÓN	127/128/131
LEPOEDOR	40
LEYRE	203
LIGONDE	177
LINARÉS	161
LOGROÑO	71/72/75
LORCA	63
LOS ARCOS	67/69/70
MAÑERU	62
MANSILLA DE LAS MULAS	123/125
MAR DEL PIRENEO	200
MELLID	180/185
MENDI-CHIPI	40
MERCADO DO SERRA	170
MERCADOIRO	172
MESQUIRIZ	44
MIRALLOS	171
MOLINASECA	147/149
MOMURRIA	177
MONJARDIN	68
MONRÉAL	200
MONTÁN	166
MONTE DEL GOZO	196
MONTRAS	172
MORAL DE VALCARCE	157
MORATINOS	120
MORGADE	171
MURAZABAL	55/56/59
NÁJERA	77/79/81/83
NAVARETE	81
OBAÑOS	55/57/59/200
OSTABAT	22
OVIEDO	189
PALAS DE REI	175/177
PAMPELUNE	49/51/52/53
PARADELA	171
PARAMO	135
PARROCHA	172
PEÑA LEIMAN	171
PEREIRINA	188
PICO SACRO	176
PINTÍN	166
POBLACION DEL CAMPOS	113/117

PODENSIS (VIA)	23
PORTOMARÍN	169/171/172
PORTOS	177
PUENTE LA REINA	22/55/58/59/200
PUERTA DE CASTILLA	67
PUERTO DE IBAÑETA	40
RABANAL DEL CAMINO	144/145
RABÉ DE LAS CALZADAS	105
RAMIL	163
REDECILLA DEL CAMINO	90/92
RENTE	170
REVENGA DEL CAMPO	113/117
RONCESVALLES	41
RONCEVAUX	37
RÚA	191
SAHAGUN	68/119/120/121
ST-JEAN-PIED-DE-PORT	37/41
ST-MICHEL	38
SAINTE-CHRISTINE (HOSPITAL DE)	201
SAMOS	167
SAN ANTÓN	191
SAN BARTOLOMÉ (EGLISE)	44/72
SANTA CATALINA	62
SAN CERNÍN (EGLISE)	53
SAN FIZ	157
SANGUESA	204
SAN JUAN DE LA PEÑA	203
SAN JUAN DE ORTEGA	94/97/99
SAN JUAN DE PADORNELO	162
SAN JULIAN DE SAMOS	166
SAN JUSTO DE LA DE LA VEGA	141
SAN MILLAN DE LA COGOLLA	83
SAN NICOLAS DEL REAL CAMINO	120/121
SAN PEDRO	62
SAN PEDRO DE LA RUA	64
SAN ROMAN	62
SAN SALVADOR DE IBAÑETA	38
SANSOL	72
SANTA MARIA (EGLISE)	72
SANTA MARIA LA REAL	79/80
SANTA MARINA (EGLISE)	50
SANTIAGO DE COMPOSTELLA	195/197
SANTO DOMINGO DE LA CALZADA	83/85/89
SAN XIL	165
SAN XULÍAN DEL CAMINO	180
SARRÍA	165/167
SETOAIN	50
SIERRA DEL PERDÓN	55
SOMPORT (COL DU)	200
SOTES	80

TARDAJOS	105/107
TOLOSANA (VIA)	23
TORRES DEL RIO (CHAPELLE)	71/72/75
TRIACASTELA	161/163
TRINIDAD DE ARRE	50
TROBAJO DEL CAMINO	134
TURONENSE (VIA)	23
URDANARRE (PIC DE)	39
URDANASBURU (PIC DE)	39
UTERGA	57/59
URETA	44
VALCARLOS	38
VALDEFUENTE	131
VALOS	177
VEGA DE VACARCE	156/159
VELANTE	171
VENTAS	176
VIANA	71/73/75
VILAFRANCA DE OCA	95/96/97
VILAR DE DONAS	176
VILÉI	170
VILLABILLA DE BURGOS	105
VILLACHA	171
VILLACÁZAR DE SITGA	114/117
VILLADANGOS DEL PARAMÓ	135/137
VILLAFRANCA DEL BIERZO	151/153
VILLAFRIA DE BURGOS	105
VILLAMAOR	68/195
VILLAMAROS DE MANSILLA	128
VILLANUEVA	53
VILLARENTE	131
VILLAVA	49/51
VILLATUERTA	53
VILLAVA	49/51
VILLAVAL	101
VILLORIA	90/91
VILLOVIECO	113/114
VIRGEN DEL CAMINO	133/137
YESA	200
ZABALDICA	49/50/51
ZARIQUIEGUES	57/58
ZOO	165
ZUBIRI	43/46
ZURIAIN (EGLISE)	51

Traveller's Notes

Traveller's Notes

Traveller's Notes

Traveller's Notes

Traveller's Notes

Traveller's Notes

Traveller's Notes

Traveller's Notes

Traveller's Notes

Traveller's Notes

Traveller's Notes

© 1990 English language edition
Robertson McCarta Limited
122 Kings Cross Road
London WC1X 9DS

This edition
Cover illustration by Alain Ricaud
Production: Grahame Griffiths
Typeset by: The Robertson Group, Llandudno

English translation based on 2nd edition, le chemin de Saint Jacques de Compostelle, 1989

British Library Cataloguing in Publication Data
Bernès, Georges
The Pilgrim route to Compostela.
1. Spain. Navarre. Christian pilgrimages to Santiago de Compostella. Routes.
Description & travel
I. Title II. Chemin de Saint Jacques de Compostelle
English
248.463094652

ISBN 1-85365-219-9

Printed and bound in Great Britain by Butler & Tanner Limited, Frome.